CHICKEN SOUP TO INSPIRE THE BODY AND SOUL

CHICKEN SOUP TO INSPIRE THE BODY AND SOUL

Motivation and Inspiration for Living and Loving a Healthy Lifestyle

Jack Canfield
Mark Victor Hansen
Dan Millman
Diana von Welanetz Wentworth

Health Communications, Inc.
Deerfield Beach, Florida
www.bcibooks.com
www.chickensoup.com

We would like to acknowledge the many publishers and individuals who granted us permission to reprint the cited material. (Note: The stories that were penned anonymously, that are in the public domain or that were written by Jack Canfield, Mark Victor Hansen, Dan Millman or Diana von Welanetz Wentworth are not included in this listing.)

Joey's Gold Medal. Reprinted by permission of Perry P. Perkins. ©2002 Perry P. Perkins.

Playing For Keeps: Michael Jordan and the World He Made. From PLAYING FOR KEEPS by David Halberstam, copyright ©1999 by The Amateurs, Ltd. Used by permission of Random House, Inc.

The Home Stretch. Reprinted by permission of Karen Sue Hayse. ©2002 Karen Sue Hayse.

Racing for Life. Reprinted by permission of Ruth Heidrich, Ph.D. ©2001 Ruth Heidrich, Ph.D.

A Marathon of Dreams. Reprinted by permission of Marcia Horn Noyes. ©2001 Marcia Horn Noyes.

(Continued on page 362)

Library of Congress Cataloging-in-Publication Data

Chicken soup to inspire the body and soul : motivation and inspiration for
 living and loving a healthy lifestyle / [edited by] Jack Canfield ... [et al].
  p. cm.
 ISBN 0-7573-0141-X (tp)
  1. Conduct of life—Miscellanea. I. Canfield, Jack, date.
 BJ1597 C47 2003
 158.1'28—dc22

2003057053

Publisher: Health Communications, Inc.
        3201 S.W. 15th Street
        Deerfield Beach, FL 33442-8190

Cover design by Larissa Hise Henoch
Inside formatting by Lawna Patterson Oldfield

Dedicated to those who strive
onward and upward to improve their bodies and
stretch their souls, those quiet heroines and
heroes who test their limits and face the
challenges of healthful and dynamic living head on.

We salute you, and wish you well on your quest.

*B*ody and soul are twins;
God only knows which is which.

Charles A. Swinburne

Contents

8. LIFE CHANGES

9. ON GRATITUDE

Acknowledgments

The path to *Chicken Soup to Inspire the Body and Soul* has been made all the more beautiful by the many "companions" who have been there with us along the way. Our heartfelt gratitude to:

Our families, who have been chicken soup for our souls!

Inga, Christopher, Oran and Kyle Canfield, and Riley and Travis Mahoney, for all their love and support.

Patty, Elisabeth and Melanie Hansen, for once again sharing and lovingly supporting us in creating yet another book.

Ted Wentworth, Lexi and Dave Bursin, Kathy and Court Purdy, and Christy and Jeff Coyne, Diana von Welanetz Wentworth's expanding circle of cherished family.

Joy, Sierra, and China Millman, for their support and creative suggestions.

No team can function properly without a team manager, and every home needs a mother (or mother figure) who serves as the heart of the household. Associate editor Bobbie Probstein has served as our team manager and heart through the years of the *Body and Soul* project. She has also functioned as editor, central clearinghouse, organizer and record keeper; and—when our sturdy little craft hit white water in the final months— Bobbie served as compass, ballast and rudder. To her we give our deepest thanks. Couldn't have done it without you, Bobbie!

Our publisher, Peter Vegso, for his vision and commitment to bringing *Chicken Soup for the Soul* to the world.

Patty Aubery, for being there on every step of the journey,

with love, laughter and endless creativity.

Heather McNamara, Tasha Boucher and D'ette Corona, for producing our final manuscript with magnificent ease, finesse and care. Thanks for making the final stages of production such a breeze!

Leslie Riskin, for her care and loving determination to secure our permissions and get everything just right.

Nancy Autio and Barbara LoMonaco, for nourishing us with truly wonderful stories and cartoons.

Dana Drobny and Kathy Brennan-Thompson, for listening and being there throughout with humor and grace.

Maria Nickless, for her enthusiastic marketing and public relations support and a brilliant sense of direction.

Patty Hansen, for her thorough and competent handling of the legal and licensing aspects of the *Chicken Soup for the Soul* books. You are magnificent at the challenge!

Laurie Hartman, for being a precious guardian of the *Chicken Soup* brand.

Veronica Romero, Teresa Esparza, Jesse Ianniello, Russ Kamalski, Robin Yerian, Stephanie Thatcher, Jody Emme, Trudy Marschall, Michelle Adams, Dee Dee Romanello, Shanna Vieyra, Lisa Williams, Gina Romanello, Brittany Shaw, Dena Jacobson, Tanya Jones, Mary McKay and David Coleman, who support Jack's and Mark's businesses with skill and love.

Bret Witter, Lisa Drucker, Susan Heim, Allison Janse and Kathy Grant, the editorial department at Health Communications, Inc., for their devotion to excellence.

Terry Burke, Tom Galvin, Lori Golden, Kelly Johnson Maragni, Randee Feldman, Patricia McConnell, Elisabeth Rinaldi, Kim Weiss, Paola Fernandez-Rana and Teri Peluso, the marketing, sales, administration and PR departments at Health Communications, Inc., for doing such an incredible job supporting our books.

Tom Sand, Claude Choquette and Luc Jutras, who manage year after year to get our books translated into thirty-nine languages around the world.

The art department at Health Communications, Inc., for

their talent, creativity and unrelenting patience in producing book covers and inside designs that capture the essence of *Chicken Soup*: Larissa Hise Henoch, Lawna Patterson Oldfield, Andrea Perrine Brower, Lisa Camp, Anthony Clausi and Dawn Von Strolley Grove.

All the *Chicken Soup for the Soul* coauthors, who make it such a joy to be part of this *Chicken Soup* family: Raymond Aaron, Matthew E. Adams, Patty and Jeff Aubery, Kirk Autio, Nancy Mitchell Autio, Marty Becker, John Boal, Cynthia Brian, Cindy Buck, Ron Camacho, Barbara Russell Chesser, Dan Clark, Tim Clauss, Barbara De Angelis, Don Dible, Mark and Chrissy Donnelly, Irene Dunlap, Rabbi Dov Peretz Elkins, Dorothy Firman, Frances Firman Salorio, Julie Firman, Bud Gardner, Patty Hansen, Jennifer Read Hawthorne, Kimberly Kirberger, Carol Kline, Tom and Laura Lagana, Tommy Lasorda, Sharon Linnea, Dr. Fabrizio Mancini, Janet Matthews, Hanoch and Meladee McCarty, Heather McNamara, Katy McNamara, John McPherson, Paul J. Meyer, Arline Oberst, Marion Owen, Maida Rogerson, Martin Rutte, Amy Seeger, Marci Shimoff, Sidney Slagter, Barry Spilchuk, Robin Stephens, Pat Stone, Carol Sturgulewski, Jim Tunney, LeAnn Thieman, Diana von Welanetz Wentworth and Sharon Wohlmuth.

Our glorious panel of readers who helped us make the final selections and made invaluable suggestions on how to improve the book:

Kathy Brennan-Thompson, Fred Angelis, Stefanie Barenblat, Matisun Barton, Sarah Bates, Liam Bauer, Joe Davis, Holly Deme, Bobby, Daisy and Aaron Eisenberg, Gloria Eisenberg, Barry Elkin, Tanya Everett, Alyssa Factor, Kathy Freudenstein, Harold and Wilma Frey, Debbie and Mike Gold, Kathryn Hall, Charley Heavenrich, Leigh Hennessy, Patricia Highland, Rebecca Law, Barbara LoMonaco, Jennifer Martin, Ron and Bonnie Murdock, Carol Parker, Elizabeth Roberts, Joanne Reid Rodrigues, Chuck and Sharon Root, Harry Strunk, Madeline Westbrook and Beth Wilson.

And, most of all, everyone who submitted their heartfelt stories, poems, quotes and cartoons for possible inclusion in this book. While we were not able to use everything you sent in, we know that each word came from a creative place deep within your soul.

Because of the size of this project, we may have left out the names of some people who contributed along the way. If so, we are sorry, but please know that we really do appreciate you very much.

We are truly grateful and love you all.

Introduction

Despite our differences in race, culture, religion, beliefs and values, we share the experience of the human body. In our physical selves we find common ground. Even our anatomical differences pale when compared to our similarities. Women and men, aborigines and members of parliament, communists and republicans, Christians and Jews, Muslims and Buddhists bleed when cut, laugh when tickled—know hunger, pleasure, pain and love.

By virtue of the human body, we are one humanity.

Our body is, in fact, the only thing we are guaranteed to keep for a lifetime; it is our only true possession, the soul's only lifetime companion. We live, learn, laugh, love, teach, fail, succeed and fulfill our destinies only through the body. It deserves our care and kindness, because without a body, where would we live?

We did not make our bodies. Our mothers served as sacred harbors as our bodies developed, handcrafted by angels. From the beginning of the dance of life—embryo growing, infant learning, toddler walking, child running, adult seeking—our body changes according to our soul's struggles, journeys and destinies.

Every human advance or achievement flows from action—doing things with our eyes and ears, arms and legs, hands and feet, mouth and head. Physics informs us that the matter of our body is made of light, energy, spirit. How can we experience the soul except through the body? When we are uplifted, inspired, renewed or redeemed—when we have an epiphany, a realization—these are physical revelations.

Chicken Soup to Inspire the Body and Soul celebrates our body—our physical life, our goals and dreams, our struggles, courage and spirit. Our challenges in the body test and teach us as we stretch the envelope in sports, work and everyday life; as we sweat and toil to get or stay in shape; as we recover after injury or illness.

For all its imperfections, all its various shapes and quirks and needs, our body remains our best friend and most staunch supporter. It can be as loyal as a dog, as supple as a cat—and take us to heights known only by the eagle. If we treat it with respect and care, it will serve us into our autumn years, and take us deep into the winter seasons until it's time to say good-bye.

Chicken Soup to Inspire the Body and Soul celebrates our soul's journey in, as and through our body. The variety of stories—from sports to self-image, from weight loss to healing—reflect our human heritage of struggles, challenges and dreams. It has been our privilege and pleasure to compile and edit these reminders and revelations. May these stories of body and soul remind us that we are in this together.

Share with Us

We would love to hear your reactions to the stories in this book. Please let us know what your favorite stories were and how they affected you.

We also invite you to send us stories you would like to see published in future editions of *Chicken Soup for the Soul*. You can send us either stories you have written or stories written by others. Please send submissions to:

Chicken Soup for the Soul
P.O. Box 30880
Santa Barbara, CA 93130
Fax: 805-563-2945

You can also access e-mail or find a current list of planned books at the *Chicken Soup for the Soul* Web site at *www.chickensoup.com*. Find out about our Internet service at *www.club chickensoup.com*.

We hope you enjoy reading this book as much as we enjoyed compiling, editing and writing it.

$\overline{\underline{1}}$

YES, I CAN!

Follow your dreams, for as you dream, so shall you become.

James Allen

Joey's Gold Medal

There are two lasting bequests we can give our children: One is roots. The other is wings.

Hodding Carter, Jr.

It was 1988 and I had just graduated from high school. It was my first summer working with the Special Olympics. I had volunteered that spring and was assigned as a trainer for a young man named Joey. He was eighteen years old, had Down's syndrome and was a delight to be with. He wore a perpetual smile and was quick to laugh and give a thumbs-up to everyone he saw, peering at the world through his thick, Coke-bottle glasses, which he polished habitually. Standing just under five feet tall, Joey was everyone's friend. His race was the long one-quarter-mile run, the full lap around the track.

At each practice, I stood at the finish line and called out: "What are we going to do, Joey?" as he rounded the final corner,

"We're gonna win!" he shouted back.

We hit the track every Saturday for the six weeks preceding the race, and his time slowly improved until he was making the finish line in just less than three minutes. We would follow up our practice with a trip to the local burger joint, where every week he would tell the waitress that he couldn't have French fries.

"I'm in training," he said proudly. He always added, "I'm going to win a gold medal and could I please have a salad?"

As summer neared, the girls at the restaurant would all come over to talk to him. "What's your best time so far?" "How did practice go?" They patted him on the back and wished him luck. Joey basked in their adoration.

The day of the race, I picked him up in my van; his mother kissed him good-bye and said she would be there for the race. We loaded his gym bag and drove to a local high school where the Special Olympics were being held. Joey was so wound up he could hardly sit in his seat, his hands drumming constantly on his knees, stopping only to polish and repolish his glasses. We arrived, parked and signed in, and received our race assignment and number. On our way to the sidelines, I realized that something was terribly wrong.

I asked, "Where are your glasses?"

Joey stared back at me, blinking owlishly, "I dunno . . ."

I got him started on his stretching and went back to search the van from top to bottom and end to end. I found no glasses. I walked back through the parking lot searching the ground, but there was no sign of them.

When I returned to the field, Joey had finished stretching and was jogging in place, keeping his legs warm. Knowing that he was nearly blind without his glasses, my heart was breaking as I sat him down on the bench.

"I don't know if you're going to be able to race today," I began as his chin began to tremble. "I just don't think it's safe," I continued. "Without your glasses, you could get hurt."

His eyes began to fill. "But we're gonna win," he said, voice cracking, "I'm going to win a medal!"

I sat there for a moment, struggling with my own disappointment and Joey's anguish. Then I had an idea. "Come with me."

We walked over to the track and I stood him in his lane. I pointed to the white line on his right: "Can you see that line?"

He peered at his feet. "Yes."

I pointed to the line on his left. "How about that one?"
"Yes."

"Okay," I said. "Now this is very important, Joey. When you run today, you have to keep your eyes on those two lines, and you have to watch very carefully, and not cross over them. Can you do that?"

"Yes."

Still unsure if he could do it, but out of options, I led him back to the starting area. He walked haltingly, squinting badly, one hand slightly out in front of him.

"Is Mom here?" he asked. I scanned the bleachers until I found her and waved. She waved back. "Yeah," I said, "She's in the stands watching."

He waved in the wrong direction.

The other coaches and I got our runners into their lanes and then headed down toward the finish line to cheer them on. The starting gun fired and they were off! Joey was doing well, holding steady in second place until they rounded the first corner. Another boy swerved from his lane into Joey's and he lost sight of his white line. I winced as I watched one sneaker catch the back of the opposite leg and send him sprawling onto the tarmac.

He had fallen before and seemed okay this time. He scrambled to his feet and, pausing to squint at the track, found his lines and started again, limping slightly on his left foot. The rest of the boys had passed him and he was about a quarter track behind. He ran doggedly around the far corner, arms pumping at his sides, and into the straightaway. Just as he was starting to gain on the last boy, his foot slipped again and he dropped to the track, rolling onto his side and groping blindly around him for balance.

I groaned and started forward, but Joey rose to his knees again. He was crying now, and almost started back the wrong way, but he turned toward the finish line as the crowd yelled to turn around. He was limping badly, worn out, arms hanging limply. Twenty feet from the finish line he fell again.

It was too much for him, and I was going to stop it. As I

stepped out onto the track to lead him to the sidelines, I felt a hand on my arm. Joey's mother, her eyes full of tears, was standing beside me.

"He'll be okay," she said. "Let him finish." Then she stepped past me and walked over to stand next to the finish line.

"Joe," she called over the crowd, "It's Mommy. Can you hear me?"

His sweaty, tear-stained face came up, searching blindly through a sea of blurred faces.

"Joey," she called again. "Come this way, honey . . ."

I watched as he rose to his feet for the third time, his palms, elbows and knees scraped and bloody, but he stood up and began hobbling toward the finish line again.

"This way, Joey," his mother called again, and his face broke into a smile like the sun through the clouds, as he crossed the finish line and fell into his mother's arms.

As I ran toward them through the roaring applause of the crowd, I could hear him telling his mother again and again, "I won, Momma, did you see me win, I won . . ."

Joey took home two gold medals that day, one for his race and one for best spirit.

He had earned them both.

Perry P. Perkins

Playing for Keeps: Michael Jordan and the World He Made

Don't fear the space between your dreams and reality. If you can dream it, you can do it.

Belva Davis

In the past, America's ideal of beauty had always been an essentially white one; American males had looked longingly in the mirror hoping to see Cary Grant or Gregory Peck or Robert Redford. Michael Jordan, shaved head and all, had given America nothing less than a new definition of beauty for a new age.

What America and the rest of the world saw now was nothing less than a kind of New World seigneur, a young man whose manner seemed nothing less than princely. He was most assuredly not to the manner born—his paternal grandfather had been a tobacco sharecropper in North Carolina. His parents were simple and hardworking people, the first in their families to enjoy full rights of American citizenship, and they produced a young man who carried himself with remarkable natural grace. Because of the loving way he had been raised and because of the endless series of triumphs he had scored over the years, his personal comfort zone was dauntingly high; he had an inner confidence that was simply unshakable.

His manner with all kinds of people in even the briefest of meetings was usually graceful, particularly for someone subjected to so many pressures, and those upon whom he smiled seemed the grander for it. He had charm, was very much aware of it, and used it skillfully and naturally, rationing it out in just the proper doses, holding it back when it served his purpose. He was easy to like, and people seemed to vie to be liked by him. Veteran sportswriter Mark Heisler once noted in a magazine article that he had never wanted an athlete to like him as much as he did Michael Jordan.

Because of all this, he had become a great salesman as well as a great basketball player. He sold the game of basketball to millions of people in different lands who had never seen it played before and to millions of others who had never seen it played *like this* before. He sold everything from Nike sneakers if you wanted to jump high, to Big Macs if you were hungry.

Each year he seemed to add a new chapter to the legend in the making. Probably the most remarkable chapter had been written in June, when he woke up violently ill before Game Five of the NBA finals against the Utah Jazz. Whether it was altitude sickness or food poisoning, no one was ever sure. Later it was reported that he had woken up with a fever of 103. That was not true: his temperature was high, but not that high, not over 100, but he had been so ill during the night that it seemed impossible that he would play. At about 8 A.M., Jordan's bodyguards called Chip Schaefer, the team trainer, to tell him that Jordan was deathly ill. Schaefer rushed to Jordan's room and found him curled up in a fetal position, wrapped in blankets and pathetically weak. He had not slept at all. He had an intense headache, and had suffered violent nausea throughout the night. The greatest player in the world looked like a frail, weak zombie. It was inconceivable that he might play that day.

Schaefer immediately hooked him onto an IV and tried to get as much fluid into him as possible. He also gave him some medication so he could rest that morning. More than most people, Schaefer understood the ferocity that drove Michael Jordan, the invincible spirit that allowed him to play in games when most high-level professionals were betrayed by their bodies and, however reluctantly, obeyed them. During the 1991 finals against the Lakers, when Jordan badly injured his toe while hitting a crucial jump shot to tie the game, Schaefer had struggled to create a shoe that would protect Jordan's foot in the next game. Jordan eventually rejected the shoe because it hindered his ability to start and stop and cut. "Give me the pain," he had told Schaefer.

Now, seeing him that sick in the Salt Lake City hotel room, Schaefer had a sense that Jordan might somehow manage to play, that Michael Jordan might, as he sometimes did in situations like this, use this illness as a motivational tool, one more challenge to overcome. He did make it to the locker room before the game, still frail and weak. Word circulated quickly among journalists that he had the flu and that his temperature was 102, and many assumed he would not play. One member of the media who was not so sure about that verdict was James Worthy of the Fox network. He had played with Michael Jordan at North Carolina and watched him emerge as the best player in the NBA, and he knew how Michael drove himself. The fever meant nothing, Worthy told the other Fox reporters. "He'll play," Worthy warned. "He'll figure out what he can do, he'll conserve his strength in other areas, and he'll have a big game."

In the locker room, Jordan's teammates were appalled by what they saw. Michael's skin, normally quite dark, was an alarming color, somewhere between white and gray, and his eyes, usually so vital, looked dead. As the game was about to begin, the NBC television crew showed pictures of a frail and haggard Jordan as he had arrived at the Delta Center, barely able to walk, but they showed him trying to practice. It was one of those rare moments of unusual intimacy in sports, when the power of television allowed the viewer to see both Jordan's illness and his determination to play nonetheless. This was to be a unique participatory experience: when before had illness and exhaustion showed so clearly on the face of such an athlete so early in such a vital game? At first, it appeared that the Jazz would blow the very vulnerable Bulls out. At one point early in the second quarter, Utah led 36–20. But the Bulls hung in because Jordan managed to play at an exceptionally high level, scoring twenty-one points in the first half. At halftime his team was down only four points, 53–49. It was hard to understand how Jordan could play at all, much less be the best player on the floor. The unfolding drama of the event transcended basketball.

He could barely walk off the court at halftime. During the break, he told Phil Jackson not to use him much in the second half—just in spots. Then he came out and played almost the entire second half. He played a weak third quarter, scoring only two points, but Utah could not put Chicago away. Late in the fourth quarter, when the camera closed in on him as he ran down court after a basket, Jordan looked less like the world's greatest athlete than the worst runner in some small-time marathon, about to finish last on a brutally hot day. But what he looked like and what he was doing on the floor when it mattered were two separate things.

With forty-six seconds left and Utah leading by a point, Jordan was fouled going to the basket. "Look at the body language of Michael Jordan," the announcer Marv Albert said. "You have the idea that he has difficulty just standing up." He made the first foul shot, tying the score, then missed the second but somehow managed to grab the loose ball. Then, when the Jazz inexplicably left him open, he hit a three pointer with twenty-five seconds left, which gave Chicago an 88–85 lead and the key to a 90–88 win. He ended up with thirty-eight points, fifteen of them in the last quarter.

It had been an indelible performance, an astonishing display of spiritual determination; he had done nothing less than give a clinic in what set him apart from everyone else in his profession. He was the most gifted player in the league, but unlike most supremely gifted players, he had an additional quality rare among superb artists whose chosen work comes so easily: he was an overachiever as well.

David Halberstam

The Home Stretch

The purpose of life is to matter, to stand for something, to have it make some difference that we lived at all.

Leo Rosten

Four miles! I've only run four miles! I stood at the side of the road, dejected, waiting for a relief wagon to pick me up. I hadn't even run a third of Kansas City's Hospital Hill Half-Marathon. Six months of training down the drain—all because of a microscopic virus.

Sprained muscles, bad weather . . . I thought I planned for it all. But strep throat?

Add medicine that had side effects like rapid heartbeat and shortness of breath; I didn't have a prayer of finishing.

Regardless, my parents met me at the finish line with an armful of pink roses. The offering was bittersweet, since I clutched them after climbing out of a van instead of after sprinting across a finish line.

I vowed I'd try again. Unfortunately, Kansas City half-marathons are in short supply, and life got busy again.

For one, I suddenly became a mom of an eight-year-old.

Cute little Mandy Porter had packed all her things, waved good-bye to her foster parents and moved into our spare bedroom. This pixie-like redhead had been passed around like most foster children. Unfortunately, her story was more disheartening than the average one. Twice, she had been placed for adoption and began calling an unfamiliar couple "Mom" and "Dad." Twice, the stress had been too much for these new parents, and they sent little Mandy back to foster care. Social workers call this an "adoption disruption." I call it a soul disruption.

My husband and I would become two more in a line of uncertain parents for Mandy. The very day she moved in, we could see why the disruptions had happened. Little Miss Mandy was a tough cookie—throwing tantrums daily, refusing to comply, being passive, being aggressive, being anything but cooperative.

Seven years had passed since my undoing at Hospital Hill at mile four, but even after all those years, I still felt empty and undone at not having finished the 1994 race. Advertisements for the 2001 half-marathon popped up again on store windows. I mulled over whether or not to try again. I had been having hip pain so badly that I was having trouble sleeping and hadn't run in years.

I oscillated between sending in an application and being realistic. I had little time to prepare. And I had a daughter, now a teenager, who still took immense amounts of time and energy.

I don't quit. I do what I say. I could hear my own words echo back to me. I thought, *This is a perfect opportunity to show this to Mandy—to let her see that I mean it, instead of just hearing it.*

I mailed my application and bought new shoes. I found running routes with big hills like the official Hospital Hill course, and I ran them whenever I could squeeze it in.

Too soon, that Sunday morning arrived. Mandy and I swung into a downtown parking spot and headed to the starting line. I told her, "I hope to finish in two and a half hours. Meet me at the finish line at 10:30."

She nodded.

I lifted her chin and looked into her eyes. "Mandy," I said, "I don't quit. Not in this race, and not on you. I am running this race for *you.*"

With my number pinned securely, I found my place in the mob of runners and lost sight of my precious daughter.

Could I do it? I had to!

I am strong, and I don't quit! I am strong, and I don't quit! It was my mantra, the words that patterned my cadence.

Oh no! Is that a raindrop? The gray sky opened up, and sheets of rain began to pelt us. My shoes became soggy and doubled in weight. The wet socks rubbed my feet, forming instant blisters.

I don't quit! I yelled the words in my mind now, picturing my daughter waiting at the finish line. My hip began to sear with pain, and the raindrops turned to torrents.

I repeated the words, louder and faster at the never-ending hills. Through the pain, I felt exhilarated. *I would do it. I was doing it!*

Sooner than I realized, I rounded a corner to discover the official clock ticking off the finish times. It read "2:13." On the one hand, I was thrilled; regardless of all the obstacles, I had finished fifteen minutes sooner than I expected! On the other hand, I kept picturing Mandy inside where it was dry, watching the clock for the time I told her to come out to meet me.

I sprinted the last few yards, planning my strategy to find Mandy in the thick pack of people inside the Crown Center.

But I didn't have to. There she was—her rain-drenched hair dripping onto her soaked T-shirt. And even through all the raindrops—and now the tears—I could see her beaming smile and her arms open fully to receive me.

"I made it, Mandy! I don't quit!"

"I knew you would, Mom," she said, holding me tightly as we stood in a deepening puddle. "I'm so glad you never quit."

Karen Hayse

Racing for Life

*To suffer confusion is the first step in healing.
Then the pain of contradiction is transformed
into the mystery of paradox. The capacity for
paradox is the measure of spiritual strength.*

Robert Johnson

Breast cancer. These two words, this cold clinical diagnosis,
were to shatter my life, then transform it. The words stirred a
cauldron of red-hot emotions: rage, fear, hatred. Now it seems
so long ago—literally another century, 1982—when the doctor
told me. I remember the day and moment of the dreaded diagnosis as starkly as if it happened yesterday; the taste and smell
of fear still lurk just below the surface of my memory.

It's 1982 and I'm forty-seven years old. I run marathons regularly and long ago gave up alcohol, tobacco and red meat. So
how could I have breast cancer? Surely it's a mistake. Other
people maybe, who don't take care of themselves, but not me,
not now. Not fair!

I hate it when I feel sorry for myself. I'm a strong, self-reliant
female—the equivalent of a lieutenant colonel in the U.S. Air
Force. I shattered the so-called glass ceiling before most people
knew what it was. I've raised two dynamic, smart and

successful children, largely on my own after the breakup of two tough marriages. I've put myself through college up to and including my doctorate. *"I am woman. I am strong. Hear me roar!"* In the vernacular, I am one tough broad. Then why am I so frightened? Why am I crying? Tears are for sissies. My value system, my identity, my whole worldview is shaking under the assault of this terrible revelation; everything is turned upside down. And I'm really, really scared. How much time do I have left? I've taken care of myself since I was fourteen years old. I've never asked for anyone's help, nor have I ever needed it. Now I need help. But whom do I ask? And how do I ask?

Anger, rage and self-pity—scalpels of the psyche—cut at my core with deep and vicious slashes, like a monster turned loose inside me. A jumble of confused and ambivalent feelings rise like bile in my belly—the beginnings of an emotional roller coaster ride gone amok. To calm this emotional holocaust, I revert to the clinician in me. As a way of denial, repression, avoidance, I cling to whatever gives me momentary relief from the maelstrom of grief.

Infiltrating ductal carcinoma—a moderately fast-metastasizing cancer. The doctors had been following it for the three years since I had first reported a suspicious lump in my right breast. Now it had grown to the size of a golf ball. I know because I saw it. I had insisted on watching the surgery when they removed the large, red, ugly mass of deadly tissue. But because the cancer had spread through the whole breast, the surgeons told me that they needed to perform a modified radical mastectomy. As soon as I recovered from *that* surgery, they would then have to remove the other breast due to its high risk of being cancerous as well. Worse yet, in the three-year period that the doctors had been "watching" the tumor, it had spread to my bones and left lung.

Devastated, feeling betrayed by the medical system and by my body, I enrolled in a breast cancer research study conducted by author and physician John McDougall. It required me to follow a vegan diet (pure vegetarian with no animal-derived products). I would have tried anything to help save my life. The only catch here was that I could not take chemotherapy or radiation because the challenge was to see if a vegan diet alone could reverse the cancer. I talked to my then-husband. He thought I was crazy to think that diet had anything to do with breast cancer, and he believed I had fallen into the hands of a quack. Furthermore, he said he was surprised I would fall for "such garbage." None of my friends or family knew what to advise. So I decided to set my own course and follow where it led.

Around the time of my diagnosis, I saw a sporting event on television called the "Ironman Triathlon." I was captivated as I watched these superb young athletes race through a 2.4-mile swim, followed immediately by a 112-mile bike ride, then a full 26.2-mile marathon. "I want to do that," I said, then remembered: *Hold on, Lady, you're a cancer patient and you're forty-seven years old—way too old to do such an event.* But it wasn't just negative self-talk; it was the voice of reason. After all, no woman that old had ever attempted the Ironman. But this idea just wouldn't go away. With my new diet, I could swear I was feeling stronger, lighter, more energetic, faster, healthier and, by God, I decided I was going to do it. I increased my running and added swimming, biking and even weight lifting to my training.

Of course, the doctors thought I was absolutely insane. "You should be resting," they said. "All that stress on your body isn't good for it—running marathons (much less endurance swims and 100-mile bike rides) will depress your immune system." That's when I stopped relying solely on the doctors for advice.

Back in those days, before most people had even heard of triathlons, there was little guidance on how to train for such grueling endurance races. So I just got out there and swam until I couldn't lift my arms, biked until I couldn't pedal anymore, ran until I couldn't run another step and lifted as many pounds as I could without injuring myself. To simulate actual racing conditions, I entered every race I could find. If there were two on the same day, so much the better, because that would force me to race when tired, a condition I knew I'd face doing the Ironman. I entered "The Run to the Sun," a 37-mile run up to the top of Haleakala, a 10,000-foot high mountain on the island of Maui, Hawaii. I remember reaching the twenty-six-mile point and looking back down at the ocean far, far below, not believing that these two legs had already carried me the equivalent of a full marathon—straight uphill. Then I turned back toward the mountaintop, still more than ten miles beyond. My internal response was *I don't have it in me; I just can't do it.* My next thought was, *Listen, Lady, if you think this is rough, just wait until you get in the Ironman!* That's what kept me going. If I quit here, how could I face the Ironman? That technique served me well in the coming months. And competing and winning first-place trophies in my age-group events added to the post-race highs.

I found myself getting stronger and developing muscles I never knew I had. I was passing my cancer checkups as well: The hot spots in my bones—once a source of despair because they indicated cancer—were disappearing, and the tumor in my lung stayed the same size, allowing me to avoid chemo and/or radiation, and to stay in the dietary study.

The only real reminder of the cancer were the two postsurgical, angry red gashes, which left a chest that resembled a prepubescent male's. Because of all my training, I was having to shower and change clothes several times a day, so the reminders of the cancer were constant. I wanted so much to have a normal body again. Enter the plastic surgeons, who gave me a fabulous choice: I could now pick my new size. "You want a 'C'?" they said. "We can do that!" I told them I wouldn't be greedy—"Just give me what I had before, a nice, average 'B'." They also gave me something else I never thought possible: breasts that will never sag. I believe you have to look at the positive side of life, and now, at sixty-eight years old, I can really appreciate this benefit.

Today, there's no sign of cancer in my body. I've continued my vegan, low-fat diet now for more than twenty years, and I have never been healthier or more fit in my life. To date I have raced the Ironman Triathlon six times, plus over a hundred shorter triathlons, a total of sixty-seven marathons, plus hundreds of shorter road races. In 1999, I was named one of the Ten Fittest Women in America by *Living Fit* magazine. In February 2000, on a Fitness Age test, my score was equivalent to a fit thirty-two-year-old's. My aerobic capacity score was that of a sixteen-year-old. My bone density has increased throughout my fifties and sixties, which is supposed to be "impossible" since most people are told they will *lose* bone density as part of the "natural" aging process. My blood pressure runs 90/60; my cholesterol is under 150; I have 15 percent body fat, and my hemoglobin—the test for iron in the blood—is at the top of the charts.

I do not share this information about my physical condition to boast (although I admit I'm proud of it), but to show what can be accomplished through dedication and discipline.

Since I'm a vegan—I eat no flesh or dairy products—I'm "supposed" to be deficient in protein, calcium and iron. Perhaps I'm an anomaly by most medical standards. And maybe a vegan diet and endurance exercise won't be a magical answer for everyone, but I stand as an example of a lifestyle change that might be worth exploring. And I'm not alone. Most people know how Tour de France champion Lance Armstrong also demonstrated the power of racing for life after his own battles with cancer.

When will this awesome journey end? Will I have to slow down gradually, let go, cut back to walking laps around a retirement community? I really can't say. But I know this: I had cancer and it had spread; I might have folded my cards back then, but I chose life, and I'm going to live as long as I can and run the good race. Maybe only a few will take the path I've chosen, but if sharing my story helps a few more to step forward and race for life, it will have been all the more worthwhile.

Ruth Heidrich, Ph.D.

A Marathon of Dreams

We've removed the ceiling from our dreams.

Jesse Jackson

In 1996, the possibility of manifesting my dreams didn't exist for me: I topped the scales at 219 pounds, food cravings ruled my life and the call for physical activity had faded to a faint whisper. Yet after reading *Make the Connection*, by Oprah Winfrey and Bob Greene, her trainer and coauthor, two outlandish dreams popped into my head: first, to achieve my goal weight; second, to run a marathon with Bob. These dreams were so far from reality that they seemed laughable.

Years of being overweight had left my self-esteem sunk in a swamp of despair. Still, I remembered the ray of hope I held when I found a private journal entry I wrote for my eighth-grade teacher. *"People think I'm undisciplined, but I know in my heart that if I wanted to run from Nome to China* (two small towns in Texas four miles apart) *I could do it."* Since my twelve-year-old body weighed 197 pounds that year, my teacher must have secretly laughed at that entry.

I had starved myself to a presentable weight three times in the last thirty-six years, but the thinness never lasted. Now a mother with three children under the age of seven, it seemed inconceivable that I could stay on a sensible eating program or train for anything farther than a walk to the mailbox.

However, after reading Bob Greene and Oprah Winfrey's book, I made the commitment to walk *past* the mailbox. At five every morning, I put on my size twenty-two shorts and walked in the darkness, too ashamed to have anyone see me. As I walked, I imagined Bob walking beside me and offering encouragement along the way. In my mind, he told me to keep my arms pumping and hold fast to my dreams, and he promised I *could* run a marathon, if I wanted it enough.

Did I ever! In high school, fascinated with marathon running and the feats of Bill Rodgers and Frank Shorter, I'd written a paper: "Long-Distance Running for Women." Inspired by what I learned, I began running around the football field, eventually covering three miles a day.

During the first week of walking more and eating better, I applied the idea that dreams shouldn't remain hidden—that one should "get them out into reality" by writing them down. On a whim, I sent a letter to Bob in care of the *Oprah* show, asking him to run a marathon with me once I'd achieved my goal weight.

It felt good to write the letter. Then I forgot about it.

Five days later a call from the *Oprah* show catapulted me back into the reality of what I had done. Although the producer didn't promise Greene would read the letter, she wanted to stay in touch about a possible future show appearance. Nothing spurs one toward a weight goal like the threat of putting a size twenty-two butt on national television. I immediately laced up my shoes and logged five miles that day.

I sent the producers an update and picture each month, but I continued addressing the letter to Bob, in hopes he'd eventually see the pictures and agree to the request. As the months passed, the weight came off. I even ran my first 5K.

The biggest obstacle to weight loss hit like a Texas twister. With a job transfer, my family needed to move from Houston to Denver. Almost as soon as I arrived, a fall from a ladder left me in a cast, with hopes of running a marathon postponed until late that year.

Then one day I heard a radio announcement saying Bob
Greene would be in town for a fitness presentation. I brushed off
the dream, called a new acquaintance to tag along and brought
the pictures and update letters about my training. I managed to
speak with Bob at the book signing. The pictures of my weight
loss while training for the marathon were quite dramatic, and he
said he'd take them back to Oprah's production company. He
added, however, that it would be their decision, not his, if anything came of it. I hoped that he'd agree to my request to run a
marathon with him, but I also convinced my friend Terri to train
for a spring marathon with me, so even if Bob didn't commit, I'd
go ahead with the goal. Happily, Terri said yes to early morning
runs, blistered feet and long hours of training.

The next day we began running, and developed a tremendous bond during eight months of training. However, the dream
began to change: no longer just *my* dream, it was now *our* dream
to achieve the goal together. We moaned through the pain, we
laughed through the runs (mostly at ourselves) and rejoiced in
each small success.

I continued to send Bob a letter and a picture each month
about my request, since he had given me his address.

Months later, Terri and I stood at the starting line of Grandma's
Marathon in Duluth, Minnesota. We'd long ago dismissed hopes
that Bob would run this marathon with us, but it no longer mattered. I stood on the verge of realizing a twenty-year-old dream,
and Terri and I had each other. We ran the race side-by-side and
finished the twenty-six miles with tears in our eyes, hands
clasped together above our heads.

Completing the marathon masked the residual pain I felt
those first days after the run. Needing to go back to work full-
time, Terri stopped training with me. I had already begun
thinking of the next race, so I turned to the support of my new
online friends, and we made plans to run a marathon together
and finally meet in person.

Four months later, I stood at the starting line of the Portland
Marathon—this time, arm-in-arm with my new friends. One of
the women had requested *Runner's World* do a story on our

group and encouraged the *Oprah* show to send a camera crew, along with Bob Greene.

It's not often that "back of the pack" marathoners have a camera in their faces throughout the race, but on this day our group became television personalities.

After going out too fast with some of the younger women, I started struggling around mile ten. But at mile seventeen my struggle ended. Not in a collapse, but in a surge of new energy. When many people are getting ready to hit the wall, I hit the afterburners, because as I trudged to the top of St. John's bridge, Bob Greene appeared alongside me and said he'd be running to the finish line with me. Tears welled up in my eyes.

Over the course of the next nine miles, Bob and I talked about our dreams. He expressed his belief and experience that once we set our mind on a course, we attract events and people into our lives to transform our dream into reality. I'm a believer now!

Marcia Horn Noyes

Marcia Horn Noyes

Photo reprinted by permission of Marcia Horn Noyes and Bob Greene.

Esmerelda's Song

*I learned to speak as I learned to skate or cycle:
by doggedly making a fool of myself until I got
used to it.*

George Bernard Shaw

In my long athletic career as a gymnast, I had trained with the best. At Stanford University I coached the top Olympians and a nationally ranked team. But my favorite students were beginners—especially adult novices, filled with doubt about their abilities, but game enough to try.

Students of all ages and abilities would show up for my gymnastics classes—little boys with oversized shorts and mismatched socks; little girls with red pigtails and matching freckles; adolescents and adults who looked warily around at the apparatus, their fear mingled with excitement. Over the years I taught them—in a rooftop room at the Berkeley YMCA, in a fancy gym club in Atlanta and in a tiny studio in San Francisco—at Stanford, Berkeley and finally, Oberlin College.

There, I remember an amazing, heavyset young man named Darwin, blind from birth, who announced that he had his heart set on learning a front flip on the trampoline. Darwin's lack of balance or visual cues led me to doubt the likelihood of his learning even the basics of trampoline, much less a somersault. But I welcomed him to class and said we'd take it one step—or rather, one bounce—at a time. After many months of preparation and many failed attempts, on the last day of class Darwin Neuman accomplished a front somersault, to the cheers and tears of everyone in the class. I remember the mixture of surprise and delight on Darwin's face; I remember the moment as if it were yesterday.

I also remember other students, of course—one is a now-famous Broadway star. And over the years, many students have made me a believer by showing, again and again, the power of persistence.

But most of all, I remember Esme.

Her real name was Esmerelda Esperanza Garcia, but she asked me to call her Esme that first day of my ten-week course in basic gymnastics at Oberlin. Esme had no particular disabilities—she could see and hear and to all appearances was in good physical health—although she was a bit thin and frail for the rigors of bars and beam. As it turned out, I had never before met a teaching challenge like Esme. Something had brought her to me and to one of the more challenging physical education classes at Oberlin. She brought with her a set of psychological baggage that included her self-image as a klutz, and she seemed determined to demonstrate that each day. Esme didn't just fall behind everyone else—she was like a golfer who played entirely in the rough, never touching a fairway.

To fully appreciate what Esme faced, understand this: each term, as new students wandered into the gymnastics area and looked around, I would call them together and demonstrate a full exercise routine on the floor and on all the apparatus. These included a variety of swings, arm changes, handstands, cartwheels, and rolls and dance elements requiring flexibility, strength, coordination, balance, stamina and reflex speed. Then, as I watched the looks of incredulity, doubt or total disbelief on their faces, I would then predict that they would indeed be able to do every one of those routines by the term's end.

One of the greatest joys I experienced as a teacher was to help my students to do far more than they believed they could accomplish. So my courses became something more than mere skill learning; in transcending their limiting beliefs in this area of life, my students were more likely to excel in other areas as well. I believe that most students returned the second day on trust alone—on blind faith that "this guy might be able to deliver what he promises." So, beginning on the proverbial wing and a prayer, on hope and dreams and the challenge I'd set before them, they began.

In Esme's case, she had complete faith—negative faith. She was certain she could not even come close to what I had predicted, but at least she would learn something. Apparently intent on convincing me of her ineptitude, she told me stories of glasses of milk knocked over on the dinner table; of slips and falls, and of being the last-to-be-picked for every team in every sport at every school she attended. She was giving it another try because she had heard that I was a "miracle worker," and said she needed a miracle at that point in her life.

I'd like to say that a miracle happened—that Esme became the star of the class and went on to the Olympics, or some such thing, but that would be sheer fantasy. Esme trailed behind the class all the way to the end, and received a "B" for persistence, effort and yes, some discernable improvement.

But then she did something no student had ever done— Esme asked if she could take the same course over again. Normally, I would decline, because the class had a long waiting list, and new students should have an opportunity to participate. This time I made an exception.

By the third week of class, even with her head start, Esme was again behind half the class. But this meant she was even with, or ahead of the other half!—a new experience for her, and one that did not escape her notice. She was like a runner who glances back to see people behind her for the first time. This struck her with the force of revelation, and something wonderful happened—Esme was stuck in a handstand. Not permanently, but for a few wonderful seconds, her handstand was so straight, and so well balanced, she just hung up there, to my surprise and to her amazement. She came down beaming, and the entire class applauded.

A light went on inside Esmerelda Garcia on that day, in that moment.

After that, she started pleading with me to spend a little extra time to help her after class—with her cartwheel, her balance beam dismount, her hip circle on the uneven bars. She asked questions, tried, fell, asked more questions, tried again, her face focused with an intensity I'd only seen in world-class gymnasts and young children. Now it was do-or-die for Esmerelda Esperanza Garcia.

By the term's end, Esme got through every single routine, with only one minor fall and a few bobbles. The class members, who had come to know and help one another in their common endeavor, had come to know Esmerelda as well, and to respect her dedication. As she completed her last routine, they gave her a standing ovation. She laughed. Then she broke down in tears.

Who would have guessed that a two-unit physical education class could change someone's life?

My only bittersweet regret in teaching was that I hadn't learned more about each of my students—their lives outside the gymnasium. They showed up, were gymnasts for an hour and a half, two days a week, for ten weeks; then they left the gymnasium and went on with other classes, other lives.

As it happens, Oberlin College has one of the finest conservatories of music in the United States. And one of the many things I had not known about Esme was that she was a conservatory student, and that her specialty was voice.

In mid-April, after the last snowfall, as the first touch of spring warmed the air—about four months after Esme's triumphant completion of my class—I was walking through Tappan Square, the park directly across from the conservatory. I noticed an announcement sign—"Senior Recital: Vocalist . . ."—an announcement I would have passed by with barely a glance, until I saw the name of the vocalist: "Esmerelda Garcia."

That night I sat in a small audience of students, faculty and friends of Esme. I sat mesmerized by her voice, her skill, her charisma and her radiant singing. Again, her performance was rewarded with well-earned applause, which I joined enthusiastically.

I believe someone told her that I had attended, because when I returned home that evening, I found a note by my door. It read:

"Dear Dan, I was at an impasse in my singing and my life, and about to give up. Then I met you and learned what I could do." It was signed:

"With love and gratitude, Esme."

I gazed out into an evening made more beautiful by Esme's song. Memories of her voice mingled with images of her in the gymnasium, blending like the spring breeze through the blossoming apple trees. It felt good to be a teacher, good to be alive.

Dan Millman

New Year's Resolution

*Nobody can go back and start a new begin-
ning, but anyone can start today and make a
new ending.*

Maria Robinson

Hello Body, I wrote in my journal and listened inwardly for an
answer. My belly growled back, *It's about time you paid some attention to me!*

How did my body and I lose rapport? It began in my agonizing year in junior high when I grew eight inches in one year and
didn't know what size my feet would be when my lanky form
climbed out of bed in the morning. *This body,* I thought, *is* way
out of control. So I began to pretend that it didn't exist. I fed and
clothed it, but hoped if I otherwise ignored it, it might go away.

Determined to heal my mind/body rift, I mustered my
courage and marched into a gym near my home, looking for a
personal trainer. I had never done any deliberate exercise other
than walking, so this was going to be a *big* stretch.

The bronzed, sculpted woman at the desk could have been a
model in a muscle magazine. Gathering my courage, I took a
breath, and on the exhale I said, "I'd like a trial session." Clearly
bored by the prospect of a midlife client, she put me through an

extraordinary number of impossible-for-me exercises, all the while pursing her lips and stealing seductive glances at herself in the mirror.

She could have the mirror. Feeling old and frumpy, I hated every minute on the torture machines, but pride kept me in the game. Muttering *this is good for me* like a mantra, I signed up for twelve sessions, and paid in advance.

Buyer's remorse descended like a dark cloud when I got home, but I vowed to do it for one month no matter what. The next day I could hardly move; every muscle in my body ached. I canceled my appointment. Still sore two days later, I called and asked for my money back. No one returned my call; the contract's fine print told me no refunds. I'd gotten myself into this pickle and I would have to live with it.

For the next few months, I vented my anger doing exercise videos at home. *It's too much trouble to go to a gym,* I told myself. *I like the privacy of working alone.* But these solo sessions at home were inconsistent, and I knew I needed weight training to get results.

One day my psychologist-daughter Lexi told me over lunch that she had begun working out at a gym and raved about the improvement in her body tone, energy level and stamina. Meanwhile, I recounted my hard luck story, getting tired of my whining litany.

Lexi offered to drive across town to join me at my gym so I bit the bullet and made an appointment with a different trainer. He and Lexi had me laughing all through the session. We clarified my goals and set a schedule of three times a week.

I attended every session, worked at a moderate pace and never suffered the soreness of the original workout again. Sure enough, I began to love the surge of energy and satisfaction that came after each session. When the month was up, I signed up for three more—then three more months after that. By then I found a trainer named Mike Krpan who came right to my house for the same price as the gym, and I've stayed with twice-weekly workouts for almost five years. I realize that not everyone can afford or needs to hire a personal trainer, but that's what works for me.

I'm amazed at how much my formerly ignored body has changed. Even though I weigh only three pounds less than when I began, weight is no longer an issue. Now when I look in a mirror, I purse my lips and smile as I see firm arms and shoulders, a slimmer waist, flatter tummy, taut and toned thighs, and straighter posture. Best of all, I feel years younger.

I was shopping with Lexi the other day, and I tried on a rather revealing dress. "Wow," she said, "guess I'll have to call you 'Buff Mama!'"

The time and effort it took to train these last few years were one of the best investments of my life. Now when I ask my body what it would like me to do, it tells me I'm doing just fine. In the place of anger and frustration is a new sense of teamwork and partnership, my body and soul.

Diana von Welanetz Wentworth

Stretch Marks

Inside every older woman is a young girl wondering what the hell happened.

Cora Harvey Armstrong

For most of my life I have pursued a policy toward my body that could best be characterized as benign neglect. From the time I could remember until the time I was fifteen it looked one way, and from the time I was fifteen until I was thirty it looked another way. Then, in the space of two years, I had two children and more weight changes than Ted Kennedy, and my body headed south without me.

So I go to this gym three times a week, and here is how it works. First I go into the locker room. On the wall is an extremely large photograph of a person named Terri Jones wearing what I can only assume is meant to be a bathing suit. The caption above her body says "Slim, Strong and Sexy." It is accurate. I check to make sure no one else is in the locker room, then I take my clothes off. As soon as I've done this, one of two people will enter the locker room: either an eighteen-year-old who looks as good out of her clothes as in them who spontaneously confides to me that she is having an affair with a young lawyer whose wife has really gone to seed since she had her two kids, or a fifty-year-old woman who has had nine children, weighs 105 and has abdominal muscles you could bounce a quarter off and who says she can't understand why, maybe it's her metabolism, but she can eat anything she wants, including a pint of Frusen Gladje Swiss chocolate almond candy ice cream, and never gain a pound. So then I go out and exercise.

I do Nautilus. It is a series of fierce-looking machines, each designed, according to this book I have, to exercise some distinct muscle group, which all happen in my case never to have been exercised before. Nautilus was allegedly invented by Arthur Jones, husband of the aforementioned slim, strong and sexy Terri, who is his seventeenth wife, or something like that. But I think anyone who comes upon a Nautilus machine suddenly will agree with me that its prototype was clearly invented at some time in history when torture was considered a reasonable alternative to diplomacy. Over each machine is a little drawing of a human body—not mine, of course—with a certain muscle group inked in red. This is so you can recognize immediately the muscle group that is on fire during the time you are using the machine.

There is actually supposed to be a good reason to do Nautilus, and it is supposed to be that it results in a toning without bulk; that is, you will look like a dancer, not a defensive lineman. That may be compelling for Terri Jones, but I chose it because it takes me only a little more than a half hour—or what I like to think of as the time an average person burning calories at an average rate would need to read *Where the Wild Things Are, Good Night, Moon* and *The Cat in the Hat* twice—to finish all the machines. It is also not social, like aerobics classes, and will not hold you up to widespread ridicule, like running. I feel about exercise the same way that I feel about a few other things: that there is nothing wrong with it if it is done in private by consenting adults.

Actually, there are some of the Nautilus machines I even like. Call it old-fashioned machisma, but I get a kick out of building biceps. This is a throwback to all those times when my brothers would flex their arms and a mound of muscle would appear, and I would flex mine and nothing would happen, and they'd laugh and go off somewhere to smoke cigarettes and look at dirty pictures. There's a machine to exercise the inner thigh muscles that bears such a remarkable resemblance to a delivery room apparatus that every time I get into it I think someone is going to yell, *Push!* and I will have another baby. I feel comfortable with that one. On the other hand, there is another machine on which I am supposed to lift a weight straight up in the air and the most I ever manage is to squinch my face up until I look like an infant with bad gas. My instructor explained to me that this is because women have no upper body strength, which probably explains why I've always found it somewhat difficult to carry a toddler and an infant up four flights of stairs with a diaper bag over one shoulder while holding a Big Wheel.

Anyhow, the great thing about working out is that I have met a lot of very nice men. This would be a lot more important if I weren't married and the mother of two. But of course if I was single and looking to meet someone, I would never meet anyone except married men and psychopaths. (This is Murphy's Other Law, named after Doreen Murphy, who in 1981 had a record of eleven bad relationships in one year.) The men I have met seem to really get a kick out of the fact that I work out, not unlike the kick that most of us get out of hearing very small children try to say words like hippopotamus or chauvinist. As one of the men at my gym said, "Most of the people here are guys or women who are uh well hmm umm . . ."

"In good shape," I said.

"I wouldn't have put it like that," he answered.

Because I go to the gym at the same time on the same days, I actually see the same men over and over again. One or two of them are high school students, which I find truly remarkable. When I was in high school, it was a big deal if a guy had shoulders, never mind muscles. So when I'm finished I go back into the locker room and take a shower. The eighteen-year-old is usually in there, and sometimes she'll say something like, "Oh, that's what stretch marks look like." Then I put on my clothes and go home by the route that does not pass Dunkin' Donuts. The bottom line is that I really hate to exercise, but I have found on balance that this working out is all worth it. One day we were walking down the street and one of the guys from my gym—it was actually one of the high school guys, the one with the great pecs—walked by and said, "How ya doing?"

My husband said, "Who the hell is that guy?" and I knew that Nautilus had already made a big difference in my life.

Anna Quindlen

You Don't Have to Wear a Thong to Belong!

Transforming yourself gives light to the whole world.

Ramana Maharishi

In the winter of 1989, I was thirty-one years old and weighed over three hundred pounds. I spent my days on a couch in front of the TV and suffered every minute, barely able to move or even breathe. I had so much to offer—as a mom, as a wife, as a person—but I felt trapped in my miserable shell. More than anything in the world I wanted help, someone to believe in and to believe in me—a friend to take my hand.

That winter I met Ellen Langley, and my life began to change. She was ten years older and nearly as large, but was calm and self-assured. That fascinated me and drew me into what became a big sister-little sister relationship, a gift of precious friendship.

Because of our friendship, I took the first steps toward actually doing something about my body. It started with a Christmas present from Ellen: a month's membership at one of the hottest fitness clubs in Lake Charles.

"Don't worry," Ellen said as she steered me toward the

plate-glass doors. "You're gonna be fine."

I wouldn't have done it if Ellen hadn't come with me. My two little boys had been shocked that morning when their mommy had actually turned off the TV and walked out the door wearing elephant-sized sweatpants and the biggest purple shirt I could find. Now I was amazed as we walked into a room filled with perfect bodies in thongs. Ellen strode in like she owned the place. I was speechless looking at her, as she acted like she was right at home and chatted comfortably with everybody. I, on the other hand, was miserable.

I had already tried the health club scene. Before I'd moved to Lake Charles, I was so lonely and so desperate to find a friendly face that I actually hauled myself to an aerobics studio and signed up for a class. I thought it would be the perfect place to find a friend, but from the minute I slunk into that workout room, the students and instructor alike edged away and averted their eyes. I was so ashamed of my size. I did what I could to keep up, shuffling my feet a little bit and praying for a break, hoping someone would at least say hi.

I had given it my best shot for over a year, only lost a few pounds and was still lonely and ignored. I retreated to food, my source of comfort, love and security. It pushed me past the magic 300-pound mark; it nailed me to the sofa twelve hours a day because I had the lung capacity of a chipmunk. I couldn't even get up to play with my little boys, who had learned not to even bother asking. My emotional fuse was so short that I was snapping at my husband, Keith, and the boys.

Still, there I was at an aerobics studio trying it again. Once the workout began, things got worse. My self-consciousness was displaced by utter despair. The warm-up alone almost killed me. Everyone had their arms up over their heads, stretching, yet I couldn't lift mine past my shoulders. They all bent to touch their toes. I couldn't even see my toes. Then the actual class began—and I just couldn't do it. Two or three minutes of faking it, tapping my toes or whatever, and I had to stop. I felt like a freak. Why was I subjecting myself to this torture?

I looked over at Ellen's strength and told myself, *No, you are not going to quit. You're going to stay here if it kills you.* And it felt like it would. It felt that way for a long time. I learned to ignore the smirks, sideways glances and looks of pity. The first six months it was Ellen's presence and attitude that kept me going. We had to drive thirty miles each way to the classes, and sometimes we'd just sit in the car before class, having what we called "mini-therapy sessions."

One day the owner of the club greeted me by name. "Hi, Dee," she said. It was as if the heavens had opened. Words can't describe what that did for my self-esteem. Here was a woman who was tall, thin as a rail, had zero-percent body fat and a resting heart rate of 42. And she knew my name.

I made that dinky little "Hi" into a mountain of self-esteem, something I could cling to until another crumb came my way. And they kept coming, those crumbs. A growing number of my classmates began treating me like I belonged, once I showed them I was there to stay. Instructors adjusted my movements to fit the restrictions of my body, and in my own way I began to bloom.

By the end of 1990, I was disappointed that I'd only lost thirty pounds, a mere sliver from my beginning weight of over 300. While it didn't seem like much, I could now do things I hadn't done in years. My mood and energy improved, and I was off the couch. I even ventured outside to play with the boys. I wasn't biting my husband's head off, and I could visit friends, shop, work out and just live.

My eating habits were different; I could stop when full and there were no more midnight refrigerator raids. I learned to enjoy the taste of the food now that I wasn't cramming it in, and I didn't lie about the cookies I ate because I wasn't eating the whole package. The change was happening gradually, naturally. I wasn't superdiligent. The place I did my pushing was in the aerobics room, and I let the rest take care of itself.

That aerobics room! Just showing up was a lifesaver. The music, the energy and Ellen—my oasis, the bright spot. Sometimes I'd run out of gas and just stop, wait a while, and then jump back in when I was ready. Sure I felt frustrated, self-conscious and intimidated. Sure I got a little pissed off sometimes. But I persisted . . . and *that* made all the difference in the world.

Then all the good fell away when, caught up in the Christmas rush, I stopped working out for three weeks. I regressed, started stuffing myself again, got cranky, began complaining. Finally, my husband even told me to get lost. "You're a nightmare," he said. He was right. I had slipped badly. I realized that my workout wasn't for my body or appearance or how others felt about me. My workout was for how I felt about *myself*, for how happy I was and how happy that made the people around me, the people I loved.

I returned to the club in January with a vengeance. I thought every day about how my life was changing and about how others could be changed.

I thought to myself, *How many other heavyweights would want to work out at a hard-body studio if they knew they'd be accepted and not too critically compared with the workout animals around them?* How I would have loved people to give me the time of day or feel the instructors reach out. And then I thought, *Why not me?*

The next day I showed up at the studio to ask the owner: "Why can't I be an instructor?" Her reaction was predictable: partly supportive, partly disbelieving.

She said, "Neat idea, Dee." I actually heard in her tone, *Gee, you might be onto something.* Some of the staff, however, thought it was beyond ridiculous.

No matter. I enrolled in a National Dance-Exercise Instructor's Training Association (NDEITA) workshop, which included a written exam. The day of the test, I arrived at the Lake Charles YMCA, one of about thirty men and women.

No one was near my size and, of course, I got the usual "good for you, honey" looks. The daylong exam was a snap, and the next morning I was at the owner's office door with a perfect score.

"All right," I said. "Let's go."

She couldn't believe it. Tossing it back in my court, she told me if I could get ten people to sign up for a month, she'd give me a room and a time slot.

So I made up my own flyers and taped them up at every Weight Watchers location, plus-size clothing shop and grocery store in town. They introduced a brand-new, very-low-intensity pre-aerobics workout specifically for overweight people, taught by an overweight instructor.

Twelve prospects signed up—all women. And so, on a Monday morning in April 1991, I walked into the studio and for the first time stepped to the front of the class.

I could see the owner and the staff watching, getting a load of the misfits. I said a silent prayer, popped my *Got to Git* tape into the machine, punched the "Play" button . . . and . . . kicked . . . aerobic . . . butt.

It was like magic. It felt so good to be in front of that class, motivating them, helping them feel accepted, comfortable, like they belonged—because they did. I watched their faces light up and laugh as they moved. It was the most memorable hour of my life, that first class—the hour went by like a minute. It was incredible.

Beyond the inspiration and identification, I gave everyone specialized attention the second she came through that door, assessing her abilities and adjusting techniques to meet her limitations. No one in that room was going to have to bail out and just watch.

Three years after teaching my first class I was awarded Nike's Fitness Innovation Award for the program I created. *The New Face of Fitness* has been implemented nationally into more than thirty YWCAs through a Nike grant. It has expanded into hospitals, corporations and fitness clubs across the country.

I weigh about 220 pounds and have maintained my hundred-pound loss for years now. I have regular checkups that confirm I've corrected my medical problems, including high blood pressure, elevated blood cholesterol and diabetes.

With all my newfound energy I even wrote a book—*Thin Is Just a Four-Letter Word: Living Fit for All Shapes and Sizes*—that is selling far beyond anyone's wildest dreams.

The last thing on my mind fourteen years ago when Ellen helped me find the courage to walk through those doors was that I could actually teach aerobics classes, much less write a book, work on my own video series, and sign up with an agent who has already negotiated three sports equipment endorsements for me.

The truth is I wouldn't be here if my students hadn't seen a woman their own size in front of those mirrors. They told me so. If I could do that, they said, then by God, so could they.

Dee Hakala

Reprinted by permission of Donna Barstow.

Soaring with Eagles

Once you greet death and understand your heart's position, you wear your life like a garment . . . you wear it lightly, because you realize you never paid anything for it; you cherish it because you know you won't ever come by such a bargain again.

Louise Erdrich

John and I strained forward as if to assist his worn Army surplus Jeep, inching up a steep hill blanketed with loose sliding rock. A heartbeat later, I was hurled to the ground. The Jeep's wheels pointed skyward, spinning dizzily. I screamed for John; then I screamed again. My cries were met with silence.

We had first become acquainted as pen pals. I so admired his struggle to become a doctor and to serve his people with no thought of personal gain. It was not just a profession for John, it was a calling. So when he invited me to spend the summer with him as an assistant and traveling teacher, on vacation from my regular teaching job, I could barely contain my excitement. Many of the families he treated lived in remote areas that often lacked roads, and the small children had no benefit of schooling.

Our first meeting at the airport held no awkwardness—John offered a warm embrace as if we'd been friends forever. Early the next morning we were off on rounds, leaving dusty white whirls behind the Jeep. Abruptly, I cried out: "Stop, John! *Stop!*"

Alarmed, he slammed on the brakes. "What's wrong?"

"Look up there!" I shouted. "Look, an eagle! Oh! It's my very first one." Overcome by its beauty and majesty, I wept.

He leaned to brush away my tears with gentle fingers. "My city girl has heard her first call of the wild," he said quietly. "From this moment on, you shall be known as 'Little Eagle.'

In that moment we fell in love.

Each morning after that, John would call, "Come, Little Eagle, it's time to soar. The children need you."

Whenever we pulled up to a cluster of tiny houses, children would run to hug us. Shouts of "Dr. John and Little Eagle are here!" were a symphony to my ears. How I loved this work. John treated his patients with respect and compassion. He listened before he spoke, and his patients' smiling eyes mirrored the trust he had earned.

I often assisted John until the children tugged at my jeans for their lessons, which I disguised as games. Their eyes grew wide when I brought oranges and cut them into fractional parts. At the end of the lesson, we sat in a circle, sang a numbers' song and ate every fraction.

John and I cared for their bodies, minds and spirits. Our pay was a shared meal, a heartfelt hug or a handshake. Grateful mothers offered to patch our threadbare jeans with bits of colorful cloth. With the small stipend we received from the government, we purchased upgraded medical supplies and nourishing treats for the children.

In a few short weeks, our friendship blossomed into a spiritual bond bred of shared service. Our hearts became one. Whenever unpredictable medical emergencies delayed our departure, we would camp out, as traveling after dark on makeshift roads was impossible. Sleeping in John's arms beneath billions of stars in the South Dakota sky was the closest thing to heaven I have ever known.

By mid-August, I called home to tell Mom and Dad that I would be staying on.

"If it makes you happy," said Dad, clearing his throat, "then I share your happiness."

Mama whispered into the phone, "I know you're young and in love, but it pains me to think you'll be dirt poor for all your life."

"Oh, no, Mama, we'll never be poor. You cannot imagine how rich we are."

These are the memories that sustained and tortured me once my dreams were shattered. John was dead and my career was over, because none of the city schools were wheelchair accessible. My principal had offered to build a ramp, but his request to have me return was denied.

In the hospital, I cried myself to sleep.

I awoke one night to see John sitting on my bed, and I heard his gentle voice as if he were whispering in my ear: "The Little Eagle that I know and love would not give up so easily," he scolded. "You have to help yourself soar again—the children need you."

"Oh, John, I can't. It's just too much. Take me with you, please!"

"That is not to be," he said. "The city children need you. Imprisoned by concrete, they know nothing of the joys of nature. Share your joy with them; bring it into the classroom. You have the gift, Little Eagle. Don't throw it away."

Then he was gone.

For the next two months, I worked feverishly in physical therapy. Every muscle and bone in my upper body screamed, but I would not stop. Struggling to hold myself erect on parallel bars, I swung my legs ahead or dragged them behind me, refusing to acknowledge their numbness.

My doctor entered the therapy room and sat down, "You've given it all you've got, Toni, but there's no improvement. I'm discharging you tomorrow."

"I *will* walk. I know it."

Cradling my face in his hands, my doctor said, "Sweetie, you're in denial; at some point you'll be better off accepting your reality."

Reality, I thought, as I drifted to sleep that night.

About 3 A.M. a voice awakened me. "Come, Little Eagle—it's

time to soar." John was standing over my bed, smiling. "Push your legs over the edge and stand up." John's softly glowing image kneeled at my feet and gently rubbed my legs until they tingled. I swear I could feel his hands touching me. Then he stood with hands outstretched and backed away. "Walk with me now."

With hesitant, shuffling steps, I followed him out of my room and into the hall. My eyes were riveted on John, coaxing every step. A stairway loomed ahead.

"One step at a time, Little Eagle. You can do it."

The sensation in my legs was almost unbearable, as I climbed one step, and then another. Suddenly, from the stair-well door, the excited voices of the resident intern and head nurse carried up the stairs.

"I'll always be with you," John whispered. With a kiss on my cheek, he was gone.

For the next two hours, doctors poked and prodded; they mumbled to each other about "spontaneous something or other," and finally left. When all was quiet, a nurse came in and sat on my bed.

"I saw the young man leading you up the stairs," she said quietly. "Is he your guardian angel?"

"Yes, he is."

"I've often heard patients speak of seeing angels. Did he tell you his name?"

"Yes," I nodded. "His name is John."

Two months later, I returned to my teaching job with a gait sorely lacking in feminine grace, but propelling me nonetheless. My classroom is now filled to bursting with all the wonders of nature. The walls are covered from ceiling to floor with colorful sights from the wild.

Many teachers bring children to my room to view live creatures firsthand. In each child's eyes, wide with wonder, I see my beloved John, smiling.

And in the quiet of night, when my day is done, my spirit soars with him in velvet skies on the wings of eagles.

Toni Fulco

Guiding Me Home

On a journey, an agreeable companion is as good as a carriage.

Publilius Syrus

I had to retreat to a place where I could feel safe and in control—my home, in a big comfortable chair in the corner of my living room. There I would sit, afraid to venture outside, in a newly darkened world I never chose.

A few months earlier, I was on top of the world: My daughter was about to leave for college, I liked my job, and Marie and I were looking forward to being newlyweds all over again. Then, at a surprise party for my fortieth birthday, I began to open all those cards that would rib me about the "Big 4-0," and found I couldn't read the words—I had to ask my wife to help me. "The first sign of advancing age," my friends joked. Within weeks I'd lost most of my sight, and the doctor declared me legally blind.

I was fortunate to have a supportive family and many good friends, some associated with Lions Clubs, whose mission involves helping the visually impaired. The Lions Clubs also support an organization called the Fidelco Guide Dog Foundation. My friends encouraged me to apply, but I wasn't a "dog person." How would I take care of a dog when I could hardly take care of myself?

One day my wife told me how hard it was for her to watch what blindness had done to me: how she hated to leave me alone at home every day and go off to work; how scared and helpless she felt, even guilty, because she could see and I could not. I realized then that blindness didn't just happen to me—it also happened to her, my daughter, my family and my friends. Not yet convinced, I applied for a dog.

In the meantime, a friend gave me a tape-recorded talk by a blind man named Tom Sullivan, speaking at a Lions convention. He told his audience that because he had a guide dog, he did anything he wanted to do and that nothing got in his way. "In this life," he said, "you have to change negatives into positives; you have to believe in your own human spirit and continually build pride in yourself." His definition for the word pride is "Personal Responsibility for Individual Daily Effort," and he talked about how his guide dog changed his life. Listening to that talk changed my life, too. By the time I played the tape for the fourth time, I stopped feeling sorry for myself.

The call from Fidelco came two days before Christmas. They had a dog for me and his name was Karl. My daughter, home on Christmas break from college, and my wife, Marie, who had taken a couple of days off for this monumental moment, were both standing at the window when Dave, the man who would serve as my trainer in using Karl, rang the doorbell. I heard the dog bounding into the room. He ran straight to me as if he knew who needed him most. I sat still as this huge German shepherd checked me out. When he seemed satisfied, Karl placed his head in my hands. I asked him, "Are you the one?" and he licked my face.

I petted the dog and "saw" him with my hands. He had a large head and soft pointed ears. We sat on the floor together, and I scratched his back. Then he rolled over so I could rub his belly. When he snuggled close, I realized this dog was a loving, gentle giant.

The training was tough and stressful for both Karl and me.

Some days went well; others showed no progress. During our second week of training we were missing curbs and failing to walk down the sidewalk in a straight line. I felt as though Karl wasn't listening to any of my commands. I was terribly frustrated, and I could tell Dave was getting frustrated as well. Poor Karl just didn't know what to do. All of a sudden Dave yelled out, "Will the both of you just stop!" I gave Karl the command to halt, thinking, *All right Karl, you're in trouble now.*

Dave said, "You two have got to be the worst looking guide-dog team I've ever seen in my life. Karl goes to the left and George, you try to go to the right. Karl tries to walk you around obstacles, and you walk into them. Karl stops at curbs and you keep going." This wasn't what I expected to hear. It sounded like I was in trouble, not Karl. Dave continued, "George, you have to start trusting your dog. Follow his lead, listen to him! Karl can see and you can't. George—you're blind."

I stood there in shock as Dave continued, "Let Karl do his job. His job is to guide you and keep you safe. If you trust him he'll never let you down."

That moment marked another shift in my life. "I'll try," I said, and picked up the harness. I put all my trust in Karl and let him be my eyes. We began walking as a real team for the first time. I could sense the confidence in his stride, and for the first time we picked up our pace. I knew we had a long way to go, but I felt reborn as trust became more important than fear.

The training continued, and with Karl at my side, we went to Boston and New York. We rode in taxis, buses and subways. We visited malls, dined in restaurants and took walks in the country. Then came the last day of my training during the worst rainstorm I can remember, but that didn't bother us—we had made it. It was official: Karl and I were a team.

Before my wife and I went to bed that night, I told her of a plan I had devised to test my new skills. Marie worked in the town where I grew up. My plan was to go to work with her the next day and walk to my parents' house (just under two miles), spend the day with them and then walk back to her office. She thought I had lost my mind. Cocky and confident, I told her I could do this walk—well, with my eyes closed. "I grew up in this town; I know every turn and every street. Besides, I have Karl, so don't worry." She reluctantly agreed.

I was soon to learn this would be more than just a walk.

As Karl and I set out, the first challenge we faced was the most dangerous thing a blind person has to do: safely cross a busy street. I picked up the harness and listened for a lull in the traffic. Hearing no oncoming cars, I gave Karl the command "Forward," and our walk began. Although he and I had crossed many streets during training, this was the first time we were alone. I could feel how focused he was, even more alert to danger. As we reached the other side of the street, he halted to wait for my next command. He stopped at every curb and walked me around every obstacle.

Everything went well until we reached about the one-mile marker. On a busy, narrow street, I second-guessed myself, but even worse, doubted Karl. A large vehicle passed us and it sounded too close, as if it were on the sidewalk right in front of us. I gave Karl the command to "Halt," dropped the harness and stood there in a panic, leash in my hand. I remember thinking, *What are you trying to do? You have no right to be out here!*

I stood there until a man came up to me and said, "You appear to be lost. Can I help you?" Instead of accepting, I thought back to what Dave had said. *Always trust the dog; he'll never let you down.* I bent over and took Karl's head in my hands and asked him, "What do you think, Karl, do you think we need help, do you think we can make it?" Licking my face, he calmed me. That simple act of love reminded me I had nothing to fear as long as he was by my side. I thanked the person for his offer of help and explained, "I'll be fine. I have this dog and I trust him to keep me safe. Well, we have to get going, because a new journey begins today." It occurred to me that my dog also represents my own body, and that I have to learn to trust it as well.

In that moment, my dream of independence became reality. Karl and I crossed each street and passed the landmarks I knew were there: the church I attended as a child, my old school and the playground where I learned to play basketball.

As we crossed our last street before my parents' house, I knew their front gate would be about seventy yards ahead on the left. When I felt we had gone about forty yards, I told Karl, "Find left inside," to find an opening that would take us off the sidewalk to left inside. I repeated the command several times and started to worry we'd gone too far. What if he'd missed the gate? That wouldn't be a huge problem—we'd just have to backtrack a little. But what if I had taken a wrong turn, or miscounted streets? If that was true, I had no idea where we were. What would I do now? I thought: *Trust the dog and we can do it.*

All of a sudden Karl turned hard to the left, picked up his head and put his nose on the gate of my parents' front yard. We had made it! I dropped to my knees, wrapped my arms around Karl, cried and thanked God for the incredible gift of this dog.

I am now Executive Director of the Fidelco Guide Dog Foundation. Once afraid to leave home, I now travel across America speaking to a variety of groups and organizations. I help them realize their own inner strengths, and I remind them that we're all here to turn negatives into positives and learn to deal effectively with our own life-changing situations. I help others realize, as I came to realize, what an incredible difference these dogs make in people's lives. I love this job!

In many ways, my life is better now than when I could see. And it's hard to imagine life without Karl; he's so much a part of me. If given the choice of sight, but living without Karl—well, let's just say I'd have to give that a lot of thought, because I can't imagine life without him.

George Salpietro

It's Never Too Late

Character consists of what you do on the third and fourth tries.

James Michener

We can all appreciate that "Behind every successful man is a good woman." But sometimes it works the other way around, as in the case of devoted husband Norman Klein. Norm is an accomplished distance runner. It wasn't always so, until one day he accepted a friend's challenge to run a ten-mile race. Norman accepted the challenge, but then he did something else: He encouraged his wife, Helen, to train with him for the race.

The rest is running history.

This story is about Helen—she takes the spotlight, which is fine with Norm. But as you read, remember the quiet hero, the strong, supportive husband (and he cooks, too!)—a dream guy, an oral surgeon whose fitness level is also the envy of many younger folks—the good man behind the amazing success story of Helen Klein.

Let's jump to present time: Helen recently broke the world marathon record in her age group—*the eighty- to eighty-five-year-old class*—completing the 26.2-mile run in four hours and thirty-one minutes. Maybe that's why she was labeled by one magazine as "Grambo." Or why Dr. Kenneth Cooper, who made aerobics a household word, calls her "legendary" and her accomplishments "unbelievable human feats."

Helen views herself as "an ordinary person with extraordinary desire."

Here are a few highlights of Helen Klein's remarkable achievements: At age sixty-six, Helen ran five 100-mile mountain trail races within sixteen weeks. In 1991, she ran across the state of Colorado in five days and ten hours, setting the world record for the 500K. She also holds a world age-group record in the 100-mile run, has completed more than sixty marathons and nearly 140 ultramarathons. In 1995, still getting younger, Helen ran 145 miles across the Sahara desert; in 1995 she completed the 370-mile Eco Challenge, running with Team Operation Smile, for a charity that does reconstructive surgery free of charge for indigent children.

As you read this story, Helen is now running through her eighth decade—marathons, ultramarathons, and the grueling twenty-four-hour runs, forty-eight-hour runs and six-day runs of 100 miles or more. That's when life teaches you a few things about yourself. For example, in the legendary Eco Challenge, endurance athletes from around the world strive to complete a grueling, ten-day, multisports event. Here is what Helen did in the Eco Challenge: rode thirty-six miles on horseback; hiked ninety miles through broiling desert heat; negotiated eighteen miles through freezing, water-filled canyons; mountain-biked thirty miles; rappelled down a 440-foot cliff; climbed 1,200 feet straight up; paddled ninety miles on a river raft; hiked another twenty miles; and, finally, canoed fifty miles to the finish line. "I would never have completed the Eco Challenge as an individual—only as a team member," Helen commented.

"Well, she's just a genetic anomaly," you might say. "One of those people born under a running star—luck of the DNA draw— one of the gifted ones. What does this have to do with me?"

As it turns out, a lot.

Helen was not always an athlete. On the contrary. Helen says, "Raised by a mom who abhorred sweat and believed that little girls must be ladylike and domestic at all times, I was programmed to believe I'd be an old lady who couldn't walk a mile, who played bridge for sport and went to luncheons. So I studied to become a nurse, married, and had four children, and refrained from exerting myself so as not to perspire." That is, until she turned fifty-five.

Helen was a nurse who had smoked for twenty-five years and never run a mile in her life. But the year she turned fifty-five, her husband, Norm, challenged her to train with him for a ten-mile run. She agreed to try it out, but wasn't so sure after running about a fifth of a mile. She was exhausted and panting from two laps on a track they had marked off in their backyard. "I thought I would die," she said. But the next day it was a little easier, and she ran one lap farther. One lap more each day, and in ten weeks she completed the ten-mile race. She finished last, but thought it was "cool." Spurred on by this success, Helen entered other "short" races, but soon realized she was not blessed with blazing speed. So she decided to try longer, slower marathons.

Since those days, Helen has crashed on her mountain bike, fallen asleep on her feet while running through the night, run through snow for twenty-six miles of a 100-mile race, faced pounding rain and 100-degree heat. Helen's mantra: "Relax and move. Relax and move." She adds, "When I had to drop out of my first attempt to run the Western States 100, I said that I would never do it again. But soon enough I struck the world 'never' from my vocabulary—except to remind others of one of the great lessons of my life: 'It's never too late.'"

During one six-day run, Helen covered 373 miles. There were plenty of times she could have quit, and many excuses she could have used. But she thought, *If I want to reach my goal, I'd better push past the excuses and think only about how great the results will feel.* Helen has often said that if she had been told years ago that she would be where she is today, she would have laughed.

And she has laughed many times in her running career. Like the time Helen and a friend were running along a mountain trail and came across two fellow runners within the span of a few minutes. The first one exclaimed, "Helen, you have the legs of a twenty-year-old!" A short while later, the second runner said, "Helen, you have the legs of a thirty-year-old!" Helen turned to her running partner and said, "I may have to give up running—apparently, I've aged ten years in the last mile."

But it's not all laughter by any means. "I've felt fear many times," she says. "I fear riding a bike, and getting on a horse. But I will not run from fear . . . I will not let myself give in to the panic stage. I know for certain that anyone without physical disabilities could do what I do. They only need a little push—a challenge. I am not coordinated and have absolutely no talent for running. All I get by on is desire and determination."

In 1982, at fifty-nine, Helen was the oldest woman in the world to complete the Ironman Triathlon, consisting of a 2.4-mile ocean swim, a 112-mile bike ride, followed immediately by a 26.2-mile run. "I had played around in the water before—I snorkeled and scuba dived and collected shells—but had not swam seriously. I only dog-paddled until last spring when I learned the crawl. I borrowed my daughter's bike to learn how to ride. My first lesson was getting on and off the bike. When I really want something, I don't give up until I collapse. It takes a lot to get this great-grandma to stop."

In 1980, Norman and Helen traveled to Nepal to trek with a Sherpa guide from Katmandu to the 18,000-foot base camp of Mount Everest. When they hit 17,000 feet, Norm experienced some altitude sickness and the couple returned to 16,000 feet. The next day, the Sherpa suggested taking Norman to the base camp and leaving her behind. He told the couple that he was sure that, because of her age, she would be unable to complete the trek, and that he could not carry both of them back. Norman and Helen stood firm: They would both go or neither would go. So they both successfully completed the trek. "I proved to the Sherpa that you can't say, 'You're too old to do this,'" Helen said.

Three years later, during a tour of Israel, Helen told their guide she planned to jog up to the mountain fortress of Masada. But he insisted she was too old and would hold up the tour.

Later, Helen challenged the guide to a three-mile run and finished ten minutes before him. He ended up taking her back to Masada for a sunrise run. "I had no idea you could do that," he said, admitting that he had learned a lesson about not judging anyone by age.

Today, Helen says, "I have such good health that I can do whatever I wish to do. I plan to live a vital life every single year. The key is very, very simple: Eat right and exercise. Apples are my favorite food, plus any fresh fruits, vegetables and all the grains. Before a race, I eat huge amounts of pasta and fruits and vegetables, but only small portions of meat, chicken and fish."

What's the secret of a thirty-year-old's bone density and a svelte figure? Helen runs ten to eighteen miles a day. She retires about 9:30 P.M. and rises at 4:30 A.M. for a cup of coffee, some stretching exercises in a hot tub, then breakfast, the newspaper and a run. "I rest one day each week," she says. "I never overtrain, and I listen to my body. That's why I don't get into trouble. I don't believe in 'no pain, no gain.'" Referring to the ultramarathon endurance events, Helen says, "It may be a little unusual, but with proper training and listening to your body, most dedicated runners could also do these events. It's impossible only if you tell yourself it is."

Here are a couple of other things Helen Klein has learned over the years and miles: "I may be over eighty in age, but I will never be old in mind or spirit . . . I just like to show what a granny can do. Whenever I'm disappointed, I look at my watch and allow myself exactly ten minutes to feel sorry for myself—to whine and cry and complain. When that ten minutes is over, I put it behind me and move on. I don't have the physical talents, but I have a natural capacity to deal with hardships. We can all develop that capacity . . . we all have more strength than we think; it comes from doing something you didn't know you could do. I detest driving; if I need to go somewhere and it's less than 100 miles, I run it. Before you decide you're too old to run across mountains, rock-climb in canyons, or take up scuba diving, remember: It's never too late—muscles never lose the ability to improve, no matter how old you are. We are raised with the idea that when you hit fifty, you should relax and take it easy. I think this is a mistake. The more energy you expend, the more you get back. I get more tired sitting all day than when I run fifty miles.

"Ability may put me at the starting line, but heart takes me to the finish. When we carry gratitude in our hearts for what we have, instead of bitterness for what we don't have, the world becomes a place of smiles instead of frowns. And whenever I lace on my shoes, I lace on my smile. I want people to see both. It's great to be living in high gear, but the most significant reward is when I hear somebody say, 'I was going to seed at sixty-five, and you encouraged me to come back to life.'

"Starting out running (or anything else) is like achieving any other goal. Start out slowly. Establish a comfort zone first before you push. There have been times that I have been tired during a long race, and when I am, I don't think about how much farther I have to go. If I do, it can feel overwhelming. I just focus on taking the next step, because I know that I can always do that. Pretty soon, all those little steps taken individually add up to 100 miles."

For Helen Klein, success is not just a race; it's a lifetime: how we live and what we do with our lives. Goals give our life meaning and purpose. "Easy goals," she says, "are not really motivating; they mean little when you achieve them. Large goals are everything, and they can change your life just by going after them. No matter what your goal, keep focused. Do not give your mind a chance to talk you out of something you want.

"I like to inspire others and I don't like the world 'failure.' I don't believe in it. If you try for something and don't get it, that is not failure. That's just a message to keep trying. The greatest gift I can give is encouragement. I hope I can encourage others with my words, but more so by my example."

Running is Helen Klein's passion, but it isn't for everyone. Her four children are all active in sports, but they only run with Mom. None have run marathons, but as Helen might remind them: "It's never too late."

Dan Millman

Learning to Love Golf

Total absence of humor renders life impossible.

Colette

I don't golf. I never learned to golf. I don't even like the basic premise of golf—hitting a small ball with a skinny stick toward a hole you cannot see—and I don't ever intend to take it up. For me, golf is an expensive way to ruin a perfectly good hike. In spite of my negativity toward this sport, I must admit that for many years—basically since 1985 when I became a single parent—I've been asking my friends to help me find a man who golfs, because after this many years of being single I want my third husband to be someone who is gone a lot. At approximately four hours per eighteen holes, plus a couple hours for celebrating at the nineteenth hole and then perhaps dinner with his friends afterward, I figure a game of golf is worth almost a whole day to myself. Now if I could just find a pilot who golfs, I'd be in married heaven.

Even though I possess no golf genes, never let it be said that I have a small mind when it comes to this strange sport. I encourage my loved ones to enjoy it with all the gusto I can muster. When my oldest son turned thirty, I took him to Florida for our first-ever, all-alone vacation. I whisked him away from his wonderfully understanding wife and three beautiful children and the two of us spent five delightful days together exploring, biking, hiking along the seashore, pigging out on seafood and—you guessed it—golfing.

Since it seemed to me that golfing with a partner would be more fun for him than going it alone with a whacked-out mother who only wanted to drive the cart, I asked my dear friend Shirley, age sixty-eight, to golf with Michael. It was a match made in heaven. She proved to be on a level of golf expertise very similar to my son's. It wasn't easy talking that man behind the counter at the clubhouse into letting me go along without paying. "Mister, I am *not* golfing. I've *never* golfed and I *never* intend to golf. I don't even like golf. I want to drive the cart. I will pay for the cart. I just don't want to pay for the golf. I promise I won't even touch one of those skinny sticks. I'm just the scorekeeper." The man wiped his brow and agreed reluctantly to let me on the course.

Gleefully I found my cart, learned how to drive the thing in ten seconds flat, and placed my purse, water bottle, sun visor and book in the various nooks and crannies I found on the dashboard. I brought a book along, figuring I'd have plenty of time to read while Michael and Shirley were doing their thing.

First of all, I *loved* that cart. Forward, reverse, right, left, spin around. I revved the little machine into world-cup competition and had more fun sashaying around that course than I did in the bumper cars at Disney World.

"Mom! Don't get so close to the green!"

"Slow down! I'm getting whiplash," Shirley hollered as I cackled demonically while pressing my foot to the floorboard.

After spinning my newfound pleasure cruiser up and down, back and forth and all around each body of water I discovered while the two real golfers dinked around the sand traps, ponds, woods and the rough edges of the course, I soon discovered that I had another duty.

"Mom, come on, you have to be the flag holder on the green."

Yes! *More fun.* More exercise. I leaped from my motorized throne, ran up onto the green, grabbed the flag, held the flag, waved the flag, marched around a little bit, started singing "I'm a Yankee Doodle Dandy," and tried to entertain myself while those two Arnold Palmer wannabes tried to get the little ball into the little hole. After listening to a few mild cuss words when the little ball missed the little hole by inches time after time, I'd replace the flag and race back to the cart so I could whisk them and their clubs to the next tee box.

No sooner were my passengers hanging on to the cart than I pressed the pedal to the metal with a yell. "Whee! Golfing is fun!" I shouted to the birds in the trees.

Shirley hissed, "Sheesh, you're giving me whiplash."

Then I noticed we'd left Michael behind. I spun that little machine around on a dime in a flourishing Mario Andretti move to retrieve Michael, only to hear, "No, go on. *Please* go on. Mom, it's okay, I really want to walk."

Terrific, I thought. *Now I have an excuse to do another 180-degree turn. Wonder if I can whip it through here fast enough to miss that tree.*

"Holy bat wings, woman, will you slow down?"

"Oh, sorry, Shirley. Can't help myself . . . I love this little cart! Hey, look, there's somebody's ball over there in the woods." I jumped out, ran into the trees, grabbed the ball and tossed it into the back of the cart. I thought, *This is more fun than looking for Easter eggs.*

"I think that was Michael's ball . . . the one he's playing on this hole."

"Oh, sorry." I tossed the ball back into the trees, hoping he hadn't noticed."

"Wow! Shirley, look! Grapefruit trees! Right here on the course. I'm going to pick some. Hey, what a perk. You don't get free grapefruit when you golf up north."

I lifted my foot off the cart's power pedal with a jerk, giving her head a balancing forward jerk and ran off to grapefruit-tree paradise. "Sure wish I had a few plastic grocery bags," I said, scurrying up the trunk of one tree whose fruit was just out of reach. I grabbed as many large yellow grapefruit as I could carry and waddled back to the cart.

"Michael, look: free grapefruit! Can you believe this? I got a dozen of 'em! I'm telling you, I just love golfing!"

At the next hole, when my son and my friend were discussing some goofy distance calculation and which club to use, I zeroed in on the fact that there were beautiful creatures around, besides the skinny-stick–wielding Shirley and Michael prancing around that golf course. I'd seen large graceful herons, egrets and the strangest, talking, squawking chicken-like bird creatures I've ever seen. Even the "Beware of Alligators" sign at each pond, lake and stream made for interesting viewing. Golfing was as much fun as going to the zoo.

All in all, it was a day to remember. Michael and Shirley remember their scores. I think they were nice and high.

I remember how much fun I had. It was like being at Disneyland, the zoo, a citrus orchard and a flag-waving parade all wrapped into one grand eighteen-hole adventure. Now when I hear someone mention golf, my eyebrows pop up and I offer to be their driver.

Golf . . . what a wonderful sport!

Patricia Lorenz

"You need more exercise. How would you like to carry my golf clubs at the physicians' open?"

Letting Go

Some think it's holding on that makes one strong, but sometimes it's letting go.

Sylvia Robinson

The orange-clad monk smiled at our blond hair.

"From where you come?" he asked.

I wondered if he could understand how far away the Rocky Mountains actually were from this Buddhist temple in southern Thailand, and yet how much at home I really felt.

"America?" he beamed, and pointed at himself: "I student of English!"

He handed me a book in English on Buddha's four noble truths. As I opened it, my eyes came to rest on a page dealing with the origin of suffering. Buddha says that the root of all suffering stems from attachment—attachment to ourselves, to our possessions, to our activities, to our opinions.

I looked at my teenage son, Eri. Here we were on our father-and-son journey to new places and new ideas, exploring the world with all our senses, finding real sights and sounds, smells and tastes—things you can't get through textbooks and television. We were taking a year off from what we thought was our life, to discover what else it could be.

Two boys, one in his forties and the other fourteen, both celebrating a rite of passage of sorts, wandering in Southeast Asia—our backpacks filled with camera, clothing and assorted "necessities."

Reading the wisdom of Buddha's words, Eri and I nodded in agreement with the principle of nonattachment. I stared at the radiant, shaven-headed monk who owned nothing, and reflected on attachment. Life does seem to get easier when I let go a bit. There are the little things like giving away old clothes or tossing out old files after years of pack-ratting. Then there are the big things, like letting go of an unworkable relationship, or a job that makes dollars, but no sense.

Driving away, we thought about the monk's smile, Buddha's words and an old mindfulness prayer:

> *Breathing in, I calm body and mind.*
> *Breathing out, I smile.*
> *Dwelling in the present moment,*
> *I know this is the only moment.*

The test for letting go was just beginning. Somehow I think God knew we were just novices and that more training was needed. Each day it was something else—misplaced keys, passports, scuba mask and more. It kept the pressure on to really let go. After a couple of arduous weeks, we thought we had it made, the principle of letting go now firmly established. We purchased a new Nikon camera, to replace the one we had accidentally ruined.

It was late afternoon some days later on the tenth hole of a jungle golf course. Eri and I are both avid golfers, and the one constant in life (besides change) is that golf can be played anywhere, even in the jungles of Southeast Asia. I was about to nail my approach shot to the green when a monkey came out of the jungle and began to cross the fairway. We had never seen a monkey in the wild before—and certainly never one on a golf course—so Eri immediately took out our new camera. As he approached, the animal growled, bared his teeth and made an ugly swipe with its hand. Eri backed up and froze. Four baby monkeys appeared out of the forest behind the monkey. The threatening gesture must have been to protect the babies. We smiled at this unique sight, something never seen on the Pebble Beach links.

Suddenly, a large male with a full beard, jagged teeth and a Clint Eastwood squint emerged and slowly began to knuckle his way toward us. Despite all my years of martial-art training, I was devoid of aikido techniques for large, hostile simians. One look at the size of his arms made me thankful I was holding a five-iron. With each step he took toward us, we backed away. He kept coming.

"What do we do, Dad?" Eri asked nervously.

I said, "Judging the lie the monkey has, and the distance to the pin, a five-iron is the club of choice."

He grabbed a three-wood. Eri rarely takes my golf tips.

Laughing, we calmed ourselves and relaxed, and the monkey seemed to relax too, and turned away from us as he developed an interest in my recently abandoned golf bag. He began touching the clubs, and picking up my ball and tossing it, as if to say, *I don't play Top-Flites. Do you have any Titleists here?*

Just as I said to Eri, "This will make some great photos," all three of us noticed the camera on the ground near the bag where Eri had left it when he had hurriedly picked up his three-wood. The monkey eyed it carefully and approached it . . . *my* camera. So much for my attitude of detachment.

I stepped forward to claim what was rightfully mine and said to the macho primate, "Hey, don't even think about it, you big . . ." But I was frozen in my tracks by one fixed make-my-day glare. The monkey reached down and swooped up the camera . . . *my brand-new camera!*

I tried mental telepathy. No response. He deftly removed the case, took the camera and held it up to one eye.

I know this sounds like too much artistic license, and I'm sure if I didn't have a witness to corroborate the story, I couldn't trust myself to repeat it. But I swear that this hairy primate with the beady eyes began to mimic a professional fashion photographer, as if working on the proper angles and lighting. I imagined him muttering to himself: *Beautiful, beautiful. You two look great!* After a couple of minutes, he wrapped the camera strap around his wrist and ambled off into the jungle.

In the approaching darkness, father and son, golf clubs in hand, followed nervously, looking for a monkey who had stolen their camera. To what strange karmic past did I owe such a teaching?

Exposing our human inadequacy, the monkey gracefully and swiftly ascended sixty feet up a tree. We agonized as he swung happily from branch to branch, banging our camera along with him. Mercifully, an idea surfaced. "Remember the book *Caps for Sale?*" I asked Eri.

It's a children's story about a cap peddler who has all but one stolen by monkeys, who each put on a cap, climb into a tree and mimic the peddler as he rages below. Finally, the peddler throws his remaining cap on the ground, and *violà!* The rest of the caps come flying out of the tree as they mimic him again. Our solution was *obvious.*

We began to throw clubs, coconuts, rocks, golf balls and sunglasses to the ground, all with one eye on our hairy friend as he studied our antics below and fingered our camera. Then, in the honored lineage of all the great masters, he opened the battery compartment, removed the two batteries, and in a frivolous gesture, tossed them at our feet.

The sun had now set. Two boys, one in his forties and the other fourteen, lay laughing on the jungle floor, looking up at a bemused, long-armed relative. The boys had been forced to let go of a killer case of the clings. Let go, let God. Relax. Release attachments. Everything is unfolding perfectly. And, after all, we did get the batteries back.

As soon as we were ready to go, what do you think happened? Did the monkey toss our camera down? No. But the principle of letting go is that it is not a manipulative technique to control the universe. As Buckminster Fuller once said, "You did not create this universe, and you do not control it."

However, if you ever stumble across a monkey somewhere in Southeast Asia carrying a Nikon camera, follow him. It was a good camera.

Thomas F. Crum

"This is the tough hole I was telling you about."

Reprinted by permission of George Crenshaw, Masters Agency.

The Week I Got My Life Back

*A talent can be cultivated in tranquility; char-
acter, only in the rushing stream of life.*

Goethe

We arrived in San Francisco early on a crisp Sunday morning
in 1998. As cameras flashed and a crowd cheered, thousands of
participants flooded the registration area to begin the 475-mile
AIDS Ride to Los Angeles.

A few months earlier, the longest bike ride I'd ever done was
eleven miles along the boardwalk. I was utterly terrified of
street traffic. On my first training run I had crashed, and I
couldn't get back on my bike for two months. When I returned
to cycling, I was the tortoise of the training pack, barely
struggling through two miles when the others had crossed the
ten-mile mark. I had four months to get ready for the AIDS
Ride and wondered if I could ever train in time. I decided to get
appropriate equipment, including a racing bike. My boyfriend,
Jim, tried to teach me how to get on and off it in my new
cleated shoes, but I never even made it out of the parking lot
that day.

Every weekend we got up at dawn and trained, no matter
what the weather was like or how we felt. Each week I faced a

new fear and pushed through it, climbing harder hills, riding farther. My lupus, which had been in remission, flared up again, and I wondered if I was crazy to attempt the strenuous ride. I almost quit, but then Jim had a bad fall, injured his knees and couldn't take part in the ride. When I thought of his brother and my friends whose memories we were going to honor, and the money we would raise for the victims and for research, I became determined. When I first became sick, I'd been angry at what had been taken away from me: my looks, energy, career and health. But these friends had lost *everything*, and I hoped that in doing this ride I would discover a new me.

On the first day we rode ninety-two miles, to Half Moon Bay. The scenery was magnificent, the traffic terrifying. That evening, I fell asleep, too tired to even eat. On day two, I tucked a wide-brimmed hat under my helmet, since lupus makes my skin hypersensitive to the sun. We rode inland, and completed another ninety-seven miles.

By day three, the euphoria was over. Life was one hot, long hill. I had never felt more alone, because Jim was out of the ride. By day four, as riders in front of me dismounted to push their bikes up a monster of a hill, something deep within me kicked in: *You're going to ride every mile.* My coach, Gregg, had said, "Cycling is good for the spirit."

By day five, I hit "the wall"—utter exhaustion. Just when I was ready to quit, I saw my friend David ahead of me. He had lost both legs, built his own bicycle and cycled with his arms. He was my hero. If he could do this, so could I. Through every ache and pain, through the sweat streaming down my face, through the heat of the sun—I discovered to my astonishment that the struggle brought out the best in me.

On our very last day, Jim was determined to ride in, despite his damaged knees. Our roles had reversed: I had become the strong one, the fast one, and now it was my turn to support him. We arrived in Malibu by lunchtime, and he urged me to ride full out as we got close to our goal. I let it rip. Cars honked, people cheered us on, and I felt I owned the Pacific Coast Highway. Four months ago I had been terrified of it.

Twenty-six hundred of us rode our bicycles down Avenue of the Stars in Los Angeles to the closing ceremony. We wept in silence as an empty bicycle was led down a platform, the missing rider another AIDS victim.

We raised $9.5 million dollars. I had ridden a bicycle from San Francisco to Los Angeles, and in the process, got my life back.

Adoley Odunton

Relax, Breathe and Flow

*Sport strips away personality, leaving the white
bone of character to shine through.*

Rita Mae Brown

It's been said that we don't remember days; we remember
moments. And there's a moment I won't ever forget. It
happened at the peak of a mountain. It happened on a bike.
I'd been training for months to prepare for the Downieville
Classic—a seventeen-mile, downhill mountain bike race.
Before the race, I had high hopes, but my training and state of
mind had felt off-kilter for the last few weeks before the
event. I was losing my focus, losing my edge, losing hope of a
podium finish, crashing in sections of the trail I'd once mastered; every workout seemed laborious, uninspired,
drudgery. I was burned out.

Still, I was committed to doing the best I could. Then, as I was
packing for the trip, I glanced at my cluttered bookshelf for a
book to read before the race. I grabbed one I'd been meaning to
read—*Body Mind Mastery*. It was written by a friend of mine
named Dan Millman. I tossed the book into my bag between
the biking shorts and downhill pants, hoping it might give a
little insight into my slump.

The race was scheduled for Sunday, and like any dedicated athlete, I scheduled a practice run on the course for Friday to reacquaint myself with the terrain. I'd ridden the course late in the spring, but I had been told that heavy traffic during the busy summer months had left the course rough and rocky.

Gearing up for the practice run, I felt jittery. I expected a lot of myself and knew that this run would likely mirror my performance on Sunday. With that thought in mind, I lined up on the top and set off. My legs and lungs burned with the elevation, and every pedal stroke took effort. As I dropped into the most challenging part, the technical section, I suddenly felt like a pogo stick. Taking the wrong line down sections and bouncing all over the place, I even had to put my foot down a couple of times to save myself from crashing. I felt like a novice—as though I had no skill—and the more irritated I got, the worse my riding became. I crashed twice, and used more swear words than I had in the last year. I had lost my rhythm, my breathing and my focus. When I was done with the run, which took well over an hour, I was disappointed with my body and my mind.

I returned to camp, bathed in the river, then sat down in a gloomy state. With only a few hours of daylight left to read, I pulled out my book and began. In the first twenty-five pages, I found the exact reminders I needed. It's amazing how that can happen. It was as if Dan had written this book for me, then and there, for this downhill bike race.

Phrases appeared like long-lost friends: "Flow like water over rocks . . . pull when pushed and push when pulled . . . use the forces you encounter . . . relaxation, breathing, and awareness are the keys . . ." After reading each section I stopped, closed my eyes, envisioned a relaxed blend of bike and rider, body and soul, flowing like water over dust and rocks. I repeated lines from the book to myself, while applying them to my present actions—focusing and flowing.

The next morning I awoke with a newfound sense of clarity. During a long wait for my turn, I chatted with other riders to take my focus off the butterfly convention in my belly as the time passed until I was poised at the start line. Then, "Three . . . two . . . one . . . GO!"

I lunged off the start line with laughter in my heart. I floated over the course relaxed as a wet noodle, light as a feather, mindless as an infant, my mind open yet focused, letting my bike do all the work. I saw each line clearly and took it. Before I realized it, I was in the technical section, and I imagined myself to be water flowing; now I was a supple willow, bending in the wind.

Then, at one uphill section, I dismounted; as I began to run uphill, the heel of my shoe came off. For an instant I snapped back into a state of shallow-breathing panic—I was about to lose it, in every sense of the word.

Then I heard Dan's voice in my mind, and I remembered to take a deep breath and relax. I slipped the shoe right back on, remounted my bike and started pedaling again. I flew over the rest of the course and crossed the finish line in 59:27—under the one-hour mark.

In that moment I understood the meaning of "body-mind mastery." I felt a joyous, peaceful sense of body-mind connection—call it flow, balance or the zone. To me it felt like pure joy. Even if I had come in with the worst time of the day, it wouldn't have mattered. I had won a personal victory.

It turned out I came in third—only one minute behind the leader. As I stood on the podium I felt like a champion. My award was a bike-stem, the piece that connects the handlebars to the frame. It could have been a rubber duck or a gumball machine—the prize wasn't the point.

Every time I look at it, I think of that race, and it brings my focus back: *relax, breathe and flow.* And I remember how it felt crossing the finish line. On that day I didn't just get in touch with my body. I touched my soul, I touched the sky.

Nichole Marcillac

Nichole Marcillac

2

HEALING AND RECOVERY

*Our own physical body possesses a wisdom
which we who inhabit the body lack.*

Henry Miller

"Rags" to Riches

There's nothing harder to stop than somebody who wants to believe a miracle.

Leslie Ford

Ragnar Arnesen's nickname is "Rags." His father, Erik, calls him this; he also calls his son a hero.

Ragnar, named after his Norwegian grandfather, was born in San Francisco and grew up near the waves in Manhattan Beach. At age eleven he learned to surf. But the crashing waves, capable of breaking his surfboard in two, posed less of a threat to Rags than his own blood-sugar level. He was diagnosed with diabetes while still an infant, and his blood sugar could crash worse than any wave, leaving him helpless in the ocean.

Nearly two decades ago, Erik Arnesen—himself an avid surfer in the sixties—took his son to San Onofre state beach for the first time. After giving Rags a lesson on dry land, Erik went into the deep water to ride some curls—alone.

"I just couldn't get out there," Rags, now thirty, describes. "I kept paddling and paddling, but that first day I could never get past the white water where the surf breaks."

While another, less insightful father might have considered his son's failure a lack of talent, Erik focused on something else.

"I saw what a fighter he was," Erik recalls. "I offered to help him, but he was determined. He wasn't going to let the frustration defeat him. And that became our credo: '*Whatever it is you want in life, you have to paddle out to get it.*'"

Rags has since paddled through storm surf and *tsunamis* (tidal waves).

His *big* trouble began when he was thirteen and diagnosed with kidney problems. The doctors said he would need a transplant within six months. Rags would hold out for an extra six and a half years.

"I refused to let my condition stop me from doing things," he says. So he surfed, he cycled and he ran varsity cross country at Mira Costa High—all with failing kidneys and a malfunctioning pancreas because of severe diabetes.

That first day Rags tried to surf is nothing compared to the time he was training to run the Manhattan Beach 10K with his father a few years later. On the eve of the race, Ragnar's blood-sugar level had a wipeout. He was rushed to the ER by ambulance. "It was touch-and-go," Erik remembers.

The scare abated at 5:30 the next morning when Rags insisted on leaving the hospital to run the 10K. The doctors strongly advised against it, but Erik knew his son.

"I knew if he allowed his diabetes to keep him from running the race, it would have damaged him for the rest of his life," explains Erik, himself a four-hour marathoner, cyclist and backpacker. "We took sugar cubes for Rags to suck on while he ran, for a quick energy lift, until he could get an insulin shot after he completed the race."

Whatever it is you want in life, you have to paddle out to get it.

The disease worsened. Rags paddled. "Even in the most difficult times," he says, "if I could go surfing with my dad I knew things were okay. And even with my obstacles, sports make me appreciate life more . . . much more. When I'm cycling, running or surfing—especially surfing—I feel totally alive."

Finally, the doctors told Rags that he had to have a transplant immediately. He and Erik went to their favorite surf spot. There, out on the ocean swells, waiting for the next set of waves, they picked a date to do the operation. On December 19, 1990, twenty-one-year-old Ragnar checked into UCLA Medical Center to get a new kidney. A fifty-one year-old kidney from his dad.

Sometimes you can't paddle alone. Sometimes we all need some help getting past the white water.

"It was a no-brainer," Erik says of his decision.

Five days later, on Christmas Eve, father and son left the hospital together. Rags felt more energetic than he had in years, and Erik was in considerable discomfort. "But I never felt better," he says.

Rags returned to Chico State, where he was majoring in biology. In six weeks he rejoined the university cycling team. He continued taking six to ten insulin shots a day to keep his diabetes under control.

Then the clouds returned—another *tsunami* hit Rags head-on.

While Rags competed at the 1995 World Transplant Games in Manchester, England, his body began to reject his father's donated kidney. For five years, the son and father had shared their flesh. Now they shared their anguish.

"I felt terrible for him," Erik says, "but I also felt bad for myself. I wanted *my* kidney to work for him—now whatever I had done for him was over."

Gone too, was Rags' fighting spirit. For the first time in his life, he didn't feel like paddling.

"My life felt upside-down. I had been a fit athlete; now I was on kidney dialysis."

The first three months were especially difficult.

"I finally decided I could do two things," Rags recollects. "I could feel sorry for myself, or I could accept it."

Whatever it is you want in life, you have to paddle out to get it.

Rags paddled. With the help of his mother, Xenia, he studied about dialysis and nutrition to better manage his condition. *And paddled:* He earned his Emergency Medical Technician degree and started working twelve-hour shifts between his Monday, Wednesday and Friday "part-time job," as he called his four-hour dialysis treatments. *And paddled:* He surfed, cycled and started training for a triathlon, which, while on dialysis, is like climbing Mount Everest carrying a 200-pound backpack.

Rags never completed that triathlon, but not for the reason you might think. He skipped it because the day before the race a kidney match was found. Christmas in 1997 came on July 11 for Ragnar Arnesen.

A year earlier, the rejection of his father's kidney had seemed the cruelest of fates. Now it turned out to be the greatest of blessings. This time, Rags was the recipient of a kidney/pancreas transplant that not only restored his kidney function, but ended his diabetes as well.

"When I woke up, I wasn't diabetic anymore!" said Ragnar, the excitement still in his voice three years later. "It has been a miracle."

In September 1999, Ragnar the Miraculous joined a contingent of international athletes who have donated organs in their bodies at the 1999 XII World Transplant Games in Budapest, Hungary.

For Rags—who competed in cycling, track and field, and volleyball—it was his eighth national/international game. He has won more than a dozen medals, all silver and bronze.

"I'm still looking for my first gold," the five-feet, seven-inch, 130-pound athlete says. "I'd like to give it to my dad."

But Erik says he already has something better: a collage of pictures of Rags at various Transplant Games, inscribed by his son with the words from Bette Midler's popular song, "The Wind Beneath My Wings."

Erik Arnesen has known great striving and adventure in his own right. But his greatest hero and treasure is his son.

A "Rags" to riches story, indeed.

Woody Woodburn

[EDITORS' NOTE: *To obtain a donor card, call the National Kidney Foundation at 1-800-747-5527.*]

Rags Arnesen

Photo reprinted by permission of Erik Arnesen.

The Little White Shoes

Miracles happen to those who believe in them.

Bernard Berenson

My ten-month-old baby daughter threw her arms around my neck and nuzzled her tear-drenched cheek against my chest, desperate to get away from the doctor who had just finished a painful examination. He was a kind man who spoke to me with warm reassurance, but his words were anything but reassuring, and it was all I could do to hold back my own tears as I stroked my child's downy blond hair. She had been born without a hip socket, and the fact that it was being diagnosed so late was crucial.

The doctor said, "I recommend two years in body casts, followed by at least one surgery. At that point, we'll be able to determine whether she will ever be able to walk normally. Most likely, she will always have a painful, heaving gait."

The essential issue was time; it was essential to begin her treatment immediately so the condition didn't worsen. But the situation was worse than the doctor knew: The cost of treatment was beyond anything my husband and I could afford. It was clear I'd never see this physician again.

In the car, I sat down and curled my precious child in my

arms. Delighted to be out of the office, she was quickly consoled and began to happily tap her little toes against my stomach. Her unborn brother, due in just a few weeks, kicked back at her from within. Distracted by their sweet tapping rhythm, I glanced down at the new white "walking shoes" I had so optimistically purchased when she had begun to pull herself to a standing position. She would never be able to walk in those shoes. I was terrified she'd never walk at all.

For the next few days, I vacillated between despair and anger. For months I'd been telling my pediatrician there was something wrong with her legs. A longtime friend, he had patiently listened to me, but had found nothing amiss. Now it seemed my child was to suffer permanent damage because of the delays. I prayed we'd find the help she needed and vowed to do whatever it took to find resources—a process that turned out to be dismal. Doors seemed to close at every turn. Banks refused to lend us the funds for her treatment. Shrine Hospitals had long waiting lists. Far too often, I felt like giving up. But then my darling child would look at me with joy and trust, and I would realize she could not afford the luxury of my discouragement.

Finally, I received a call from the physician who had made the diagnosis. He had been concerned about us. How were we doing? Were we ready to begin the treatment? Embarrassed, I reported that our efforts to raise the funds had failed. After a pause, he said, "When I didn't hear from you, I feared that might be the case. So I took the liberty to make a few phone calls. I've learned that young families such as yours can often qualify for assistance from the Crippled Children's Services in our state. I think you should call them right away." I felt a soaring sense of optimism for the first time.

The ensuing weeks were arduous, but we were carried along on a wave of renewed hope. During that time, I gave birth to a wonderful new baby boy. I also waded through mountains of bureaucratic red tape to get the approval to go to the Children's Hospital for an evaluation.

Sitting in the waiting room of a hospital for "crippled"

children turned out to be an extraordinary learning experience. The little children, faced with all manner of physical challenges—wearing braces and casts, on crutches and in wheelchairs—seemed to embody the spirit of optimism so necessary for their healing. They played, laughed and babbled with one another. In contrast, the parents wore worried, tired expressions. We all were burdened by "the facts" and had to work much harder to maintain a sense of faith.

When our turn came, I picked up my two babies and walked in to meet the physician. My initial reaction was that this beaming man must be a lunatic. "Young lady," he bubbled, "I have absolutely wonderful news for you. I have reviewed your daughter's X rays, and we are going to be able to provide her with state-of-the-art care. A young physician in a nearby state has been specializing in a new treatment for conditions like hers, and he has had incredible success. He has just made the decision to come to our hospital for a year and provide care here." The "door" had opened wider, and the future held even greater promise than I had imagined.

The visiting physician's treatment was indeed revolutionary. His surgical procedure was to put a chip of bone where the missing hip socket should have been, and after the surgery my daughter was put in a body cast and sent home with us. Unseen, beneath the thick layers of plaster, a miracle began to grow. Every time they took an X ray, I could see that the small chip of bone was gradually growing and shaping itself into the form of a perfect hip socket.

The surgery was 100 percent successful. After the cast was removed, my little daughter walked pain free and without a limp.

I still remember the visiting nurse coming to our home for a follow-up visit a year later to see the child with the hip dislocation. I pointed to our daughter as she ran through the room squealing after her brother. "No," the nurse said patiently. "I'm here to visit the child who had surgery for her missing hip socket." Then the light dawned and she said, "This is amazing. I've never seen a child recover so fully and in such a short period of time."

My daughter is now a grown woman with a family of her own. We rarely speak of her experience. The only reminder is a small scar on the front of her hip, a scar so insignificant she has been able to successfully pursue a career in modeling. Recently, she and I went roller-skating with her young daughter. As my granddaughter launched herself confidently onto the skating floor, my daughter and I began our somewhat wobbly, but valiant effort at merging with the other skaters. When they called for a "couple's skate," she and I joined hands as we had so often when she was little. As I watched our feet gliding along, I was suddenly struck by the sight of her skates and remembered the little white shoes of the child who could not walk. As we skated along, they began to play "Just the Two of Us."

I, too, have been forever changed. Out of my despair of not knowing where to turn, *I learned to trust.* I appreciate the importance of listening to my own instincts. From persisting in the face of adversity, I discovered that many of life's possibilities are unseen, yet may be ready to materialize in the next moment. Despite appearances to the contrary, our bodies carry within them great wisdom and the ability to heal in miraculous ways, and somewhere there are always caring and capable people who are willing to lend support. Out of challenges that seemed too heavy for my twenty-one-year-old shoulders to carry, came lessons that have carried me throughout my life.

Catherine Monserrat, Ph.D.

Mending the Body, Healing the Soul

The body is a sacred garment.

Martha Graham

In the peace of June 1941, I was drafted for a one-year stint in the army. After desert training in California, I shipped out to Alaska for infantry duty. By the time war erupted on December 7, 1941, the Japanese already occupied the Aleutian Islands— the stepping-stones to Alaska.

Our outfit was so short of men that each of us had to patrol five to ten miles of Cook Inlet alone. One frozen day I took what I thought was a shortcut, and jumped six feet into the snow below, unaware that just beneath a thin covering of snow lay a frozen river of ice. My left leg was torn apart.

The lower part of my left leg stuck out at a right angle to the upper half; my kneecap was pushed up near my groin. In excruciating pain, shivering with shock and cold, I tried to hold my leg together as the pain became unendurable. As the hours wore on and hopes of rescue faded, I decided to kill myself and inched toward my rifle, a few feet away. But as my finger touched the trigger, I blacked out.

When I recovered consciousness briefly, I found myself strapped to a cot in a medic tent somewhere in the forest. My leg was bound with two tree branches. When I opened my eyes again, I discovered my leg in a cast from toe to hip.

After months in army hospitals, and more surgeries, the army was so desperate for men it declared me fit enough—no matter how badly I limped—to serve three more years fighting the Japanese in the Aleutians.

In the Aleutian Islands, where the fog was often so dense we couldn't see each other until we were a few feet apart, I fought Japanese soldiers in hand-to-hand combat. I have no idea how I survived those horrors, but I did. Still, there were many scars: some showed; others lay hidden.

My knee never healed well. Despite additional surgery, ten years after my initial injury I still felt constant pain in my shortened leg. For years I searched for relief through medical clinics and specialists, but no one could help. Then, forty years after the injury, I heard of a gifted surgeon—a Dr. Robert Watanabe—who was famous for treating athletic injuries, particularly knees. When sports medicine was still young, he had been chosen as the physician for the U.S. Olympic track team in 1984.

In time I was to learn much about his life: His parents were both American citizens, but when war broke out, nine-year-old Robert and his entire family were sent to a detention camp where they remained for years. Young Robert felt deep pain, despair and then fury at such injustice. As time passed, he would vent his frustration by running around the perimeter of the camp's enclosure until he collapsed from exhaustion. By the time the war ended and his family was finally released, he had developed into a champion runner, driven by volatile and dangerous fuel.

Back home in Los Angeles, Robert met a family doctor who encouraged him to turn his rage into constructive activity. Robert followed his mentor into the medical world.

By the time we met, Robert Watanabe had become a sports doctor renowned for his innovative research and surgery. But due to my own horrific war experiences, it seemed a terrible irony that a Japanese-American might help me.

Hesitantly, I told him of my reservations. He understood. I sensed that he had his own past and his own reservations. Nevertheless, he said, "Sanford, I am a doctor and your case is a great challenge. I will do my best for you." He operated on me three times over a period of several years. My leg lengthened and straightened out under his brilliant reconstructive surgeries, and he was as excited about my progress as I was. At one of my appointments, a visiting British surgeon examined my medical records and watched in disbelief as I walked down the hall without a limp, both legs now the same length, my body erect and obviously pain free. Dr. Watanabe embraced me as a coach might embrace a victorious athlete. We all agreed it was a miraculous healing—but the greater healing was yet to come.

In the course of my medical odyssey, Robert and I opened up to each other, sharing our wartime experiences—his imprisonment and my combat horrors. We had long transcended a doctor-patient relationship to become dear friends. We came to understand our wartime anguish and shared our youthful vows to make the world a better place. And we both have tried our best to do just that in the ensuing years.

On what was to be our last medical appointment, Robert did the most astonishing thing. He took down his most cherished treasure—his Olympic gold medallion, earned as team physician—from its honored place on the wall amongst his diplomas and citations. He placed it around my neck and spoke words forever seared into my heart and soul: "We are both winners, because we have made peace within ourselves and have helped heal each other."

We bowed to each other in respect, embraced as lifelong friends and sat together exchanging silent blessings.

Sanford Drucker

My Favorite Injury

You save your soul by saving someone else's body.

Arthur Hertzberg

I've always believed that life provides a series of experiences that serve our growth, insight and wisdom. That philosophy was tested—and ultimately deepened—during a series of surprising and challenging incidents at the age of twenty-six in the year 1979.

The previous year I had run my first under-three-hour marathon and, armed with the goal of improving that time, I intensified my training. By midsummer I was running seventy miles per week and keeping up with much faster runners for the first time in my racing career. My training partners included elite-level runners whose presence and encouragement contributed to my progress. They told me I could run a 2:40 marathon (two hours and forty minutes), with the potential to reach 2:20, given the progress in our training. Running had become both a physical and spiritual passion in my life, and I was riding a wave of rising excitement and bliss.

That all came to a grinding halt when I developed a painful injury in my knee. From running an effortless twenty miles at a fast tempo in the mountains, I could now barely run one mile. The pain increased until I couldn't even run a few steps without sharp pain. I decided to rest a few weeks, expecting to return to my training. As the weeks passed, however, my body experienced no improvement and my spirits sank. The doctors were unable to predict when I might recover. With each passing day, I could see the benefits of my hard, progressive work of the last six months ebbing away, and I grew increasingly disheartened.

I had to find some way to sustain my fitness as my knee healed. My body had grown accustomed to the rigors of training for two or more hours a day. It felt imperative that I keep my cardiovascular system strong and not lose the gains of the last half-year. I bought some swimming goggles, joined the local YMCA and set about duplicating my training regimen, assuming I'd soon be able to swim for several hours a day. I was about to receive my second difficult lesson in dealing with challenges and setbacks.

I had a smattering of swim lessons as a kid and believed that, as a marathoner, I would have no problems with a transition to the pool. But the first day I plunged into the water, it was painfully apparent that my expectations far exceeded my ability. After swimming only one length of the pool, I stopped and clung to the edge, gasping and winded. I tried a second lap with the same result. This continued for about twenty minutes, one lap at a time. I was exhausted.

I recalled that while growing up in New York I had little exposure to swimming. I didn't really like being in the water. In fact, the ocean frightened me. I remembered when a camp counselor forced us to stay out in the ocean for "our full thirty minutes," despite the chilling water temperature. A poor swimmer, I found the waves intimidating. Even as an adult I had rarely ventured into the sea.

In early July, determined to solve my dilemma, I befriended the lifeguard who spent many hours a day by the dimly lit, indoor pool in the YMCA basement. He patiently guided me seven days a week. I worked hard, determined to improve, but progress was slow. I would swim every day until exhausted;

then I'd wait a few minutes and try a few more laps. Week by week, my effort and his coaching and encouragement began to pay off.

By August I was swimming nearly forty laps a day. In September I swam a mile a day, learned the breaststroke, backstroke and crawl, and even started lifesaving lessons. Feeling more competent, my confidence grew and I pushed onward. By December I could swim two miles a day and felt as comfortable in the water as I had running on land.

By the Christmas holidays, my knee had improved, but it was not yet ready for running. So I decided to travel to Hawaii, hitchhike around the islands and camp on the beaches. This seemed an idyllic break in my past routine—and besides, my budget didn't allow for much else.

I learned soon after my arrival, however, that during this period in the islands, tensions between locals and tourists had reached a peak. Recently, newspapers and radio reports had related several incidents of campers being burned out of their tents and visitors being assaulted at night by locals. As I made my way around Maui, I was repeatedly warned to be cautious when hitchhiking and especially careful if sleeping on the beach.

Hearing this news, I remember standing on Makena Beach late that afternoon, feeling vulnerable, depressed and alone, when a distant scream pulled me out of my dark reverie. It was a voice crying "Help!" from the ocean. I looked out to see several figures bobbing in the ocean beyond large, crashing waves. Without thinking, I threw off my shirt and shoes and raced into the water. Swimming through the rough surf I found two men in their twenties holding up a terrified, much older man. They said they were exhausted from the riptide and had no strength left to bring him in. They asked me to take over so they could swim to the beach and get help.

The older man started panicking, grabbing my neck and pulling me under as huge waves thrashed us. I grabbed him firmly, looked directly into his terrified eyes and said, "Do what I tell you and I promise I won't let you die." He nodded and stopped struggling. I turned him on his back, held him with my left arm and, using all the strength of my right arm, started to swim against the riptide. The surf was terrible. A fierce storm two days earlier had shifted the sand and left behind enormous waves and an even more ferocious undertow. Sharp coral to the east precluded swimming at an angle to the beach. I would have to overcome the waves and swim straight in, against the riptide, towing the weight of an exhausted elderly man.

At first I swam with all my strength, thinking my fitness would be enough. I quickly tired, however, in the strong surf and undertow, which repeatedly pulled us out back into the sea as if we were weightless corks. I realized I had to conserve my energy—not only to make it back in with this man, but to save my own life as well.

Little by little, I neared the beach, trying to ride each wave and swim when propelled forward. A group of rescuers had locked arms and formed a human chain in the shallow water, reaching out toward the crashing waves. After an eternity, I pulled the man within thirty feet of the beach and placed him into the arms of the other rescuers.

I staggered out of the water and collapsed onto the beach, breathing hard. Then I stumbled away from the rescue group and the elderly man, to sit alone with my thoughts, which were rushing back in like the tide. Only minutes earlier I had been standing on the beach consumed by my own problems. Now, a few paces down the beach lay a man whose life I had saved. My past concerns disappeared. His cry for help had pushed me to a place far beyond my inward troubles and personal predicaments—past my fear of the ocean into an act of courage and strength.

I never again spoke to the man I saved. I never even learned his name. It wasn't necessary. He was safe now, surrounded by the group. I was consumed by a revelation . . . free and liberated. Life's incredible lessons and opportunities had again worked their magic.

The same knee injury that seemed to end my marathon dreams had catapulted me into choices and events that had a profound effect in my life—and had saved the life of another human being. It struck me then how the interconnected threads of our destiny are profoundly tied to one another. I used to wonder if things happen for a reason. Now I believe I understand: When things happen, it's our job to make the best use of the events. Everything that happens is a chance to grow, to create something positive out of a negative. When one door closes, another always opens. It's our job to pay attention.

I work as a sports chiropractor now, and when my patients struggle with an injury, I sometimes share the story of my favorite injury—one that saved a life, and maybe two.

Leonard Stein

Angel to the Bone

We are each of us angels with only one wing.
We can fly only by embracing one another.

Luciano de Crescenzo

When I met Cindy, she seemed like any one of us women dropping our children off at school: thirty-something, a wife and a mother of two with a minivan, a dog, a house in the sub-urbs—a middle-class woman living a middle-class life. But things aren't always the way they seem.

Shortly after I met Cindy I found out she had leukemia. Her appearance gave no hint, nor did her attitude reflect it. If it weren't for the fact that she was listed with the National Bone Marrow Registry, I wouldn't have believed it.

While days for the rest of us passed with relative normalcy —kids with stuffy noses, trips to the vet, grocery and dry clean-ers—Cindy continued with business as usual too—except that her young life was slipping away as each day passed without word of a donor match. She went to the market, drove carpool, baked cookies for her youngest daughter's preschool and cheered as she watched her seven-year-old daughter perform gymnastics. She even went on daily, one-hour power walks with her friends, met us gals for the occasional lunch and managed to laugh during our many silly get-togethers. When I think back on it now, I marvel at her strength. Cindy set an example for all of us.

The only time I can remember her broaching the subject of her illness is when one of her young daughters asked Cindy if she was really dying, or whether it was just a bad dream.

Those were the hardest days, when she thought about her children. She was a mother and wife first, and a cancer patient a distant second.

Overcoming the odds was Cindy's specialty: one match out of 20,000 possible donors was located in a few months. The donor had passed the initial screening and follow-up tests; all systems were go. Cindy's husband could breathe again, her children had fewer nightmares and her family and friends rejoiced.

But this was real life, not a medical television drama.

After seven months of indecision, the donor backed out. It was as simple and as devastating as that. (The names of all donors are confidential until a year after the transplant.)

The agonizing awareness of the odds in finding another matching donor was almost too much to bear. As much as Cindy tried to hide it, the strain was beginning to show in her beautiful eyes. Her laugh, when it came, was no longer as easy or as deep. Days now seemed like weeks, and we all knew that time was the enemy, and the enemy was closing in.

Lightning rarely strikes twice in the same spot, but in Woodland Hills, California, one winter afternoon, a second miracle appeared in the form of a telephone call. Another donor had been found. And because of what had happened the first time, the registry had waited to make sure this donor was committed.

Most angels are easily identifiable, given away by their gossamer wings and opaque halos. But sometimes they live here on Earth—even disguised as a twenty-eight-year-old married mother of a two-year-old daughter from New Hampshire. Although Cindy didn't know anything about her donor—her angel—she received a note as she waited in her hospital room for the gift of bone marrow from this perfect stranger.

It said simply:

"I know this marrow will help you. My mother will be watching over you, Patty."

Patty was released the next day after the bone marrow aspiration. Cindy had a six-week hospital stay. After a fever and an additional week in the hospital to remedy that, as well as some drug modifications, the first year of Cindy's recovery went well. The doctors explained that the biggest hurdle was the first hundred days; after that, if the disease stayed in remission for one year, the prognosis would improve significantly.

At first, her friends handled Cindy like fragile crystal. We networked on the telephone, confirming with each other that she seemed to be getting stronger, looking better, acting like herself again. But before long, as we were swept into the business of our own daily lives, Cindy's illness faded into history.

Then, exactly one year to the day after Cindy's transplant, that harbinger of life-altering news—the telephone—rang again. Cindy's husband answered the call and handed her the phone.

"It's your sister," he said.

When Cindy put the receiver to her ear, the voice on the other end was not familiar to her. "This isn't my sister," Cindy mouthed to Hal.

"Oh yes it is," insisted her husband, his voice trembling.

Then she realized it was Patty.

Tears ran down Cindy's cheeks; on the other end, Patty was crying, too. They spent an hour on the phone, swapping information through the telephone lines back and forth between New Hampshire and California. Cindy learned that Patty had lost her mother to cancer, and although she couldn't help her mother, she was determined to help someone else. She had originally registered as a donor with the City of Hope to help a little boy. She called every two weeks to inquire about the status of her compatibility with him. Ultimately, she discovered she was not a match for the boy, but she was for a woman in California: a wife and mother named Cindy.

Patty had recently given birth to another daughter—but she

had waited to get pregnant until she was able to donate her marrow to someone in need. Cindy described her battles with the life-threatening disease and how she eventually emerged victorious due to Patty's generous and loving act. They made plans to meet the following month.

Cindy and her family flew to Boston, then drove to Portsmouth, New Hampshire. Patty arrived at their hotel with her tiny daughter. When the door opened the two women fell into each other's arms like the long-lost sisters they had now become. Between tears and laughter, these two women, once strangers, who now shared identical bone marrow, forged a permanent friendship and bond.

Five months later, Patty and her family made the trip to California to meet Cindy's family and friends, who all wanted a chance to personally thank the woman who saved Cindy's life. They met at a local restaurant—a modest setting for the thirty people who gathered to celebrate the kindness of strangers and to renew their trust in the goodness of people.

When Patty was introduced, some guests raised glasses and some broke out in applause; others wept openly as they beheld the face of an earthbound angel and everyday saint.

Every year, on October 14—the anniversary of Cindy's transplant—Cindy places a call to Patty and says the same heartfelt words: "Thanks for another year, angel." Eight priceless years of memories and cherished time have come and gone since the paths of these two remarkable women crossed: a story of love, character and courage. A gift of healing and hope.

Lori Shaw-Cohen

Inner Windows

When you cannot see what is happening, do not stare harder. Relax and look gently with your inner eye.

Lao-tzu

One morning just after dawn, I sat quietly, trying to meditate. It's often hard to stop the mind chatter and become peaceful, and so it was in the gray silence of the room that I decided to use some imagery. I often visualize my "sanctuary"—an imaginary room with a small stage in front—where I can summon in my mind any part of my body I have questions about. Most often, I call on my immune system to fight a cold I've been exposed to, and I imagine a funny little creature dressed in silver, adorned with stars, and holding a laser gun to zap any germs. I think, *You have my permission to keep my body totally healthy!* I don't care if it sounds weird; I rarely get colds anymore.

This morning something else came first. Yesterday I had noticed a very small, dark gray spot in the bottom of my field of vision that didn't move when my eyes moved, as "floaters" do . . . those spots that nearsighted people like me often get. Floaters are generally harmless.

There was no pain at all, and the small spot seemed odd but

insignificant. I had gone to bed without giving it much thought, but when I awoke, I'd noticed it again. I decided to go to my sanctuary and ask my eye what was going on.

I was not prepared for the answer I sensed. *This is very serious. Get to a doctor immediately.* That was it. I don't "hear" voices. I just get information—an awareness—in some way I can't define. It doesn't feel spooky to me at all, and I trust this intuitive knowledge at a level deeper than mind.

I was quite shaken and called the eye doctor when his office opened. "Come in tomorrow," the secretary said, "but be prepared for a long wait. The doctor has to see three times as many patients as usual because most of the doctors here at the clinic are leaving the day after tomorrow to attend the big annual conference."

The next morning, as I prepared to go to a previously scheduled early morning meeting before my 11 A.M. doctor appointment, I found myself packing an overnight bag. That seemed ominous; I couldn't imagine why I would need it, but threw it in the car anyway.

After the meeting, I drove seventy miles to the eye clinic to wait for hours in Dr. Miller's reception room, relieved that the gray spot had not moved, enlarged or darkened.

When the ophthalmologist dilated my eye and looked into it, he asked the most surprising question. "How did you know to come here with such a tiny spot?"

I told him the story of the inner dialogue with my eye, and of the peaceful times when I can ask such questions and receive answers. He seemed unnerved, and made no response; I understood it didn't fit the medical model he'd been taught.

"Bobbie, it's a miracle you're here," he said. "You have a hole in your retina, and a detached retina as well. If you had let this go you could well have been blind in a very short time—a couple of days. I'm going to call a retinal specialist in right now, and I'm sure he'll have you in surgery today as soon as he can schedule it. I don't really understand how you knew to get in here so quickly, but I'm grateful you did so we can fix the problem."

Waiting more hours to have the surgery, I alternated

between fear of going blind and thankfulness I had listened to my inner wisdom and made it in to a world-renowned eye clinic in time to have treatment.

The surgery was mercifully brief. My eye socket was injected with a local anesthetic, and I was conscious, but wishing I weren't.

The surgeon said, "I know you weren't expecting to have this done, but you'll need to stay in a local hotel overnight so I can see you first thing in the morning. My plane leaves at ten, and I want to make sure you're doing well before I go."

I did very well indeed, and still thank my eye for warning me of the problem when it was solvable. I continue to imagine my sanctuary, and to appreciate my body for bringing me this far in life. Most of all, I'm filled with gratitude for the inner voice of wisdom I've come to trust so deeply.

Bobbie Probstein

The Last Attack

Human experience would lose something if there were no limitations to overcome. The hilltop hour would not be so wonderful if there were no dark valleys to traverse.

Helen Keller

As a child I was stricken with severe allergies and asthma, which kept me from having, holding, tasting, touching and smelling a variety of foods, most plants, trees, grass and flowers. And keeping a pet—especially a dog or a cat—was completely out of the question. All my childhood doctors had agreed: I needed to avoid everything I was allergic to, remain sedentary and visit the doctor every Saturday morning for my weekly allergy shot.

"Do *not* exert yourself," he told me. "It will probably trigger a dangerous asthma attack."

Often disregarding his advice, I played hard, ran everywhere, rode my bike like a demon, swam every summer and trained in gymnastics year-round. I became the top gymnast in my grammar school and also set the 50-, 60- and 100-yard dash records. At eleven, I told my parents that I would no longer be taking the allergy shots each week—a subjective decision based not on information I read in any book, nor on the advice of any experts. Rather, my body told me I didn't need them anymore.

My parents, though doubtful, agreed to a trial period. "We'll see how you do without them," they said.

But I wasn't through. I begged, pleaded and finally convinced them to get a dog—a furry little Pekinese we all grew to love—and I began to immerse myself in all the things that used to make me sick (or had been told would make me sick). I cut the grass for neighbors who didn't know I wasn't supposed to be near lawns. I smelled flowers and climbed trees. I even began to eat strawberries, which doctors said "could possibly be fatal."

I don't remember my first asthma attack, but I vividly remember my last. I was eleven years old; it was a humid, hot summer day in Chicago, and I was running hard through the African jungle—in reality, the alleys behind our house. There were many beasts and potential predators I needed to outrun. Sometimes while running, especially on a sticky day, my lungs would swell and squeeze off my air supply. That day was no different. Reluctantly, I decided to leave the jungle and return home to rest.

The house was empty, a true blessing that allowed for undisturbed, quiet focus. In the stillness, I came to a new awareness and found my cure.

As I lay on my parents' bed gazing up at a ceiling fan, I stared at the shiny silver bolt that held the sharp blades together. I focused on what seemed like the still point in the center of the fan's great vortex and held my attention there, while listening calmly to the chorus in my chest. I heard the rapid, rhythmic crackling sounds of blocked lungs, accompanied by high pitched whistles, which marked the trail of the few puffs of air struggling to make their way through narrow passageways. I remained calm, content to listen to my body.

Then came the sudden, dazzling realization that altered my life forever: a simple thought that penetrated to my core: *I have all that I need.* I understood, for the first time, that the little bit of air getting through was all that was necessary to sustain me. It was enough. When I realized *I have nothing to fear, I will always have enough air,* my lungs opened fully.

Wayne Allen Levine

Maureen's Fears

There is nothing to fear but fear itself.

Franklin Delano Roosevelt

My niece Maureen was a nervous child almost from the moment she was born. She was lovely, in a doll-like way: long, curly, fair hair and a delicate stature. When she was little, her shyness and wide-eyed alarm at strange things was endearing, but as she grew up it began to hold her back. In her teens, she remained shy and fearful; at college, mixing tentatively with kids was initially an ordeal.

She came to me in tears the night before her first job. "Oh Joyce, I am so scared I won't be able to do what I'm expected to and that I will let people down!"

Fortunately, Maureen was clever and bright, and so she settled in just fine. It was clear to us all that once Maureen found a job where she felt comfortable, it would take heaven and earth to move her out of it, and we were right! She did make a few friends there and that made her mum and me happy.

One day Maureen met Douglas and he took to her straight away. He was a gentle lad, and she gradually got over her shyness and they started dating. In a year they were engaged. She was so happy, but very nervous about her wedding, even if it was a couple of years away. That was Maureen.

One morning, she looked in the mirror and noticed a lump on her breast. She told her mum and off they went to the doctor.

He said reassuringly, "We'll take a biopsy, of course, but most lumps of this kind are nothing to worry about." Of course, Maureen worried. When the results came back, they showed the lump *was* cancerous. Maureen would need to have a breast removed.

No one could describe what this did to Maureen; she was so filled with fears already that she had no reserve of courage on which to draw. She was convinced she would die during the operation, or—if she managed by some miracle to survive—that it would not be successful, and she would die a little later. After she survived the operation, she was terrified of the treatment, ill quite a lot and still convinced she was going to die. I knew one of Maureen's doctors, and he took me aside as I left her one afternoon.

"I fear for your niece, not physically, since her treatment is going really well. We caught her cancer early and there is every hope she will go on and live a normal, healthy life. I worry for her mentally: She is giving up hope and reacting very badly to the treatment because she thinks it will kill her. As a doctor, I cannot ignore the power of the will to live, and Maureen almost has a will to die."

I spent most of that night praying for my niece. I asked the Lord to give her strength to overcome this, give her faith and send someone to help her.

Typing manuscripts for authors left me lots of free time to be with her, and I was in her house, next door to mine, when the bell rang. I opened the door and Robert Adam stood there, his big burly frame almost filling the doorway. "Sorry to bother you, I guessed you might be here."

"Come in," I ushered him in, and Maureen stared in alarm as he walked into her living room. Robert is in his fifties, an imposing man, 6 feet, 2 inches tall, and broadly built. He smiled at her and in his deep, lovely voice asked, "How are you today?"

"Not too well," she said in a voice he could barely hear.

"Sorry, Maureen, this is Dr. Robert Adam," I said.

She looked up at him, "You're a doctor?"

"Oh yes, so come tell me what you mean when you say you don't feel too well," he said.

He sat down beside her and took one of her tiny pale hands into both his big hands as she spoke. She told him how sick her treatment made her and to her surprise he nodded. "Good, good!" he said. She talked about how weak she felt, and again he nodded and smiled, like it was a good thing.

Finally she ran out of words and he said, "Well that all sounds pretty good to me, young lady. There is every indication in the world you're going to make a complete recovery—well, almost complete."

My heart dropped at that comment, and Maureen's face fell as she repeated, "Almost complete recovery?"

"Well, I would have been happier if you felt a bit dizzy now and then, almost as if sometimes you were in the room only in spirit, not really a part of life itself."

"Oh, but I do feel that!" she protested. "I feel that quite a lot of the time."

"You do? Oh good, then I can't see that you have any problems," Robert Adam told her. "Day by day, every one of your systems will ease a little, not sick so often, not dizzy so much, and your appetite will come back a little at a time. Finally, one day you'll look in the mirror and say: 'That's it, I'm back. Now I can tackle the world!'"

Maureen laughed up at this big man smiling down at her.

He began to call on her a couple of times a week. Just like he said, Maureen began to pick up, little by little. Everything he said to her came true, simply because Maureen believed in him. Her mind believed him, and her body followed right behind it.

I thanked God for pointing me in the right direction. I also asked his forgiveness for deceiving Maureen as well. Although Robert Adam was indeed a doctor, I hadn't told her he was a Doctor of Divinity and not a medical doctor!

Two years down the road Maureen is fine, married to

Douglas and expecting her first baby. Robert Adam has already been asked to be godfather to the newborn. When he finally said to Maureen that he was not a medical doctor but a man of God, she just hugged him and said, "Well. You're God's doctor, so no wonder I got better once I met you!"

Joyce Stark

Input and Outcome

*I have learned to use the word "impossible" with
the greatest caution.*

Wernher Von Braun

I was frightened, terribly frightened. In my situation, who
wouldn't be? The last time I'd gone under a surgeon's knife I
had nearly bled to death. Now I was about to do it again. This
time, they would open my abdomen to determine whether I
had cancer.

I'd done a lot of reading since my first horrific experience.
This time I would not be a passive patient lying helpless on a
table. This time I had a plan.

Surgery was scheduled for 8 A.M. Tuesday at a major Los
Angeles hospital. I was told to check in on Monday afternoon.
That night, the anesthesiologist visited me in my room—the
usual procedure for a brief, presurgery meeting. I could hear
the anxiety in my voice as I questioned him: "Doctor, last time
I had surgery, I felt horribly nauseous afterwards. Could you
give me a different anesthesia this time?" He agreed and said
he would if possible.

I added, "I've read a book called *Healing Now,* by Bobbie
Probstein, which proposes that even when someone is totally
sedated, their subconscious mind records what's being said,

and that those words take on the power of hypnotic suggestions. I believe this is true and respectfully ask that you repeat
the following statements to me: 'Sheri, you are allowing perfect surgery . . . You're doing fine! . . . Keep up the good work!
. . . You have the ability to heal perfectly . . . You will give us a
clear field [as little blood as possible at the surgical site] . . .
Your healing will begin immediately!' Would you be willing to
read me these statements?"

He made a few brief notes on my hospital record, looked at
me strangely and said, "Are you serious about this stuff?"

"I'm absolutely serious about it. And I'll only accept an anesthesiologist who will cooperate with this. Are you willing?"

He looked away and twiddled the pen in his fingers. He
started to say something, apparently thought better of it and
looked at me without saying a word.

"Doctor, whether or not you happen to agree with my
view, I'm the one under the knife. And it's my strong belief
that saying these positive things will help. They certainly
can't hurt. This is my body and my health. I need your assur-
ance, your word that you'll do what I'm suggesting, even if
you do it just to reassure or humor me. I know the surgeon
doesn't have time, and you'll be standing at my head, keeping track of my vital signs."

"All right," he said. "I'll do it. I've never said things like this
in surgery before, and I don't agree with your belief that an
anesthetized patient can hear *anything*. But if you feel *that*
strongly about it," he said, a wry grin on his face, "you have my
promise I'll do what you want."

"Thank you! Oh, one more thing, please. I don't want any
negative talk from anyone while I'm under, no matter what
you may find. Okay?"

"Okay."

He then asked me to repeat what I wanted him to say, wrote
it down and left the room. The nurse came in a few minutes later.
"You're lucky to have that doctor tomorrow morning," she said.
"He's the head anesthesiologist for this hospital. He's very good."

When I awoke after surgery, I had no idea what day or time
it was. I wanted to get up and move around, with a little watchful help. I felt surprisingly good. It suddenly dawned on me

that I wasn't nauseous at all, and I vividly remembered the uncontrollable sickness from the time before, and the fear that the stitches wouldn't hold.

My surgeon came in later that day. "You're doing great!" he said. "You exceeded my expectations. Given the procedure I performed, you've come through in better shape than anyone I can remember. I understand the staff is delighted, too; you've been up sooner and getting around with far more ease than most patients. And I've been saving the best news for last: Your results are all negative. In this case," he added quickly, "negative is good—absolutely no sign of a malignancy."

The next day the anesthesiologist dropped by, a big smile on his face. "Well, I'm impressed. You did so well and had little bleeding, so I'm going to repeat the same positive suggestions for all my patients from now on."

"Oh, I'm delighted, Doctor. Thank you for doing what I requested." I was thrilled beyond words. "What anesthesia did you use instead of the other one? I didn't have a problem this time."

"The truth is, Sheri, I used the same one, because it's the best there is." He laughed out loud. "I didn't give you anything to prevent nausea because I didn't want your system to have to deal with an additional drug—I just kept saying, over and over: *you will have no nausea.*"

Our partnership had clearly worked.

Now I appreciate that I have the power of choice in my medical care—even when I'm apparently unconscious. I read somewhere that the quietest and most compliant patients don't do as well in their healing as those who are more assertive. So I believe in taking matters into my own hands, working with my medical team rather than just letting them work on me. Why not go for the best results possible? I may sound a little odd, but who cares what people think? It's my body, my health and my life.

And after my second surgery, I have a newfound appreciation for the combined powers of my body, mind and spirit. What a team they make!

Sheri Borax

3

ADVENTURES

Self-discovery is the secret ingredient that fuels daring.

Grace Lichtenstein

Mountains to Climb

It is not the mountain we conquer, but ourselves.

Sir Edmund Hillary

The day begins like any other. A bird chirping good morning to its mate breaks the silence of the woods. A squirrel scurries through the leaves nearby. I slowly stretch my legs and begin to work the kinks out of my back, which is protesting, as usual, sleeping yet one more night on the ground. My belongings are within reach—backpack and clothing to the left, hip pack and gear to the right, flashlight and candle at the ready near my head—essentials to carry me through another day.

As I wriggle out of my sleeping bag inside the tiny tent, the air is already warm and humid, promising a steamy July day ahead. I change from nighttime shorts and T-shirt into my day-time duo. No decision about what to wear today—or any day. Within minutes, everything is stuffed into the backpack and I zip open the tent, poke my head outside and welcome the new day.

A year before, I couldn't have imagined spending a night, much less six months, alone on a mountaintop. I had been liv-ing the traditional life of a career woman in a Midwestern city. Fifty years old, I was neither a camper nor a backpacker. I liked my outdoor activities to end before sunset, so I could snuggle comfortably into bed for a good night's sleep. My challenges had always been mental, not physical. My two sons were grown and launched on successful lives of their own, and I was easing into the empty-nest years quite nicely.

Then one day, my world shifted.

I read an article about a young woman who had hiked the entire Appalachian Trail—all 2,155 miles of it—from Georgia to Maine. She carried a backpack, slept on the ground, waded through rivers, trudged over some 400 mountains. She pushed on through rain, snow, bugs, heat, humidity, sore muscles and blisters. *Why would anyone want to do that?* I wondered. *Aren't the days of questing long gone in this modern world of ours?*

Evidently not. The Appalachian Trail immediately started to call my name. Surprising myself even more than my friends, I decided to attempt my own thru-hike of our nation's longest wilderness footpath. A year later, I was heading north.

I've been on the trail now for four months; it feels like forever. The air is calm and clear, no sound save the occasional animal, nothing to break the spell of a perfect morning. I head toward a tree about fifty yards from my tent, untie a rope from around it and slowly lower my food bag from its swinging perch in the air, away from prowling bears and other forest critters. Time for breakfast: two-week-old cold tarts. At least they're tastier than yesterday's granola cereal with powdered milk, eaten out of a plastic bag. *Mmm, cinnamon frosting.*

I pull out the map to decide how far I'll hike today. The days are measured in steps: the ups and downs of each mountain; making it to the next stream for water; finding level ground to pitch a tent.

Anticipating the heat, I drink a quart of water. Before starting out, I filter two more quarts into plastic bottles from a clear eddy in the stream. I swallow a couple of ibuprofen to keep the constant pain in my knees at a tolerable level, hoist the pack onto my back and pick up my hiking stick. I ruffle up the leaves, allowing no trace of my presence to remain in the woods. The task of the day—hiking eighteen miles—begins.

The forest spreads out in every direction. Crests and valleys shimmer in the morning sunlight. Every view is different: Every tree, plant, flower and rock has its own shape, color and

position on the forest floor, and each catches or casts a different shadow. Halting occasionally to take it all in, to let the
sights, sounds and smells seep into my consciousness, I wind
up and down mountains, watching for the ever-present rocks
and roots, the stuff of hikers' nightmares, and skirt a pasture
where several cows stare blankly at me as I pass by.

At midday I stop for lunch, easing myself onto the shaded
ground under a tree. I've been sweating since early morning,
and the temperature is still climbing. I lean back on my pack,
take off heavy boots and massage my always sore feet. The
lunchtime menu is the same as yesterday: peanut butter, crack-
ers, granola bar.

A thru-hiker burns between 5,000 and 6,000 calories a day,
and I'm constantly trying to quell my body's insatiable
hunger. One of life's little ironies: Here, I can eat calorie-laden
food with abandon; unfortunately, the only food available has
been crammed in my backpack for days and was selected not
for its taste, but for how little it weighs.

Flies buzz incessantly around my head. I wet a bandanna
and spread it over my face to bring a little relief from the bugs
and the heat. When gnats join the fray, I know any relaxation is
over and press on. The insects follow along.

I hope I'll meet some of my thru-hiker buddies this afternoon. One of the unexpected pleasures of this journey has
been the growing friendship with others who are making their
own attempt to hike the Appalachian Trail. Most are young
men in their twenties and thirties. A few are in my midlife age
range or older. We're a community with the bonds of shared
experience.

Most thru-hikers have a trail name that identifies them, and
often I don't even know the real names of my comrades, but
when you meet someone who calls himself Bad DNA, Shelter
Boy, Scrap Iron or Model-T, you're not likely to forget his name.

Each year more than 2,000 backpackers attempt to hike from
one end of the Appalachian Trail to the other; 10 to 15 percent
make it all the way. The trail tests its hikers mercilessly. Thru-
hikers face two distinct challenges. First, we have to be equal to
the physical endeavor. During the most rigorous of the steep
mountain climbs, we concentrate on the task at hand, for

without focus there is the danger of injury. Adrenaline kicks in and helps us through the roughest spots.

As the months go by, the other challenge is endurance. Day after day, week after week, month after month, we have to find the mental and spiritual fortitude to keep picking up our boots step after step, mile after mile. The trail defeats more people with its daily grind than its most difficult mountain.

The day presses on. My backpack grows heavier, the knee pain intensifies and the bugs keep up their merciless bombing missions. The views remain unparalleled, but I just put down my head and hike. My water supply is low; dehydration is a constant danger in this heat. At a spot that should have provided water, only a tiny trickle is creeping over the nearly dry rocks, not even enough moisture to wet my bandanna, let alone offer a drink. Discouraged, I slowly hike on, knowing I'll have to conserve the little water left to make it to the end of the day.

By six o'clock I trudge up yet another steep mountain, still dripping wet, my bandanna draped over my face to keep the gnats out of my eyes. The stream promised by the map, where I intend to spend the night, must be right around the next bend, or the one after, but the last mile of the day is always the longest. Gritting my teeth and fighting back tears, I start down a steep decline, knees grinding.

There are days when I want to quit this strange odyssey and go home. I can't, though, because everyone at home is cheering me on, encouraging me in my adventure. Sometimes their support grates, and I think: *Well, why don't you come out here and take over this grand adventure! I'll gladly take my place in the armchair cheering section.* But this is *my* quest, not theirs, and I can't disappoint them any more than I can fall short of my own expectations. Thankfully, the times I want to quit are never when there is a road nearby.

At last I hear the gentle rippling of water against the rocks of the stream and see the riverbank ahead with level ground nearby. Another day's hike is done.

The relief is instantaneous; within seconds, my body begins to shrug off the exhaustion and pain. It's a good campsite with enough pine needles to make a soft cushion for my bed, a nicely flowing stream and trees overhead to enclose my home for the night with a comforting coziness. With my gear spread out on the ground, I pitch my tent, shake out my sleeping bag and mattress pad, hang a clothesline between two trees and take my water filter to the stream to fetch water for dinner. My bandanna now becomes a washcloth as I wash away the grime and sweat of a day on the trail.

I set up the stove and start boiling water for my meal: another night of Ramen noodles and instant mashed potatoes. Snickers candy bar for dessert. Typical backpacker fare.

Dusk falls. I enjoy the solitude of the forest and watch the shadows lengthen and disappear into the darkness. Nighttime sounds take on their usual cadence: the insistent sawing of the crickets, the slight rustle of breezes skimming the tops of the trees, the occasional far-off hoot of an owl. The mountains gradually work their magic. A sense of peace settles over me as my mind wells up with a feeling of good fortune and gratitude to be a student in Mother Nature's classroom.

Although this journey is the hardest challenge I've ever undertaken, it is teaching me more about life than I could have imagined. I see the constant, daily blend of rigor and rewards, and how one so often leads to the other. I've come to realize that the important lessons of life aren't learned within the comfort of a safe cocoon. Some days are difficult; others less so. It's important to carry on, to find dignity in simple perseverance. And whether I'm nestled into a warm, cozy bed at home or trying to get comfortable in a sleeping bag on the hard, cold ground, it helps to take a few moments to savor the joys as well as the hardships, and to appreciate the lessons.

I lie in my tent as the stillness of the night air fills the space. I blow out my candle. Its soft glow is the last thing I see before the darkness surrounds me and I settle into sleep. Tomorrow is another day, and there are mountains to climb.

Jean Deeds

Exploring Limits

*To be tested is good. The challenged life may be
the best therapist.*

                                        Gail Sheehy

Can I actually do it? What if . . . ? I forced my mind to focus on
what I had to do: pump tires, fill water bottles, bring food.
Today, for the very first time, I would attempt to bicycle 100
miles—alone. A century ride! Since the heyday of cycling in the
1880s, a "century" has meant 100 miles, and a feather in the cap
of anyone who completes it. At forty-seven, was I seeking new
horizons or denying my age? *Just think of it as another training ride,*
I said to myself. Then the critic chimed in: *But your longest ride has
only been fifty miles. Are you crazy?*

At 5 A.M. it was light enough to begin. The city was sleeping, the
air still chilly. *Maybe I should have worn something else. Fat people
shouldn't ride bicycles and shouldn't wear tight spandex shorts. But it will
be hot later. Maybe I should have . . . could have . . . would have.* My inner
critic was obviously more awake than I was. Though embarrassed
by my thunder thighs stuffed into padded stretch shorts, I wore
them anyway because they were so comfortable. Another inner
voice piped up: *The hell with you, you rotten critic!* I mounted the bike.

How I wished I were thinner! I believed *nothing* I did had

true value because I was so fat: not my job, not my twenty-four-year relationship, not even my friends. I felt inadequate because that's how I thought others perceived me.

Maybe this is stupid—a fat broad like me, 200 pounds of flab, squatting over skinny tires. I glanced at my bike computer. One mile done. *It's begun! If I do 100 miles then I'll feel worthy. Worthy of what?* I didn't know. *Maybe of just allowing myself to be me.*

After a few more miles, I settled into a familiar, comfortable pace. I paused after each hour to drink water, eat a fruit bar and stretch. *Don't think twenty miles down, eighty to go—you'll get discouraged.* After thirty miles, the sun had warmed the land. Red-winged blackbirds and meadowlarks flitted gracefully over the fields, and the smell of bacon frying drifted from a nearby farmhouse.

I knew from previous rides that the first half of the route was mostly flat and easy. I cycled along and tried to ignore the inner critic's whine that repeated: *If you were only thinner, you'd go faster and be farther along by now. If you were fitter, you'd be cycling in a group and not out here alone.* I couldn't always fight the voice that drove me to doubt my abilities, tenacity and worthiness. I had prepared mentally and physically for this challenge. I had put in 900 training miles in twelve weeks. *Hey, I'm coming up on fifty miles!* It had taken four hours.

At mile sixty-two—a metric century—I took a real break, refilled my water bottles, had a bagel and a banana, and got back on the road refreshed, concentrating on maintaining a smooth, steady rhythm. The landscape began to change as cornfields became rolling hills sprinkled with livestock.

Just shy of hour six I reached seventy-five miles, and stopped and stretched. *Wow, I've done three-quarters of a century, and it isn't even noon.* I sat by the dusty roadside and took notice of my swollen feet and aching neck. Pushing up the hills was definitely taking a toll, although the wind was still at my back. *I've already gone farther today than I have ever ridden before!*

I looked down the road and saw only more hills. I remounted, pushing hard on the pedals to get going. The spin was gone. *Why am I doing this? Cycling is freedom: a chance to explore my limits. This is my journey—not knowing what's down the road, yet creating a way to get there. Why have I let weight stop me from doing things?*

More hills. Heat. I was nearing my physical limit, and my legs felt leaden as my face flushed with the effort to keep going. I poured water over my helmet to cool my head. Around a curve I saw yet another hill, long and steep. *I can't possibly make it up that!* Fatigue echoed in my bones, voices echoed in my head: *I want to get off and walk up. No! That's cheating! Just quit! Eighty-three miles is nothing to be ashamed of!*

I got off the bike, stood there and started to cry, feeling exhausted, deflated, stunned. *Why am I doing this?* Then it dawned on me—*this* was my test. My personal version of the Boston Marathon's famous Heartbreak Hill—where some people failed. *Damn it, I'm not quitting. I won't. I just won't. I'm tired of feeling like a failure.*

I climbed back on my bike, shifted to an easy gear and started up. Midway, I began to run out of easy gears and enough oxygen for my lungs. I stood on the pedals and lifted myself off the saddle as I heard heavy, ragged breathing and felt the sweat in my eyes. I was barely able to push the pedals as my quad muscles burned.

Finally, the road flattened out a bit before the last steep pitch. I got off and sat down for a moment to relax my muscles, then rose again. *I'm no quitter.* I kept going. *I'm no quitter! Arrrggghhh! Yes! The top!*

Elation quickly turned to exhaustion as I realized it wasn't the top at all. If fact, all I could see were more hills. My jelly legs said *stop!* My whole body said *stop,* but I knew I couldn't, because my spirit had somehow resurfaced. I felt the strength in my mind, crisp and clear. I kept pushing at the pedals. No finesse, no power, just bloody-minded determination.

Mile 91: Seven hours and fifty-three minutes. *Well, I won't do it in my eight-hour time frame, but I am going to finish.* I pedaled slowly, letting the idea sink in. *I'm going to finish this! Wow!* A rush of adrenaline hit my legs.

Mile 93: *I'm through listening to my inner critic!*

Mile 95: Cheshire-cat grin, fist pumping the sky.

Mile 97: *I've been wasting my life waiting for the "thin" me to arrive.*
Mile 99: *So what if there's fat under my skin? Deeper inside there's a winner.*
Mile 100: Self-acceptance.

Sheila Ascroft

Living Life to the Fullest

It's never too late to become what you might have been.

George Eliot

At seven one autumn evening I slipped my kayak into the water, knowing it was late to start another leg of my dream voyage. I was nineteen years old, and one month into a kayaking journey around the southern half of North America from Vancouver to my home in the Saint John on the east coast of Canada via Lake Nicaragua and the San Juan River. Today's destination: the town of Westport, Washington, five miles due west.

A westerly wind gusted in my face, pushing huge waves at me as if to say, "Go back." A half-hour later, as the sun began its plunge into the sea, I was a mile from land—exhausted, wet, cold and aching. I kicked myself for not wearing my protective waterproof suit. *If I make another mistake, it will be my last,* I thought. With the wind and waves smashing against my face, it took all my strength to make any forward progress at all. Every few hundred feet, posts marked the channel. Several times a minute, I'd look back at the last post to check for any signs of progress.

I paddled on with a surge of power beyond my normal capacity. Fear gave me strength, and there was real fear here, real danger. Now my fatigue seemed strangely irrelevant. To stop paddling simply wasn't an option. So I sang to distract myself from my aching body and burning arms, but songs could not stop the fading light.

A half-mile from Westport, a massive mud flat blocked my path. I couldn't stay here—the flat would be covered with water when the tide came up. But the only way around would take me two miles out of my way, and I didn't have that kind of time left. It would soon turn dark, and I would be too far out to make it to shore. I desperately needed dry land.

I dragged my kayak up onto the slab of mud so I could assess the situation. To my surprise, I found myself standing not on a mud flat, as it had appeared in the dusk, but on an island. With my spirits recharged, I pulled on my waterproof suit and headed back out immediately. I was warm now and knew where I was going. Fatigue had turned to elation.

As I paddled around the lee side of the little island, hundreds of pelicans rose into the sky above me. With their large wings and long beaks these birds resemble pterodactyls, flying reptiles from eons ago. The sheer numbers of them filled me with awe. As the pelicans ascended, their silhouettes seemed suspended against the brilliant pink and orange sunset.

Before long, I arrived at a marina and began looking for a large boat to dock beside. I searched for a friendly soul—someone who would let me sleep on deck aboard his vessel. I paddled alongside a large yacht on whose stern was painted "Mystic Rose—Vancouver." Through a porthole, I saw a man inside browsing nautical charts. Soon after docking, I boarded and presented my request. The man—in his thirties, traveling alone and not a Canadian as I had assumed—lived in Vancouver, Washington.

While I was cooking supper in the cabin, Kerry made a suggestion that would change the course of my entire voyage: "How about pulling your kayak on board and sailing with me down to Astoria? Sailing solo is tough, and I could use the help."

"I'd really like to," I replied, "but I can't. I'm aiming to paddle the entire distance by myself." The truth was that I wanted to learn how to sail and wished to join him. Still, I felt driven by pride and independence—and a need to prove that I could set a course and stay with it. I wasn't someone who chose the easy way out. I wanted to be someone admired and respected for his courage and determination.

"I need to do this alone," I repeated. Hearing my own words, I realized that I sounded like someone trying to convince others—and maybe myself—that I was cool.

I asked myself why I took this journey, and why I had to paddle the entire distance. This journey wasn't just about kayaking, I realized. It never had been. It was about meeting people, having experiences and learning from both. It was about living life to its fullest, not waiting until I was too old to have a great adventure, to appreciate that every day I'm healthy and free is precious.

I had vowed to paddle the whole way because of pride—so I could say, "I did it by myself." But at what cost? What was pride worth when I paddled alone through the waves, miles from the nearest soul? When all I prayed for was my safety? Was my self-image more important than making a friend, learning something new and having fun in the process?

Kerry let me sail the yacht most of the way. He even let me take the wheel as we sailed through the Columbia River bar, where many ships have gone down (one of the most dangerous places to sail in North America).

We arrived in Astoria at four o'clock that afternoon. For supper, Kerry took me out for Chinese food. At the end of our meal, I opened my fortune cookie.

It read: *"Now is the time to try something new."*

Cory Richardson

A Fall from the Sky

When you look back at the anguish, suffering, and traumas in your life, you'll see that these are the periods of biggest growth. Many years later, you will be able to look back and see the positive things—togetherness in your family and faith that came out of your pain.

Elisabeth Kübler-Ross

One day, some years ago, my friend Beverley and I decided that we'd each like to experience the thrill of a tandem sky-dive—when a novice leaps out of an airplane without a para-chute while attached to an experienced jumpmaster who is wearing two, just in case. The jumpmaster keeps everything safe and stable so that even novices—in this case Beverley and I—can experience thirty seconds or more of weightless free fall.

We had heard about Kevin McIlwee's skydiving school—named after his war heroes, the Flying Tigers—and about his excellent reputation. Yes, even on a small island called Jersey, fourteen miles off the north coast of France, one can leap out of airplanes. As it happened, Kevin was presenting an introductory skydiving seminar at a local hotel, and so we eagerly attended. He was most impressive—a professional skydiver for twenty years who had completed over four thousand jumps, and the first British qualified tandem instructor.

During that first meeting, Kevin won our confidence, so Beverley and I signed up for our first tandem skydives. As time passed, Kevin won more than Beverley's confidence; he won her heart.

In the spring of 2001, Kevin and Beverley married. And now Mr. and Mrs. McIlwee prepared for their honeymoon. They packed their suitcases—and of course their skydiving rigs—and they set out on their journey. Kevin piloted their light aircraft from Jersey to the parachute center in Vannes, on the south coast of Brittany in France.

By this time, Kevin and Beverley had completed over fifty tandem skydives together and were looking forward to their long weekend in Vannes. The French parachutists welcomed them and invited Kevin to participate in some big formation skydiving. So the first two days of their honeymoon were spent doing tandem skydives together and making new friends.

On their last day in Vannes—Sunday, June 3—they decided to do one last tandem skydive before flying home to Jersey.

During their free-fall, they marveled once more at the spectacular view across Brittany. Then it was time to pull the ripcord and open the chute at 5,500 feet. Kevin looked up and saw that the parachute hadn't inflated. Kevin had to take *immediate* action. Built into his parachute rig was an automatic opening device that operated the reserve parachute. If Kevin didn't act quickly, the reserve would be released automatically, and it would almost certainly become entangled with the main chute. The result would be fatal.

Kevin yelled to Beverley to put her arms and legs back into free-fall position while he attempted to jettison the main chute. It wouldn't release despite Kevin's repeated efforts. Meanwhile, the ground was approaching at over 100 miles an hour. Kevin made a life-or-death decision—he deployed the reserve parachute with the main parachute still attached to the rig. It was an extremely dangerous maneuver, but his only chance of slowing their fall.

The chutes didn't entangle, but the reserve parachute started to spin, almost colliding with the main parachute. Kevin worked furiously to keep the two parachutes apart, knowing that they mustn't become entangled or the parachute would go out of control—and that would be the end.

Beverley stayed calm. In that moment, it was the only help she could offer. She trusted her husband to protect her as best he could. Meanwhile, Kevin was extremely busy: The parachutes would almost collide, then separate, then almost collide again, which sent Kevin and Beverley in and out of dives, their speed varying from a float to a plummet. The odds of their survival were not great. He decided to tell Beverley in case she might wish to say a prayer.

"Beverley, I don't think we're going to make it. I love you."

"I love you, Kevin," she replied. "Very much."

Beverley relaxed into her fate, whatever it might be; she felt no sense of panic, although she did say a quick prayer. Kevin prepared for a crash landing. The ground raced up at them, and he was horrified to see that they were coming down among trees, buildings and combine harvesters at work. By sheer luck, or the grace of God, they fell clear of any obstacles, but they hit the ground with massive force.

They woke in a nearby hospital where a team of medical experts set to work. Beverley had broken both legs and her feet as well. Kevin's lower left leg bones had broken and shattered his kneecap. The surgical team in France provided lifesaving initial emergency care, but it was decided that they should be flown home by air ambulance to Jersey since they were going to need extensive long-term treatment. There, the surgeon said that Beverley's feet were so severely broken that she might never walk again. Kevin's kneecap was shattered in so many pieces that it couldn't be saved. The surgeon told Kevin that he would walk, but that he would never be able to run or exercise to any great extent. Thus began a long process of operations and rehabilitation.

One year after the accident, a party of us celebrated Beverley's birthday at a local restaurant. Her ankles aren't so flexible anymore, and she has metal pins in her feet, but she looked stunning. And I saw something that night that will stay with me always and remind me what strength of character really means. When she was walking towards me, her heel pressed down on one of the metal pins and for an instant, I saw her wince in excruciating pain. Then she smiled, straightened her shoulders and said, "Oh, it's nothing. Have you all got enough to eat?"

Kevin has shown his own special brand of courage. Since leaving the hospital, he has worked out every day in the gym, without exception. He goes to spinning classes, and he works on the leg press to increase the flexibility in his left leg and strengthen the muscles around his knee. He cycles to and from work every day. His work has paid off. He passed his physical and got the all clear to pilot planes again.

According to the surgeons in France and Jersey, their injuries indicate they must have hit the ground at around sixty miles per hour. That they survived at all was a miracle —a honeymoon miracle. God must have known that they had more life to live together. And the paramedics who first arrived said that it was "good luck" that Beverley landed on top of Kevin, which prevented him from moving. Any slight movement could have severed the main artery of his leg that was still connected, and he would have likely died.

That day in Vannes, when Beverley and Kevin fell from the sky, lives that might have been lost were changed forever. Beverley's radiant blue eyes still shine as she reflects on how that accident opened her to new insights. "I can't wear high heels anymore, or run the way I used to—and I'll probably never ski again. But I've developed patience, acceptance and a new sense of perspective. The day we married, I would never have believed that we could be even closer, but we are. My brave husband saved my life, and this experience has bonded us forever."

Joanne Reid Rodrigues

Starting Over

Feel the fear and do it anyway.

Susan Jeffers

My husband of twenty-five years had died only three weeks before, and I was alone—running a business and worried about keeping house and home together. Everyone remarked how well I was doing. I looked composed on the surface and was comforted by the convincing role I was playing. But frightening questions arose when I didn't expect them. Could the business support my daughter Lexi and me without Paul helping us run it? Where would we move if I had to sell our house? Most frightening of all, I was terrified that if I surrendered to my grief, let myself really feel it, I would be sucked downward into a dark, bottomless spiral from which I would never return to sanity. I knew I had to do something.

Several years earlier Paul and I had been very impressed by a man named Tim Piering. He helped people work through their deepest fears by leading them through the very things they were most afraid of. I decided to make an appointment with him.

The following Saturday, I drove to Tim's office in Sierra Madre, located in the foothills of the San Gabriel Mountains in

Southern California. Tim, a tall ex-Marine with a big heart, asked me questions and listened to me for a while, then asked if Paul would want me to grieve for him. I thought about it.

"No, I can't imagine that he would. In fact, I think he'd strongly object."

"I'm sure he'd object, and I really think I can help, Diana. I think we can process some of the grief you're feeling, and lessen it. Would you like to try?"

"Y-yes," I managed to say. It was as if I wanted to hold onto my hidden grief out of loyalty to Paul, although I knew he'd want me to do everything I could to move ahead.

"Notice the thoughts going on in your head," Tim said. "All your fears, your considerations, sound like radio voices, don't they? Of all these thoughts, fear is the most debilitating. Not only does it sap your energy, but it also will cost you many great opportunities. Just think of how many times you have held back from doing something because of fear. If you are willing, Diana, I'm going to give you a quick course in stretching your ability to do anything you want to do. Basically, what will happen is you will have a completely new image of yourself, and you will see how you can take any action—any action you want—regardless of what your mind is saying. Your mind can be yakking away, even screaming, and you can go ahead and do things in spite of the racket going on in your mind."

Tim drove me in his truck high into the nearby mountains. He pulled onto a shoulder and parked. Carrying ropes and other equipment from the back of his sports utility vehicle, he led me out onto a bridge that spanned a dry wash several hundred feet below. I watched as Tim attached a pulley to the bridge railing and to his body and threaded the pulleys with ropes. Suddenly, he climbed over the railing and lowered himself slowly to the bottom of the canyon. Climbing back up the hill, he called, "Want to try it yourself?"

"Not on your life!"

Tim went over the side once again, showing me how he could maneuver up and down with the pulley, and how a safety rope was in place just in case. It did seem very safe, and

I began to feel I could do it, and said I might try it someday.

With that small crack showing in my armor of fear, Tim wasted no time strapping the gear on me and attaching the rope to my rappelling ring. He showed me how to gradually roll the pulley and come to a complete stop during the descent. He attached the safety rope to himself.

"Okay, now just step over the railing."

"Ha! Easy for you to say!"

"It's a metaphor, Diana, for how willing you are to really 'go for the gold' in your life."

I've never, ever felt more terrified. Since childhood I've been afraid of heights and had recurring nightmares of teetering on a cliff or window ledge. I trembled at the mere thought of standing on the outside of the railing. Very, very slowly I eased one leg over the railing, saying, "Oh, my God, I am so scared!"

Tim held both of my hands firmly on the railing as I lifted the other leg over, leaning as far toward him as I could for protection. My heart was pounding and I began to whimper.

"Let's just forget the whole thing!"

"It's your decision, Diana. You don't have to do it."

No one was making me do this, I realized. I'd come to Tim for help. I had a hunch that if I could only do this, it would make all the difference. Again, I resolved to try.

"Okay, I'm going to do it. I'm committed."

"Let go with one hand and hold the rope tightly so you won't start moving until you're ready."

I was bleating like a terrified sheep, I was so frightened. But I did what Tim said—I let go of the railing with one hand. Then came the crucial moment. I released the other hand—and there I was, swinging in small arcs over the canyon.

So far, so good.

"Now—very slowly—inch your way down a foot or two."

I did. At that moment, my fear was transformed to excitement. It was easy for me to operate the pulley. I took a long time lowering myself to the bottom, relishing the view and my victory over the terrified voice in my head. Tim ran down to meet me.

"Look what you did, Diana! You did it!"

And so I had. Li'l old me, exactly like a U. S. Marine! Wow! *If I could do that, I could do anything!* I thought to myself. I felt elated and more powerful than I ever had before.

Then Tim took me to a firing range and had me fire an automatic revolver repeatedly, another thing I would never have dreamed of doing. I realize now that Tim wanted me to feel a different kind of fear than what a woman—suddenly alone—would normally feel. Survival in a physical sense—not an emotional one. I could feel my life beginning again.

"Diana, you've stretched your reality of what you thought you could do. This is a benchmark that will allow you to rise to new levels of action in spite of fear. Whenever you feel confronted by an action you need to take, you can think back to this experience, and whatever challenges you face will seem easy in comparison. This one short event—committing to the action of going off the bridge—will propel you years ahead in how you operate in scary situations. And it will stretch your limits for all the things that frighten you. Regardless of your thoughts, you can do almost anything just because you commit to doing it. You've opened the door to the possibility of achieving all your dreams, Diana.

"In the beginning, you may spend most of your time fighting the negative comments of the radio voices that try to justify all the reasons why you shouldn't do something. But, as you remember what you accomplished here today, Diana, keep this thought in mind: The world owes you nothing. You've landed on the playing field of life. The only question is: will you play?"

Diana von Welanetz Wentworth

Into the Unknown

I believe in God, only I spell it Nature.

Frank Lloyd Wright

I've crashed motorcycles on race tracks, jumped out of air-planes in the pitch of night over heavy-canopied jungles and been narrowly missed by lightning strikes. But death came closest to me on a sunny October afternoon high in the Rocky Mountains of Colorado. On this particular autumn day I stared into the face of death with full awareness of its nearness, and knew my survival depended not upon luck, but on skill, judgment and faith.

I rode out of Boulder about 8 A.M. on my Ninja race-tuned motorcycle, heading for the high country of Rocky Mountain National Park. My objective: the granite spires above the town of Estes Park, to collect information for a climber's guidebook, which involved photography, location drawings and extensive climbing. Intending to complete charts of climbing routes, I would be climbing alone—free-soloing some of the easier routes to ascertain their difficulty and to determine the best line of ascent. (Free-soloing refers to climbing without a partner, or rope, or any other paraphernalia: one wears climbing shoes, a bag of chalk to keep fingers dry, clothing and that's all. It's just you and the rock.)

As I flew along, some little part of my mind drifted to a character called "Knulp," in the last pages of a novel of the same name by Herman Hesse. Knulp is dying alone in the snow outside his village. He laments to God that his life was wasted, that he had hurt all the people who loved him and had failed to achieve anything of substance. At that moment, a gentle and loving voice speaks to Knulp, saying that his life was not a failure, that every moment he lived, every joy and sorrow he felt, every song he sang and every woman he loved, was experienced and felt by God. Through Knulp, God had known and experienced another facet of this world. *God is here*, I thought—not only in churches, temples or monasteries, but also in the Earth and in all living beings.

When I arrived at the Twin Owls parking area, a warm wind whirled bright aspen leaves high into the air, and the soaring spires of Lumpy Ridge seemed to pierce the deep blue sky. I found no cars in the lot—not a soul present—most unusual. The day was dazzlingly bright and warm; still, a chilling, eerie loneliness ran through my bones.

As I scanned the crags above me, my gaze fell upon an unnamed rock tower with no recorded routes. I could see a long crack in the lower right side of the buttress. I decided to climb this spire, feeling I could definitely manage the initial crack and then choose whether or not to continue up the *arete* (its rounded prow of stone).

Most climbers will not free-solo, even routes they know well, because there is no margin for error. It's much like swinging on a circus trapeze without a net—no rope to catch a person who makes a mistake. Once off the ground, as I climbed ten, then twenty, thirty, forty feet and beyond, almost any fall could mean death. But I tend to be one of those who revel in the uncluttered freedom of ropeless ascents. This is not to say I carry a death wish—on the contrary, I approach each climb with the clear intention of succeeding; while I take a risk, it is calculated and planned.

Most free-soloists adhere to a few rules of thumb. First rule: Never climb up anything you can't climb down; in other

words, never make a move you can't reverse. Even great climbing athletes have broken this rule in their focus on completing
a climb, and have met early deaths as a consequence. Second
rule: Never climb near your maximum ability; that is, maintain
a reasonable margin of control. Third rule: Never free-solo a
route that you have not previously climbed with a rope. Most
important, *never* free-solo a route that no one has climbed
before.

I broke this final rule that day because I don't like rules in the
first place—and because the climb appeared well within my
range of ability. The crack was easy enough, getting more challenging toward the top. I soon found myself 200 feet above the
ground; the smooth, crackless *arete* loomed overhead. I paused
here to examine the possibilities and decide whether to climb
up or back down to the ground—knowing I could down-climb
all I had ascended so far.

Sudden gusts of wind began to blow me off balance, and I
had to expend extra energy gripping the tiny handholds. A
small, sloping foothold some three feet up to the left looked
reachable and tempting. My experience told me that once I
made the move and stood up on it, I would thereafter be able
to reach a sequence of holds with my hands.

But I knew that if I made this move, I could not hope to
reverse it. I would be committed to whatever lay above—there
could be no turning back. Some deep and unaccountable voice
in me said, *Go!* And my body obeyed. With both hands flat
against the smooth wall, I balanced up onto the little hold, large
enough only for the big toe of one foot. To my shock, the handholds I was counting on were too sloping to be of any use, and
my throat was suddenly dry. I could feel adrenaline surging
through my veins, my heart pounding. Then the feeling one
should *not* have while free-soloing poured over me like a cold
waterfall: *fear.*

I wrestled panic—fighting to extinguish the red lights and
sirens going off in my head—as my fingers groped for even the
most insecure hold, any hold at all to keep me from falling
backward into the maw of oblivion with the next gust of wind.

Another blast of wind ripped at my fragile moorings as I realized I had about sixty seconds before the few muscles supporting my body would give way, and the life I had known would be over.

I went deep inside myself—deeper than I had ever been. I knew if I gave into fear I would die. I told Spirit I wanted to live, and I wanted to prevail. I remember thinking, *May the Force be with me* as I started upwards.

To this day I have no idea what I did, or how I found those tiny holds, but I kept moving and kept believing. With attention focused upwards, I turned my back on the idea of falling and after what seemed a great distance, my fingers wrapped around a handhold that felt like the rung of a ladder. When I found that, I just hung there by one arm, knowing I was saved—that I had prevailed over something that had appeared impossible. The "Force" had indeed been with me that day— the "Force" and a few guardian angels as well. *Hesse was right*, I thought: *God is here, in the earth and in all living beings.*

Richard Rossiter

Zen in the Art of Survival

There is often in people to whom "the worst" has happened an almost transcendent freedom, for they have faced "the worst" and survived it.

Carol Pearson

Seven years ago, when I decided to take a woman's self-defense program for purely practical reasons, I was far from realizing the importance martial arts would make in my life. People come to martial arts for different reasons. For me, after more than ten years of traveling the world alone and finding myself in sticky situations more often than I wished, learning what I thought would be a few practical moves was the only smart thing to do. At the time, I didn't have any special interest in martial arts, karate movies did not appeal to me and my daily training consisted mainly of high-intensity cardiovascular workouts. Surprisingly however, what started as a self-defense program soon turned into a lifetime commitment. The practice of martial arts was a revelation to me the very moment I discovered it. It transformed my views and goals, became a new way of life, and ultimately happened to save my life in a rather unexpected manner.

When I awoke one beautiful fall morning, I didn't know I was at the start of what would be one of the most intense and fascinating days I had lived. The only anomaly was, for once, I had absolutely nothing planned. I had recently acquired a new sport bike, but the motorcycle was still in the process of being registered and I could not legally ride it. I decided to spend the day relaxing and catching up on work. My plans quickly changed when the phone rang and my friend Mike offered to pick me up for a ride to the Santa Monica canyons. The temperature was already warm and I hesitated whether or not to wear my racing leathers (something I no longer consider an option). Luckily, I opted for safety. Shortly afterward, I was flying along the beautiful Pacific Coast Highway on the back of Mike's Suzuki GSXR 1000 motorcycle.

After the long ocean-side stretch, we hit the familiar canyon roads with their narrow turns. The scent of the pines in the sun permeated the air, slowly succeeding to the salty breeze from the coast. At our favorite café on Mulholland Drive we met two friends of ours, Kate on her Honda CBR 600 and Rob on his Yamaha YZF. After a light convivial brunch, the four of us left in a single formation on our motorcycles. Just moments later, on a straight line of Topanga Canyon, death faced us. Kate was in the lead, Mike and I shortly behind, and Rob had just waved us past him to take the tail end. The road was clear, there was nothing ahead on that stretch of Topanga, not even intersecting roads or paths to be aware of.

How could we have possibly expected that a car had backed up into the dense bush behind a large tree on our right hand side? How could we have foreseen that the driver was drunk and would choose the very moment we reached the tree to shoot out of the bushes and barricade the road in front of us? No one could have anticipated the danger, and when the car suddenly blocked our way, it was too late to avoid it. Thinking I was about to witness my friend Kate coming full speed to her death right in front of my eyes filled me with the most horrifying terror I had ever experienced. I screamed as I saw her motorcycle smashing through the car with the most horrific sound of crushed metal, and her body flying through the wreck. I kept screaming as our front wheel hit the car, and as it dawned on me—only then—we were going down exactly the same way. In my all-consuming fear for Kate's life, it hadn't even occurred to me that Mike and I were condemned to the very same fate.

The instant of eternity between the moment of first impact and the time when my body finally lay still in the middle of the road, a hundred feet away from the wreck, will remain one of the most memorable experiences of my life. I had always wondered how I would react in a life-threatening situation. No matter how much we may train for it, we never know until—without warning—the moment is upon us. I often thought I would freeze in panic, or be overwhelmed by emotions. Instead, the impeccable functioning of a human brain working to save its life simply amazed me. From the very instant our front wheel hit the side of the car, all my fears and emotions vanished to be replaced by a cold, detached, data-processing mind frame. As the incredible force of the impact sent both our bodies flying through the tumbling vehicles, my scream turned into a martial arts *"kihap"* that lasted for the entire length of the accident.

My eyes remained wide open as I flew through the air, allowing me to register an image-processing moment that seemed to last forever. In the midst of the chaos, I became the calm spectator of a slow-motion slide show unfolding all around me with unmatched clarity. From our front end crashing into the side of the car to the shock—an impact incomparable to anything I had experienced—all the information I needed appeared to me in the form of snapshots: being propelled forward over the bike at full speed; the red of the car all around me; my shoulder hitting the roof; my body bouncing back and flipping over the vehicles; my helmet smashing against Mike's; colorful images of metal debris flying all around us. In this life-size kaleidoscope, projected though metal, glass and plastic, flying between life and death, and contemplating the moment free of any form of emotions, I lived an unforgettable instant of eternity.

When I saw I was going to hit the road head first, there was no hesitation as to what I had to do. Placing my left hand ahead and tucking my chin in, I landed on the pavement with a forward roll. The entire time I could clearly hear the repetitive commands of my martial-arts instructors: "Be like a beach ball . . ." "Relax your body . . ." "Let yourself roll smoothly . . ." "Be like water; fluid, flowing . . ." Also present in my mind was the advice of all the riders who had trained me in crash survival, some of which I had no idea I still remembered: "When you tumble on the pavement, never try to stand up. At some point, you will have the illusion that you have stopped, standing up then would break both your ankles and knees. . . ." "Let yourself roll as relaxed as possible until you know for sure that your body is still."

My forward roll sent me tumbling a hundred feet down the road. I didn't find out until hours later that my left hand (my first point of contact with the road) had sustained multiple fractures. Several of my metacarpals were in bone debris and required three months of consecutive reconstructive surgeries. However, not another single bone in my body was fractured. The paramedics on the scene admitted they could not comprehend how I was able to survive being projected at such height and tumbling on a pavement road for such a distance, without sustaining any damage to my spine or back. Miraculously, all of us survived. We each endured multiple surgeries and rehabilitation, with the exception of Rob, who had escaped the crash because he was last in line.

I believe I was supposed to die that day, exactly thirty days before my thirtieth birthday. However, somehow death must have been taking a break at the very moment I was flying through a car and tumbling on the road. Or was it that my forward roll was so powerful, I slipped right through my fate into another life, one I would have never known if it weren't for my dedication to martial arts?

Each year, as I celebrate another anniversary of this new life, I mentally thank all my talented martial-arts instructors for offering me that incredible gift.

Genvièv Martin

$\overline{4}$

EARNED WISDOM

*R*evelation is the marriage of knowing and
feeling.

Marya Mannes

Growing Old Disgracefully

To me old age is always fifteen years older than I am.

Bernard Baruch

I owe my life and liveliness to Grandma. If it hadn't been for her, I would have died of boredom . . . and I never would have learned the basic principles for growing old disgracefully.

My intensive training began at ten, the year I got some kind of weird skin disease on my feet. It was thought to be contagious and I couldn't go to school, so I spent all day, every day, at Grandma's house. The first time the doctor came there to look at my feet was a day I'll never forget. After carefully painting my toes with Mercurochrome, he wrapped each foot in miles and miles of gauze. He told me that I must sit very still all day so I wouldn't bump my feet, and that he'd be back the next day to take another look.

As soon as he left, Grandma turned to me, and, shaking her head, said, "That doctor may know medicine, but he sure don't know kids."

Patting my shoulder, she smiled down on me. "Don't you worry none," she said. "I know you can't sit still all day. We'll figure out a way for you to get around and still not bump those feet." And she did.

A little later, she slipped my feet into two shoeboxes lined with a layer of fluffy cotton. She tied them in with strips of sheeting and drew on the boxes so they would look like cars in a choo-choo train. Because it hurt to pick up my feet, she taught me to shuffle along and say. "Choo-choo, choo-choo, comin' through," so I would laugh and forget the pain.

But that night when I went to bed, the pain was so bad I couldn't forget it. I cried and cried. Grandma heard me and came to me. Instead of telling me not to cry, she encouraged me to cry louder. It helped somewhat, but not enough.

Then she bent down over the bed and whispered in my ear.

"I know some magic words that always take away pain. I think you are old enough to hear them. But you mustn't ever let anyone know you know them, 'specially your mother."

Peering over her shoulder on one side and then the other, as if to make certain nobody was listening, she continued, "Remember these words are to be used only in an emergency, after you've tried everything else and nothing works. And once you've started saying the string of words, you must keep repeating them over and over until the pain goes away."

Then softly she said these words in a sing-songy chant, and we practiced saying them together: "Hell, damn, shitty, poop, farty, pee. Hell, damn, shitty, poop, farty, pee. Hell, damn, shitty, poop, farty, pee."

And what she said was true. It was magic. After saying the words over and over, the pain did go away, and I went to sleep.

The next day, when the doctor came, he found me sitting quietly in the place he had last seen me, and the shoebox choo-choo trains were hidden in the closet. Grandma warned me not to tell the doctor what we had done.

"Honey," she whispered, "there is just one way to treat the wise guys in your life who tell you what to do: Listen carefully to 'em, and then do what you think is best."

Grandma's sister lived next door to her. She was humorless and crotchety and so different from everyone else in our family I used to wonder how she ever gained admission. While Grandma was round and soft and looked as though she ate sweet rolls every morning for breakfast, my great-aunt Lee was tall and bony and looked as if she sucked vinegar through a straw. At least once a day, every day, she would bemoan the fact that, "Growing old is no laughing matter."

If anyone seemed to be listening, she'd go on to complain about her rheumatism and how much it hurt to move and how she couldn't "see nor hear so good no more." Sitting at the kitchen table, dunking a doughnut into her coffee, she would recite a lecture I soon knew by heart.

"You'd better enjoy yourself while you're young because when you get to my age, you won't be able to any more. You had better obey your parents and make it easy for them because they are getting older too, and life is difficult for older people. Growing old is no laughing matter!"

One morning, after I'd heard her repeat that favorite phrase of hers for maybe the fifth time, I started to laugh. Pretending to have a fit of coughing, I ran from her house, for I knew she'd hit me if she thought I was laughing at her. And, of course, I was.

While watching her jerky movements and listening to her rasping voice and endless complaints, I suddenly had a fantasy of her on the stage, like a character in a play, a female Scrooge. I laughed because I realized she *was* a character in a play—one of her own making.

When I ran from my great-aunt's house, I sped next door to Grandma's. Still laughing out loud as I ran in, I let the screen door slam shut behind me. Grandma came out from her room to ask what was going on.

When I explained the situation, she started laughing too.

"You're quite right," she said. "That old lady is a character in a very dull play."

She took my hand and led me toward the kitchen, which smelled of freshly baked bread.

"Let's talk about it while we enjoy some hot bread. Remember, though, it's not good for your stomach to eat bread while it's hot like this. But a person has to do something now and then that's not good for them. Just do those things in moderation.

"You know, I think 'God's favorites' are those persons—

children or adults—who are slightly wicked—not bad-bad, but just a little naughty now and then. You can tell they are God's favorites because he gives them better dispositions, and people like to be around them more than they like to be around the saintly ones!

"I think people who try 'not to rock the boat' and try to make everyone happy are to be pitied. Their brain gets damaged by a too-tight halo that prevents the circulation of interesting thoughts."

At Thanksgiving and Christmas, Grandma, Mama and Aunt Emma would work together for days getting ready for the big family gathering, preparing the house, the table and the feast. Then, on the big day, after everyone had stuffed themselves, Grandma would announce to her daughters and the other women present, "I know you'll do a good job clearing away the dishes and cleaning up the kitchen. You don't need me now. I've done my share. It's time for my reward."

Then, taking all the men with her, she'd go into the living room and wait. As soon as the table was cleared, the tablecloth removed and the women cloistered in the kitchen with the dining room door closed, Grandma and her entourage would return, re-cover the table with an army blanket and proceed to play poker or craps. Sometimes she'd even smoke a cigar.

I would sneak into the living room and curl up in one of her overstuffed chairs, my arms around my overstuffed stomach. Half dozing, I'd watch, listen and marvel at my grandmother—who didn't act at all like other kids' grandmothers. I knew that I wanted to grow up and be just like her—I wanted to grow old disgracefully!

I'm eighty-five now, older than Grandma was when she died. And I've caused more than a few raised eyebrows along the way. It's been a life full of heart and humor and irreverence—just the very kind of legacy I planned so long ago on Grandma's couch.

Emily Coleman

Mirror, Mirror

Our bodies are our gardens to which our wills are gardeners.

William Shakespeare

As a student in the sixties, Janelle had traveled to Denver in search of the promised "Rocky Mountain High." She found it in some poetic scribbles on a powder room wall in Larimer Square, in these famous lines by Edna St. Vincent Millay:

> *My candle burns at both ends;*
> *It will not last the night;*
> *But, ah, my foes, and, oh, my friends—*
> *It gives a lovely light!*

The times were risky and the dangers real when she first read, memorized and adopted this simple poem as her credo.

In the shop next door she had come upon an old candleholder with a twisted brass ring. The ring held a candle before a curved reflector in a special way that allowed the candle to burn on both ends—thereby doubling the illumination. Janelle seized the odd lantern, paid too much for it and declared it her magic mirror. When faced with trouble or indecision, Janelle lit both wicks. Gazing into her distorted image above the dual flames, she reflected upon her options until a decision, or sense of inner peace, came to her.

Inner peace had become a rare commodity in Janelle's life. Like the candle burning at both ends, she habitually drove herself to the ragged edged of her time and energy, reaching her daily objectives with the help of caffeine and nicotine. Food came at random, as time allowed; rest came when the body could push no more. She often laughed about her schedule and quoted the poem that reflected her own race to achieve goal after goal without ever asking "Why?"

With time, Janelle finished college and swiftly soared to successful heights in her career. Marriage followed and, some years later, a family of two adorable babies brought her near-perfect joy. She pushed onward, mixing career with motherhood, and still kept a perfect house. She cut back on her caffeine and nicotine during her pregnancies, but almost as soon as each baby bounced beautifully into the world, Janelle returned to her subsistence on coffee and cigarettes.

As the evidence against smoking mounted, her husband hinted that her health was in jeopardy. Her mother nagged. When her friends began to kick the habit, one by one, Janelle—quoting her poem—consulted her meditation mirror, which reflected the candle burning at both ends. Gazing into the strangely quivering reflection from the distorted glass, she considered the brief span of our lives and weighed the boost from her friendly stimulants against her own mortality and quality of life. To continue smoking meant accepting the health threats in exchange for the promise of staying thin and enjoying chemically induced energy boosts. She repeated yet again, "This candle does indeed give a lovely light," and with that thought chose to continue her dubious lifestyle.

She proclaimed to friends and loved ones that she had made a conscious choice to smoke. It was her decision and her business. And smoke she did—at her desk, in the car, on the boat, in the house—even while she cooked, cleaned and read. The only time she did not smoke was when she tended the children, for somehow she could not totally shake the possibility that the smoking might not be good for them.

One day, as she drove home from work, a cigarette wedged between her fingers as she maneuvered the curves toward home, a voice came over the radio. "So you have chosen to smoke and to risk dying from lung cancer?" the voice asked.

"I surely have," Janelle sang out and took a deep drag from her cigarette.

The radio voice continued. "Did you know that 50 percent of the children whose parents smoke will also smoke?" The voice paused, then continued, "How many of your children have you chosen to die from lung cancer?" Janelle gulped and choked on the smoke in her lungs.

Janelle slammed the radio knob to quiet it, then quickly hit it again to bring it back, but the dial had moved and she could no longer find the awful man's voice. Tears stung her eyes as she desperately searched the stations.

Shaking, she pulled into the driveway. Her husband would arrive with the children in a few minutes. She had to pull herself together before they got there. From habit, she pulled deeply on the cigarette in her hand, now barely more than a filter, and the hot air burned her throat as it lunged into her chest. She flicked the butt to the driveway and ground it with the toe of her high-heel shoe.

Dropping her purse on the kitchen counter, she fled to the quiet of her office. There, she sat before the mirror and lit the two-ended candle. Staring into her own reflection, she repeated the question posed by the radio. If smoking parents caused half of their children to smoke, then odds were that one of her two would smoke—or maybe neither, or . . . maybe both. Even after she had preached to them so often against it. She shook her head. The cold, inescapable reality dawned on Janelle—because of her example, one or both of her beautiful children might smoke.

Janelle imagined she heard the mirror ask, *Which child will you choose to die?* And she began to cry as she had not cried in years.

When her sobbing finally ceased, she wiped her eyes, leaned forward and with a breath, extinguished the flames from the candle. Taking the twisted brass ring, she pulled until it turned and the candle, squatty from the dual flames, stood upright. Never again, she swore, would her candle burn at both ends. Her children would die someday, as we all do—but not from lung cancer, not from smoking.

Janelle was quieter than usual as she served dinner to her family that night. Afterward, she took the little ones aside, sat down with them and asked, "If I promise to quit smoking, will you promise never to start?"

Two warm hugs embraced her in an indelible promise. Janelle choked back the tears as she began a difficult but rewarding path toward a smoke-free life.

Janelle smoked two more cigarettes—but not until seven years later, and none since. Now, the magic mirror, silenced forever, has moved to the attic, to lie among other relics of the past. The candle retired, never again to burn from both ends.

What Janelle would not or could not do for herself, she did for her children. They have since grown up and made their own choices. Neither child smokes.

Joy Margrave

Reprinted with permission of George Crenshaw, Masters Agency.

Rite of Passage

Teachers affect eternity; they can never tell where their influence stops.

Henry Adams

When my son Chorus was in the sixth grade, his mother and I were divorced. No one suffered this parting of ways more than he. His whole body—the way he moved, as if carrying a hidden weight—revealed the extent of his wound. I wanted desperately to heal his pain, but felt powerless to do so.

When Chorus entered the seventh grade, he suffered from extreme sensitivity and low self-esteem. Fighting back tears, my son confided to me that no one liked him. I knew I had to do something for him—I would not fail him again—so, on his behalf, I began to investigate vision quests and other rites of passage in traditional cultures. I believed that some transitional ceremony might serve Chorus's confidence as he made the transition from boy to young man. I wanted him to experience a powerful rite of passage that would test his mettle and have real meaning for him. Since I was an experienced martial artist and instructor of Seibukan Jujutsu, it seemed that martial arts training might be a natural solution if he was willing.

Chorus's interest in martial arts was mostly relegated to the slam-bang movie fight scenes in action films, rather than to authentic training. So it required a leap of awareness and maturity on his part even to consider formal practice. I gave him the choice between learning some basic self-defense tactics, or committing to a serious training process that might one day lead to black belt ranking. Much to my delight, he chose the gauntlet of genuine training. Chorus remembers, "Back then I was extremely shy, small and easily intimidated. I didn't want to be this way—I wanted to be outgoing and powerful, but I felt as if a weight on my chest held me down. Then, when I began my practice, I realized for the first time that with a little help from my instructors, I might throw that weight off for good."

Each time we stepped on the mat, I became *Sensei* (teacher) to him rather than "Dad." Some days Chorus acted sullen and punky with me, ready to collapse and quit. But he stuck with it. Weeks turned to months. A year passed, then two. Chorus persisted through the peaks and valleys of training—through the bruises, the mistakes and falls, the fatigue and pain. Progress was slow and difficult sometimes, but he learned that sweat and discomfort are part of the process. There were times he was too tired or sick to train, but he still wanted to do so. Once he insisted that we keep going despite a painful injury. During his years of diligent and faithful training, his martial arts ability improved greatly. But more importantly, I watched my son mature into a fine young man with growing confidence and physical ease.

When Chorus progressed to the brown belt level, Kancho Julio Toribio, the chief instructor and I planned more intensive training for him, including several trips to Seibukan Jujutsu headquarters in Monterey, California. There, he trained in every aspect of the art required for the *Shodan* (first-degree black belt) level. Chorus recalls, "It was during this time in Monterey, while training and relating to people a lot older than me, when I first noticed changes in my personality: I started speaking to people more, and making my own decisions. I noticed that I wasn't as shy as I used to be."

One weekend in May shortly after his fourteenth birthday,

the time came for Chorus to take his black-belt test. It was both significant and unusual for one so young to have advanced in the art as he had done. I believed he was ready, but the pressure encountered in this moment of truth, in a test of this nature, can make people respond in unpredictable ways. I could not know for certain if he would prevail. We traveled to Monterey to the main school, where Chorus spent all day Saturday practicing with advanced students and receiving constructive comments from the instructors, including me.

On Sunday morning, Kancho Toribio called Chorus to a special gathering. He sat in the middle of a circle of men much older and more mature than he. There, we each told Chorus about two events in our respective lives—one in which we were proud of our response to a difficult situation, and another where, in our own eyes, we failed and felt shame or regret about how we had behaved.

Each man spoke his truth openly and honestly, sometimes with great emotion. The stories ranged from heroics to cowardice in violent situations, from abuse experienced as a child to the pain of losing a loved one to death or a parting of the ways. I believe this was one of the most powerful events in my son's life—maybe in all our lives. It seemed extraordinary to see a group of men show such vulnerability for the sake of a young man's development. This sacred event had significant impact on my son. Following this gathering of men, Chorus was instructed to clean the *dojo* (school) in a traditional manner, and prepare for his test.

On Sunday afternoon, Chorus stepped on the mat to perform his black-belt demonstration. As his father, I was pleased that, despite everyone's obvious affection for my son, they did not go easy on him during this ordeal. It was a full-out test at the black-belt level, with attacks by individual and multiple assailants—empty-handed and with live, bladed weapons. It was an exhausting trial for him both physically and emotionally. I knew, because I had passed through it myself years earlier.

As his successful demonstration ended, my tears reflected the great pride and happiness I felt for my son. And when he received his black belt with great ceremony, Chorus said, "I cannot tell you all how grateful I am to my father and to those who helped me complete this process and attain the rank of black belt. This has been the most important learning experience of my life."

Something changed for us both during this whole process. The healing that I had prayed for had occurred, but even more, there was a new bond between us. We agreed we would never hold back secrets from each other and established a deep level of trust that is rare between fathers and sons in these modern times.

Recently Chorus turned seventeen, and I had the privilege of seeing him pass his test for an advanced level of black belt outranking my own. This was a proud and happy day for us both. My boy has truly become a man. I have since retired from teaching the martial arts. My son Chorus is now the primary instructor for Seibukan Jujutsu of Marin County, California.

Robert Bishop

"Know what's a good exercise, Daddy?
Reaching down and liftin' somebody up."

Of Needs and Wants

To leave footprints in the sands of time, better wear work shoes.

LeGrand Richards

I was thirteen. It was 1967, the year I started hanging around with a handful of kids a grade older than I was. The year I learned to smoke and swear. The year my baseball coach told us to take a lap around Cloverland Park and, halfway around, a bunch of us just quit and walked. The previous year, I had made the twelve- to thirteen-year-old all-star team as a rookie. This year, as a "veteran," I not only wouldn't make that team, I wouldn't *care* about not making it.

Around me, the revolutionary sixties swirled, ushering in an invitation to freedom, to experimentation, to breaking away from the shackles of authority and boldly going one's own way. I was poised for a summer of nothingness, the idea of irresponsibility happily wallowing in my teenage brain.

At which point I learned that my mother, in all her wisdom and foresight, had arranged for me to spend the next ten weeks mowing a fraternity lawn with her father—my grandfather—an ex-Army officer.

"Now, Bob," he said, looking at me and my tattered tennis

shoes on the first day of work, "what you really need is a good pair of work boots."

What I really needed, I felt, was to be back in bed, not mowing a lawn the size of the Arlington National Cemetery in ninety-degree heat while being watched by Sgt. Perfectionist. This lawn job, you see, was not some here-and-gone task that could be completed whenever I had a spare couple of hours. This was a full-time job. I was expected to show up virtually every day at 8:00 A.M.—not to be confused with 8:05 A.M.—and complete a list of jobs that my grandfather had written on three-by-five index cards the previous night: mowing, edging, watering, weeding, fertilizing, sweeping, pruning, planting, trimming, painting, sanding, scraping, taping, chipping and clipping.

For this, I was to be paid $1.50 an hour.

Boots? Get real, I wanted to tell the old man. It was bad enough that I'd be spending my summer trying to scrape unwanted grass from sidewalk cracks, but did I have to wear a ball and chain in the process? Boots restricted. Boots were clumsy and time-consuming. But more importantly, in the mind of a thirteen-year-old boy who was knocking on the door of sixties coolness, boots simply looked—well, stupid.

From the beginning, it was clear my grandfather and I were separated by more than two generations; more like two universes. We saw the world differently. We saw this job differently. We saw proper work attire differently. He showed up each morning in a uniform that was part U.S. Army, part Home & Garden: well-pressed beige pants with cuffs, a long-sleeve shirt that often buttoned at the top, an Oregon State University (OSU) baseball hat and, of course, boots. Well-oiled boots.

At sixty-eight and retired, Benjamin Franklin Schumacher presided over the grounds of the hallowed Sigma Alpha Epsilon (SAE) fraternity at OSU, where he was treasurer and self-appointed "guardian of the grounds." To him, this was not a fraternity. It was a block-wide, split-level shrine. Nearly half a century before, he had been a member. After college, he had

continued to be involved in the fraternity, becoming affectionately known around town as "Schu of '22." In the years after
World War II, my father and uncle had been SAEs here, too.

"Now, Bob," he once said, "tell that daughter of mine [my
mother] that she should invest in some good boots for you. Get
the ones with the steel-shanked toes. They'll protect you." Then
he laughed his *hey-hey-hey* laugh, a kind of laugh that sounded
like a lawn mower that sputtered but wouldn't turn off, even
when you hit the stop button.

Yeah, yeah, yeah.

Needless to say, he wasn't all that pleased when I overfertil-
ized the Harrison Street quadrant and the grass turned the
color of beef Stroganoff—nor when, upon returning from a
weekend camping trip, I realized I'd accidentally left the sprinklers on for three solid days and created Fraternity Lake. But as
the days turned into weeks, I noticed something about the man:
He never got mad at me.

"I'll tell ya, Bob, nobody's perfect," he said after the sprinkler
incident. Instead of berating me for doing something wrong, he
would simply take whatever tool I had used inappropriately
and show me how to use it right.

"When you do a task," he'd say, "do it as well as you can,
even if nobody is watching. When you try to fix something and
find yourself stuck, improvise; use your imagination. When you
take out a weed get the whole root or 'the guy' will be back in
a few weeks."

He always talked about weeds as if they were human and
part of some top-secret military operation, as if dandelions had
generals who devised intricate plans to invade and capture,
say, eastern arborvitae (a type of evergreen tree).

He led, I followed. While I did my work, he did his. Only
when he did his work, it was with a certain enthusiasm that I
couldn't muster, as if he found a deeper purpose to the job.

One day, when I was changing the southeast sprinklers, a
guy in a car turned onto Harrison Street, rolled down his window, and said, "Hey, looks great."

After he drove on, I looked at the landscaping and realized

the man was right. It did look great. I realized people actually noticed the job we were doing here. I realized, as deeply as a thirteen-year-old can realize, that I was somehow part of something. Something good.

Gradually, I began caring about how the SAE place looked almost as much as Schu did.

For three summers, I helped my grandfather take care of the SAE grounds, and I came to realize ours was the best-kept fraternity or sorority in Corvallis, probably in the entire world. But I learned more than how to keep grass green, sidewalks swept and trees trimmed. I learned that work was good and honorable. I learned that what something looked like on the outside said a lot about what it was like on the inside. I learned there is a right way and a wrong way to do something.

More than anything, I learned how to grow up. To care more and swear less. Just like the Gravenstein apple trees along 30th Street needed pruning so the fruit would be better, so did I need some pruning, Schu figured. And he was right.

In February of my sophomore year in high school, I was sitting in Mrs. Shaw's English class when an office worker brought me a pink-slip message. All eyes turned to me. My heart pounded. It read: "Your grandfather is waiting for you in the office."

The possibilities swirled in my mind as I hurried down the hall to the office. My father was dead. My mother was dead. But there stood my grandfather, and nobody was dead. "Bob," he said, "I've arranged to take you out of school for a short time."

"Why?" I asked.

"Let's just say it's a little birthday surprise," he said, laughing his *hey-hey-hey* laugh. We got into his gold Oldsmobile, which was roughly the size of the *USS Teddy Roosevelt,* and drove a mile down Buchanan Street to a one-stop shopping store. I slumped low so nobody would see me.

I couldn't figure out what was going on, but he led, so I followed him into the store. We stopped in the sporting goods section.

Some kids get cars on their sixteenth birthday. Some get

stereos, ten-speed bikes, skis or skateboards. But my grandfather cared too much to give me something I wanted. Instead,
he gave me something I needed.

"Now, Bob," he said, "take your pick." And he gestured
toward a huge display of work boots. The kind with the steel-
shanked toes.

Bob Welch

"I need an allowance that reflects my self-esteem."

Tears and Laughter

Every child is born with the message that God is not yet discouraged of man.

Rabindranath Tagore

Through misted eyes I gazed at my little son as if for the first time—and perhaps for the last time. He lay sedated, fighting for his life, with two holes in his heart and pneumonia. Doctors questioned whether my two-month-old baby with Down's syndrome would live.

I wanted to remember what it felt like to be his mother. I wanted to savor my inability to distinguish where my flesh ended and his began. As I softly pressed my cheek against his, our connection calmed my fears. I wanted to remember the wisp of curls that twirled behind his ears, and the feeling of life fulfilled when his almond-shaped eyes drifted to look into mine. Mostly, I wanted to remember the inexplicable warmth that filled my heart when I held him.

I had dreamed of days when we might build sand castles at the beach together; when Eric would swing so high in the park that he'd feel like he was flying; when he would play catch with his daddy and cuddle with me. I begged the doctors to keep him alive. I pleaded with the nurses to feed him more. And I prayed to a God that I didn't know well to let me keep my baby.

After one special conversation with my husband, Bob, I came to realize that Eric's soul would choose whether to stay with us or let his body go. We stood on either side of his cold metal hospital crib and told him we would stay with him, love him and nurture him if he chose to stay with us. My mind trusted whatever his soul chose, but my heart ached with the hope that he would choose to stay.

Meanwhile, desperate to remember what it was like to hold my baby when it might last only these two precious months—to remember every moment—I decided to write it all down so I could never forget anything. From that moment of resolve, words flooded my thoughts. I formulated chapters in my mind between conversations; phrases appeared as I slipped off to sleep; and whole pages might appear to me upon waking, while driving or at Eric's bedside.

During his second week on life support, I strode into the hospital, past the reception desk to the bank of elevators, all the while transmuting emotions into words, mixing hopes and prayers. I stood before the elevator doors and stared up at numbers blinking all too slowly—5 . . . 4 . . . 3 . . . 2 . . .—until the soft bell rang and the doors parted to reveal smiling grand-parents, nurses and orderlies from the pediatric ward. They passed within a few feet of me, but we were worlds apart. I entered and leaned against the cold wall, returning to my sanctuary of words as the elevator rose, and then I walked slowly down the long hallway to the children's ward.

Before Bob arrived, I whispered to my baby about plans for our book; it would be our secret. Then I remembered that I don't keep secrets, especially when opening up is essential, so I told my husband and some close friends as we gathered near Eric. I began writing that very evening at my kitchen table, occasionally turning to gaze upon the empty cradle in the living room, a reminder of my baby still in the hospital. It felt like a part of me had been pulled away.

Eric triumphed through those six weeks of life support, but

over the next two years, he had numerous bouts of pneumonia, respiratory viruses and digestive problems. He was dependent on a breathing tank for his oxygen. We always knew where our little guy crawled to by following the fifty-foot oxygen tube that trailed from the breathing tank at the end of the hall, wound around the kitchen table and into the living room, and ended attached to Eric's face, allowing the prongs to let purified air flow into his nasal passages.

When he was seventeen months old, the doctors told us it was time for Eric to have his heart repaired. They said, "He's as healthy as he can be under such conditions. If you wait much longer, it will be too late." But they couldn't guarantee that his fragile heart and weak lungs would make it through the grueling surgery.

Forty-eight hours later, I stood by his crib and gazed past the tubes and wires to his angelic face, looked down and watched as he opened his eyes and focused on me. His smile illuminated the room. I let out a cry of relief. I knew Eric was here to stay.

Through it all, the writing has carried us through the recurring life-support crises as Eric's legs dangled again and again over death's pier. I recorded every experience, every emergency and breakthrough, every painful moment and every miracle as love carried us deeper into ourselves, peeling away our resistance, teaching us to rely on faith.

Our son needed cardiologists, pediatric nurses, therapists and specialists to repair his heart; we needed Eric to repair ours. Our lives were opened up to a degree I never knew existed. In the midst of these past years, I found myself sitting at the large table in the corner room of the Unity Center, where we held our Up with Down's meetings. I sat across from a brand-new mom and dad. She held her one-month-old, blond-haired, baby with Down's syndrome protectively against her chest, while her husband wrung his hands in his lap. "We haven't told our parents yet," she said. My eyes fixed on the young father's face as she spoke. His tears never stopped.

Then it came to me that my book should not be a secret from *anyone*, because we have known great pain and found miraculous healing. It comes from Eric's heart and mine. After more than four years, his valiant little heart beats stronger with each passing day we are given.

Today, we can't keep our son out of the playground. It's either monkey bars or basketball, soccer or T-ball. We've since built many a sand castle together, discovered new parks and playgrounds, have taken turns reading and rereading his books—yes, he is reading now! We have pretended to be manatees in our swimming pool and have eaten too much popcorn at the circus. We have a special boy who lives a joyful life.

Eric has his heart checked once a year, but his laughter washes away my fears. When I look into his bright eyes and feel the warmth of his bear hugs, I know his loving heart is going to be just fine. And so is mine.

Kimberly Thompson

Diary of a Yoga Retreat

The present moment is a powerful goddess.

Goethe

Saturday—Departure Day: I wonder how much we'll be "rough-ing it." The hotel in Maya Tulum, Mexico, where I will celebrate my fortieth birthday at a yoga retreat, is far off the beaten path—no minimarts, phones, televisions, radios, e-mails or faxes.

Except for our yoga teacher, Suddha Weixler, our group is all female. I wonder, *Will we compare thighs and flexibility?* By the time we reach Cancun airport, one woman complains of thirst and fears drinking the water; another camps out in the ladies' room; still another holds vigil at the baggage carousel for what has to be suitcase number five; yet another comments that the resort "better have lunch ready for us." Group travel irritates me. I ask myself, *Am I surrounded by self-indulgent, ladies with more money and leisure time than manners? Am I one of them?* I exhale loudly and close my eyes.

Gretchen, my friend and roommate for the trip, has promised that, "Yoga really does put you in another place." I hope so.

Sunday—New Realities: Our room is a little round hut called a *palapa,* with a conical thatched roof, twenty feet high, which creates a sense of space and openness. It is supported by walls of hand-cut limestone with bits of red coral and fossil patterns. Dried palms delicately scent the room with a light herbal fragrance. There are four large unscreened windows held open by sticks, and two beds draped in mosquito netting.

After dinner, we are told we may sign up for a healing session with a medicine man. We're told he prays over each person and pushes on your navel; we are advised not to eat for two or three hours before seeing him. I am skeptical, however, and have questions: What does he heal anyway? How does he know what to heal when we don't speak the same language? I'm told he's in touch with a different reality and senses what each person needs. Okay. Sure.

Monday—Inner and Outer Worlds Awaken: Gecko lizards cling to our ceiling and twitter to life at the first light of day. This lizard alarm gets me up in time to see the sunrise. Yoga class begins at 7 A.M. I gulp down coffee before hurrying off. We work hard, synchronizing our breathing and movement. Teacher Suddha demands precision and alignment, and by the end of the hour-and-a-half session, my body tingles. A childlike joy arises, and I giggle aloud as I walk back to my hut through the soft, tickling sand.

Tuesday—A Closer Look: The yellow leaves shine in the sun's glow as Suddha explains that yoga is not about perfecting a pose, but about awareness. Today I feel confused and ignorant. I know nothing of yoga or meditation, but sense a new kind of humility, a beginner's mind. "Listen to and respect your body," our teacher reminds us. This advice saddens me, because I realize how abusive I've been to my body. I don't feel as badly about the occasional drink or smoke or junk food—but rather, how I dislike my own body, especially my hips and thighs. I feel guilty.

I yearn to make a lasting peace with the body I've judged harshly in so many ways, remembering a proverb that says, "Tears are for the soul what soap is for the body." I cry cleansing tears.

Wednesday—Day of Silence: We have all agreed to a vow of

silence today. Our mandate from Suddha: "To attend only to that which is uplifting." During this meditative day, I begin to notice my constant mental chatter and instead turn my attention to the breeze, and to how the wind gives motion and life to leaves, to loose clothing, to hair.

I walk three miles or so to another beach, feeling the burning sun on my calves, complaining to myself: *I wish I'd taken a taxi; it's hot, it's too far.* Then something stirs in the bush: I watch a large bird lift into the sky as a yellow-white butterfly flutters across the road; I listen to the water bottle make a *slug-slug* sound as I walk—a primitive rhythm for the journey. I'm suddenly surprised—I realize I have all I need.

I climb down a cliff to reach the beach, taking time, making sure my grip and step are secure. This is new for me—taking my time, listening to my body, trusting its slow, calm pace, embracing slowness. I realize this is my rhythm; I am finally allowing it to guide me.

Thursday—More in the Moment: Indulging my body, I expose my upper half to the sun until my whole body longs for its warmth—so free, so open, so uninhibited to swim naked in the sea. This is pleasure: the water soft, warm, salty, wavy, caressing, pushing, pulling, rising and falling in a languorous rhythm. We begin the next yoga class with chanting, then move briskly through the poses. I keep up, doing my best, remembering to breathe, focusing my attention and therefore improving my balance.

After class, a little tired and hungry, I fall into the rhythm, flow and awareness of my body—stretching, inhaling life, exhaling what is unnecessary, feeling my strength, accepting my limits, not competing with myself or others. That's true power, true beauty, true peace.

Friday—Things Are Not What They Seem: Today I celebrate forty years of life and enter a new decade. The sun brings a new day in a sliver of fuchsia sun peeking behind a blue-gray cloud. A pelican splashes into the sea and bobs up quickly.

I finally have a session with the healer. He lifts me up like a little doll in his large callused hands. He embraces me many times, holds my hands and face, and chants, *"sanctus, sanctus"* ("holy, holy") over my sacrum and ovaries. I want to cry as he blows on my body with compassion and then inhales as if absorbing any negativity. He also pushes on my navel, massaging my internal organs—a bit uncomfortable, but not too bad. At the end, he takes an object in his hands and tenderly lays it on my belly. It feels cool. *Something healing,* I think. *A banana leaf? A small, special rock?* He leaves the room, and I hear him exhale heavily outside the door. I rest happily with the object on my belly, trying to absorb whatever healing power it might have. I finally look at it. It is my watch.

Saturday—Departure Day: Last night we shared a birthday cake with candles and song. I've grown to love these women for their kindness and generous spirits. And I love my own spirit, my own body, in new ways.

Some of us shed tears at parting. We spend our final afternoon roaming the beach, focused on the joy of the immediate reality.

Sunday—Home, and Keeping the Inner Peace: I sort my mail, surprised by the onrush of "stuff" that bombards each day, and the media clamoring for attention. I'm no longer tempted to open the envelopes touting "free offer," or "hurry—expires soon!" I recall Suddha's words: "No future, no past, just now." I pat my dog lovingly, and watch the changing morning light.

JoAnn Milivojevic

A Matter of Weight

You just give folks a key, and they can open their own locks.

Robert R. McCammon

Ever since grade school, when being the biggest girl in class landed me more than a fair share of snickers, I've had a difficult relationship with my weight. Kids called me all sorts of names—Pork Ball, Porcupine Rind, Jam Pudding and worse. I pretended to laugh along with them, but went home and drowned my anger in food.

It wasn't until I turned eighteen and fell in love with a tall, soft-spoken boy from Massachusetts that the weight slipped off. And when I married him six years later, I was a svelte 103 pounds. For someone who enjoyed food as much as I did, this was no small feat. Those were the Twiggy days, when being knitting-needle thin had become a cultural obsession; the fashion industry was relentlessly unforgiving towards natural bulges and buxom shapes.

But "skinny" didn't last long. Within two years I gained over ten pounds, and with the birth of our first child three years later, I added another forty. The old grade school angst returned, and I decided to wage my own holy war against the bulge. I took up running, beginning with a brisk walk around the block, and then doubled my efforts until I was able to run comfortably for two miles without stopping. By the end of the year, I had shed thirty pounds and was permanently hooked on running. It made me feel brisk and clean, like a colt; it allowed me to eat what I wanted and it kept the weight manageable. As long as I pounded the pavement for fifty minutes, five times a week, I was able to keep my weight within an acceptable range.

Still, I fretted over every bite. My husband, much more relaxed about body shape, said, "I wish you could just enjoy being what you are. You carry so much guilt about what you do and what you look like that you aren't enjoying life at all!"

"But I feel so fat!" I countered.

"I have a suggestion. Get rid of your scale."

I did—and miraculously discovered that my body had its own way of finding balance. I moved from "how much I weigh" to "how I feel." For several years, I ate when I was hungry and ran not because I had to, but simply because I loved the sense of exhilaration it gave me. I didn't choose one activity to cancel out the other, but did both because they fed my soul. And although I didn't know exactly how much I weighed, I was content because my clothes remained a comfortable fit.

Then everything changed the year I turned fifty. My husband passed away after an eleven-month battle with cancer. Food became a different kind of issue during his illness, when his body refused to eat because the radiation had scorched his throat and he couldn't swallow without pain. Day by day, I watched him shrink to a shadow.

After his death, I was plagued by a terrible loneliness. In the silence of an empty home, I ate, wept and ate again. I noticed my body becoming dumpy and thick. Despite a daily run, pockets of flesh flapped under my arms and my belly jiggled like Jell-O. A year later, my obsession with weight returned.

I bought a new scale, joined the local fitness club, placed myself on a high-protein diet and squelched my natural enjoyment of food. I ate only what was permitted: egg whites, cheese, onions, tofu, seeds, nuts and lentils, and drank designer whey drinks. I ran six days a week and did an hour of resistance training three times a week. I worked out this way for four weeks, like a soldier, then I stepped on the scale. You could have heard my scream ten miles down the road: I had gained three pounds. How was that possible?

An older friend had once said, "You just wait—the day will come when your body will stop performing for you. It will bloat, swell and gurgle; it will rise and spread and do all the nasty things you exercise freaks are trying to keep under control. Just wait and see." Her eyes gleamed with venom.

I would have believed her and turned the rest of my life into a lament had it not been for a vivid dream, which came like a message from my body:

> I was on a dark, stuffy train. Several people were with me, and we were on a mission of some kind. They had wrapped me up in long sheets and placed me in the aisle. When the train stopped, the sheets peeled off, and I followed the crowd out the gates and down winding stairs towards some kind of underground cavern. The journey was long and tedious, but we finally emerged from the last flight of stairs into the depths of a cave. There, in the center, was my husband, lying on a hospital bed. He was bone-thin, cheeks sunken, eyes hollow. I walked up to him, placed my hand over my hip and complained to him, "I can't stand it. All this work coming down here and I haven't lost a pound."

Then I woke up, and it hit me: that dream showed the absurd irony of my situation. My husband could barely eat at all, and all I could think about was losing weight.

The next morning I threw away the scale.

Life, I decided, was too short for weights and measures. I would run and I would eat. I would take pleasure in both. I would neither deny my body nor starve my soul. I was going to love my body in whatever shape and form it took. My body was here to serve a higher purpose, my soul's purpose, and my soul was not here to be shaped or stuffed into a standard mold.

Mary Desaulniers

Granny's Last Cartwheel

Self-respect is the fruit of discipline; the sense of dignity grows with the ability to say no to oneself.
                                                    Abraham J. Heschel

Being a family today is complicated, but it hasn't always been this way. When I was growing up in a small town in the fifties, life—and family—was simple. Like all my friends, I lived in a house with two parents, and Mom was there every day when I came home from school, filling our home with the cozy smells of something cooking. Dad worked long hours and came home exhausted, but not too weary to watch my tricks when I performed somersaults, handstands and my favorite of them all—the cartwheel.

He would sit on the porch in the evening trying (I now understand) to have a few moments of solitude, yet he would always have a cheer for me as I performed my one-woman, amazing circus act on the soft, green lawn of our front yard. A somersault got a nod. With handstands, he helped me count the seconds I could remain upside down, legs splayed, balanced on those skinny little arms. But it was my cartwheel—my amazing, back-arched, legs-perfectly-straight, toes-pointed-to-the-sky cartwheel—that won his applause.

My grandmother was a gray-haired, elderly woman who lived halfway across the world in another country called Minnesota. She wasn't fond of noise or noisy children. When she came on the train for a visit, I was reminded that children "should be seen and not heard." My grandmother never saw my cartwheel.

Yes, life was simple then. Everyone knew the rules, and everyone knew their roles in that choreography we called "family." But life changes, with twists and turns along the way. I grew into adulthood and created my own family. By midlife, I found that I was not only grandmother to my own children's children, but to the progeny of my new husband's children as well. Family was no longer simple.

Even the question of "What should they call me?" was complicated, because they already had the ideal number of two grandmothers. I dubbed myself "Granny Nanny" and hoped that it would take. It did.

I didn't want to be the granny who lived on the other side of the world and didn't like noise when she visited. I didn't want to be the granny whose visits they feared or dreaded. I wanted to be the granny who listened and laughed and loved and played with her grandchildren. In short, I wanted to be a "cool" granny.

On one trip to our granddaughters' Alison and Melissa's home, we visited a beautiful park. It was the very same one I had often taken my own daughters to when they were children. It was here that my children and I had spent many weekends frolicking in the park. Just like I had performed for my father as a child, my children would also run, skip, jump and somersault with glee, shouting, "Watch me! Watch me, Mommy!" Then I would join in and amaze them with my perfect, back-arched, legs-straight, toes-pointed-to-the-sky cartwheel.

On this sunny summer day, Alison and Melissa were bursting with the joy of youth. They began to run and jump and amaze us all with the gymnastic feats they could accomplish. No mere somersaults or cartwheels for these two young gymnasts: They twisted and whirled with back flips, round-offs and amazing multiple cartwheels. I applauded in awe.

When they paused and walked back toward me, I couldn't resist. I knew better—or should have—but I was caught up in the excitement of the show. "I can do an amazing perfect cartwheel," I announced. Both girls grinned at each other as if to say, *Granny—a cartwheel?* "I don't think so," Melissa even snickered.

Of course, I accepted the challenge. The sun was bright, the sky was filled with puffy cumulus clouds and there was just a little breeze. In the distance, birds were warbling to each other. I inhaled deeply and with a drum roll playing in my head, began the running skip that introduced my cartwheel. Arms raised overhead, I catapulted heels over head, back arched, legs perfectly straight, toes pointed to the sky. I was flying! I was still amazing!

I was in pain! The centrifugal force of the circular spin of the cartwheel became too much for my middle-aged joints. With a loud *Crack!* my left leg, the trailing one, came out of its hip socket. As I ended my circular descent, however, with both arms raised overhead—the way you always end the show—my left leg slammed back into its socket with a dull thud. *The pain! Oh the pain!* But not wanting to frighten the children, I blinked back my tears.

"Wow! Granny, you really *can* do a cartwheel!" Alison exclaimed, and Melissa beamed at me with a newfound respect for her granny. I vaguely remember mumbling something about how we should always warm up before exercising, and that I had forgotten to do it that day.

The next morning, my husband had to help me get out of bed. Every joint in my body ached with a vengeance. Warmed-up or not, I knew that yesterday had taught me something. That was Granny's last cartwheel.

Yes, family today is complicated, but I can still visit all my grandchildren, those related to me through blood or by marriage, and be called Granny Nanny. We can still listen and laugh and love and play together because, be it through shared DNA or shared history; that's what family is.

One day in the park the sun was bright, the sky was filled with puffy white clouds, and I heard the birds call to each other. A soft breeze blew just enough, and for a brief moment in time I soared, back arched, legs perfectly straight, toes pointed to the sky, performing Granny's last cartwheel for my granddaughters' pleasure. And they absolutely knew that their granny was cool.

Nancy Harless

One Price

There is only one price:
You pay for this experience with your life.
You can paint on a canvas
one inch square.
You can paint on a canvas
one mile square—
Or any size or shape in between.
The price is the same:
One life, due and payable;
One payment, in full, at the end.
And, you die knowing the scope of your choice:
Timid or expansive,
Cramped or capacious.
Listen to me!
One price.
One price buys all the rides,
or none.
The price is one life:
Spectator or player,
In or out of the arena.
One life.
Time is the only unknown,

And time matters not.
The price of admission—
for one minute or for one eternity—
Remains one life.
Hoarding adds not one second.
Giving subtracts not one breath.
Living itself is the defining action,
The shaping force;
Brave, fierce living,
In the body,
Heart open,
Arms open,
Eyes open.
The act of being shapes and sizes the canvas.
Carpe diem?
Not nearly enough.
Seize life!
Wring from it the payment's worth.
Spread out.
Unfold.
Stretch wide.
Paint in broad strokes
with bright colors.
Man or mouse,
A line or a six-lane freeway,
Gray or a rainbow,
A point or a universe.
Dance on a pinhead or across the stars.
The price remains the same:
One life.

Roberta R. Deen

5

COURAGE
AND
PERSISTENCE

Life shrinks or expands in proportion to one's courage.

Anaïs Nin

From Prison to Ph.D.

Never tell people how to do something; let them surprise you with their ingenuity.

General George S. Patton Jr.

The odds were not in favor of my sister, Grace Halloran, when it came to much of anything.

She spent most of her teen years in and out of juvenile institutions for minor offenses, but at eighteen, she hit the big time when she stole a car and traveled across state lines. Arrested, she was sent to federal prison for breaking yet another law— this time, a felony. After three years behind bars, she was released. The guards didn't bother to say good-bye; they were sure she'd be back soon.

Only a few years later, she was given a sentence far worse than the last one: blindness. Grace was summarily told she had two incurable, progressive disorders: retinitis pigmentosa, complicated by macular degeneration. The doctor added coldly, "I hope this will have a maturing effect on you. There are no cures, and nothing can be done to help you. You are legally blind now, and will soon be totally blind."

Grace was also happily pregnant—but terrified she would never see her child's face. How could she raise a child? She believed she had the love, determination and patience to succeed as a mother, although "success" had not been in her vocabulary before. When Ruchell, her son, was born, she managed well despite fading vision, and her son flourished.

Grace kept consulting specialists about her eye problems. She was given even more devastating news when one famous eye specialist said her son would also be blind by the time he was a teenager. She vowed to find something, anything, to prevent her boy from facing her fate. She appreciated the irony that she refused to accept the prognosis for her son that she had so readily accepted for herself.

Conventional medicine offered no hope at all, so Grace embarked on a personal quest. She enrolled in classes at a local college. The office for disabled students arranged to have her reading assignments put on cassette tapes so she could listen and learn. She began studying anatomy, physiology and other health sciences. Fellow students called her "Sherlock," because of her detective skills in ferreting out information, and because of the extra-large magnifying glass she had to use. She followed any and all leads about therapies for eye disorders, including a report from China on the success of acupuncture in improving retinitis pigmentosa. The article gave her a glimmer of hope, and over the next seven years, Grace investigated many alternative therapies—including nutrition, herbal medicine, color healing, yoga, acupressure and acupuncture—adapting many of these modalities for herself and her growing son.

She began to realize that what she was learning related to the health of her whole body, and Grace became a certified Touch for Health instructor, a technique for keeping the body in balance. She also explored sports medicine, which introduced her to the world of bioelectrical stimulation. Everyone who knew her was astonished at her persistence to educate herself, restore her vision and keep focused on her highest priority: to raise a son who would have perfect eyesight.

Grace earned her Ph.D. in Holistic Health. She was awarded the degree for her successful work in improving serious eye disorders. Despite the dire medical predictions, Grace's eyesight had slowly improved so much that she was able to qualify for a driver's license.

Word spread of Grace's success with "impossible" cases, and

in January 1983, a national magazine featured her story. The response was so great she put together a formal program to present her ideas. Independent assessors were hired to evaluate the data from 100 participants who used her program, and after two years, the results were overwhelmingly positive. Because European communities are more open to alternative theories than the American medical community, she was invited to teach her program overseas.

Grace was on her way to Sweden the day radioactivity entered Swedish airspace after the Russian atomic power plant exploded at Chernobyl. That fateful flight would become the trigger to a devastating downward health spiral that almost took her life. By 1991 she could no longer work, and her vision was again failing. For two years, she was either in the hospital dealing with radiation exposure, or home struggling to write her autobiography, *Amazing Grace—Autobiography of a Survivor,* and praying she'd live to see it published.

A month after completing the manuscript, Grace lost all her sight and entered a school for the blind to learn independent living skills. She was grateful, though, that after all their work, her son had 20/20 vision and was accepted into the Air Force.

Attitudes toward alternative healing have changed drastically since Grace began her studies. Some American eye specialists have now begun to acknowledge her work and dedication. A leading ophthalmologist, Dr. Edward Kondrot, dedicated his book *Miracle Eye Cure: Microcurrent Therapy* to Grace, recognizing her as a pioneer in the field. In November 1999, Old Dominion University of Virginia invited her to be a keynote speaker at the First Annual Natural Vision Improvement Conference. Professionals and lay people from all over the world attended, heard her speech and gave her a standing ovation.

She is more determined than ever to regain her sight, and keeps practicing the principles she teaches others in her training seminars.

My sister is slowly regaining her own sight for the second time. She truly is "Amazing Grace."

Kathleen Halloran

Dusting Off

You don't live in a world all your own; your brothers and sisters are here, too.

Albert Schweitzer

I have an important friend named Trey, who is exactly ten years older than I am, yet he lives the childlike life of one who is many years younger. When I was six, he was part of my Sunday school class. He seemed huge and intimidating at first, sitting crammed into a small wooden chair, but we became best friends on that first day after he broke a cookie in two and with a large grin handed me the smaller half. I thought of him as a protector, a special friend. It didn't matter that he was mentally handicapped, for I saw him as a grown-up who understood me. As years went by, however, I began to outgrow Trey. I grew up and Trey just grew. Sometimes I would watch him and wonder: did he notice that I was no longer in his Sunday school class? Did he realize I had moved on with my life as he treaded water? Did he ever miss me?

One Sunday, just a year before I began college—where I planned to participate in many sports as I had in high school— Trey's mom asked me if I would like to earn some extra money by being his "special Saturday friend." I wish I could say I accepted for altruistic reasons, but the truth was, I accepted because I needed money for tuition. Trey and I went to the library, to the pet store or for walks in the park. I mainly worked with him on socialization.

To my embarrassment, I quickly learned that this 200-pound man-boy liked to shake people's hands. In spite of his ear-to-ear grin, he could be daunting when he galloped up to strangers and stuck out his large hand in a hearty greeting. It was hard to teach him this behavior was inappropriate.

"Stand next to me and do not go up to people," I spoke tersely. "No one likes it."

"Ochay," he obediently replied, as if he hadn't a care in the world, and nothing was important.

When Trey learned to ride his bike, I watched as he ran off curbs and toppled over about a dozen times. Sighing deeply, I would impatiently tap my foot on the sidewalk and tell him, "Dust off and try again!" I assumed I was the smart one, the one with all the answers. That was about to change.

That summer, while playing in the city's softball tournament, I was sliding into third base when my cleat caught in the ground, pulling my foot to the right and backwards as my body fell forward. My parents, sitting in the bleachers, heard two loud cracks. I was rushed to the hospital by ambulance. X rays revealed a broken leg and a foot that was totally twisted off my ankle and hanging, saclike, in my skin. Emergency surgery lasted into the wee hours of the morning. A pin was put in place to hold my foot to my ankle and screws were inserted in the broken leg.

In the early morning, groggy from anesthesia, I awoke to see my father, my mother and Trey at my bedside. He waited for me to jump up and do something with him.

"Hi!" he grinned as he shoved his hand in my face.

"Hi Trey," I weakly shook his hand. My leg hurt and my mind was dense from pain medication.

"Dust off . . . try again," he said, repeating what he had heard me say so often.

"I can't."

"Ochay," he sweetly nodded and galloped out of my room in search of a hand to shake.

"Trey, don't shake hands," I whispered. "No one likes it."

Before leaving the hospital, my orthopedic surgeon said I might never regain the same mobility in my ankle—mobility essential for a champion sprinter and jumper like me. Not allowed to put weight on my leg for eight weeks, I wobbled about on steel crutches. Now Trey was the impatient one. He wanted to go places that I couldn't manage. He sat with his arms crisscrossed over his large belly and stared at me with a pouty face.

We read many children's books and drew pictures, but it was plain to see he was bored. He wanted to go to the pet store to see the white mice and feathery birds. He wanted to go to the library and count all the books on the shelves. He wanted to go to the park and have me push him on the swing. I couldn't do any of this for a while.

Meanwhile I was plagued with questions and self-doubt. Would I be finished with physical therapy in time to run track? Would I ever run at my capacity again? Would I do well in the 300-meter hurdles, the race I had lettered in the previous season? Would it still be my event? Or would the doctor's prediction be correct?

I worked hard at my physical therapy. Afterwards, I packed my foot in ice. At times, Trey came along to watch me work out and he laughed and laughed when he discovered the stationary bike didn't move. "No dusting off!" he'd say. How simple life was for him. How complicated it had become for me. I tried not to cry in front of him.

Finally off my crutches, I pushed myself hard to regain my former mobility. Trey ran laps with me around the black tar track at my high school, running slightly askew. Sometimes he tripped over his own feet and fell down hard.

"Dust off!" he would tell himself with confidence as he rubbed dirt from his legs and knees. I watched him greet each defeat with determination. He never gave up.

After many months, I somehow managed to qualify for the

300-meter hurdles. Mom, Dad and Trey sat in the stands to cheer me.

Stay focused, I told myself as I mentally prepared.

The starting gunshot split the air. Running, I could feel the tautness in my legs. My legs hit the hard track one after the other, in a quick rhythm. My breathing was even. I could feel some of the other runners around me, next to me, passing me, ahead of me. I ignored the rising pain in my foot and ankle as I prayed away the thumping fear taking hold inside my chest. On the other side of the track, I ran into a wall of cheers. No time to react or think—just time to run and run hard.

More runners passed me, then another and another. Over the hurdles they flew easily like great birds stepping over stones.

"Look at that new girl move. Go Tiffany," I heard someone shout to the other runner. Last year it was my name they called.

Once I had sailed over the hurdles. Now I felt as if I were pulling myself up and over. Then something shifted inside me—I thought of Trey and what he had had to deal with. Suddenly my problems seemed minor. With a new sense of determination, I sprang forth. I wish I could say that through a superhuman effort I passed the other runners. But I didn't. In fact, I limped across the finish line, dead last in an event in which I had once set a record. Then I looked up into the stands. Trey and my folks stood cheering for me harder than any time I had ever won.

As the season progressed I did improve, but I never placed first, second or third. I never set another school record. My hopes for a track college scholarship were dashed. Yet I learned a lesson more valuable than any medal. And it was this: "Dust off and try again." I also learned that courage comes not in the easy times, but when it's hard to go on—when others pass you, regardless of how hard you work. Now I finally understand Trey's courage, as he shakes the hands of complete strangers, risking laughter or rejection.

Today, I no longer grieve for the athlete I might have been, or the races I might have won, or the records I had hoped to break. I see a world filled with possibilities as I walk (not run) down new paths to explore.

Now, on Saturdays, when someone stares at us, I pull on Trey's sleeve. "Go shake his hand, Trey." My crutches gather dust in a musty corner of the garage. In contrast, Trey's handicap remains fresh as the day he was born. And every day he is braver than I could ever be.

Kimberly Ann Shope

Faster and Higher

The ordinary person takes everything as a blessing or a curse. A warrior takes everything as a challenge.

Carlos Casteneda

Dan was a man on a mission.

Climbing onto the treadmill, he eyed me suspiciously as I programmed the speed and elevation. Obviously not happy with my selection, he shook his head and proclaimed, "Today, I go faster and higher."

"We'll see how you do in the warm-up," I replied tersely, positioning myself behind him on the treadmill. This battle of wills between client and trainer had become a frequent occurrence in our sessions, and I relished the sparring. When I started training Dan four years ago, our sessions were marked by an awkward silence because his injuries had initially frightened and intimidated me. After all he had been through, I was terrified of failing him.

Dan Santillo's life had taken a tragic turn on an unseasonably warm November afternoon in 1990. He and a few friends were tossing a football in the street in front of his parents' house in Rochester, New York. Then an innocent prank went terribly wrong: A young acquaintance steered her car toward him, pretending for a moment that she was going to run him down. Somehow, she lost control of the car and slammed into him, hurtling him headfirst into the windshield.

Dan lay in a coma for three months. His physicians weren't optimistic about his chances of waking. But he surprised everyone by waking up, and then enduring ten months of intensive physical rehabilitation. The injuries to his body were severe; the damage to his brain was permanent. He rarely left his wheelchair during the first two years. But he managed to stand up on his wedding day, when, propped up by his brother, he painstakingly managed his way slowly down the aisle and into the arms of his bride, Kris, who had stayed by his side during his long ordeal.

Told by his doctors that he had gone as far as he could with physical therapy, Dan was urged to seek out the services of a personal trainer who could develop a fitness regimen around his limitations. That's when he found me.

During my initial consultation with Dan and his wife, Kris, I silently prayed they wouldn't select me. As a new trainer, I felt woefully inadequate to handle someone with such severe limitations, much less a brain injury. But they did select me, and thus my journey with Dan began.

Due to the nature of Dan's physical limits, we were prohibited from using most of the equipment in the gym. Since he had done some walking on the treadmill in rehab—and despite my fears that he would fall—I agreed to station myself behind him and hold on to his waist—a bear hug would be a more accurate description. This was extremely taxing on Dan's body, not to mention my nerves. His frequent stumbles always prompted me to cry out, "Are you all right?"

"I just tripped a little," he'd answer. Then we'd chuckle over my nervousness.

Eventually, Dan started walking faster and steadier on the treadmill, and we were able to add some elevation.

Over time, I developed creative ways for him to use some of the gym equipment and invented new positions on the machines to accommodate his limited range of motion.

Dan also began opening up to me more, even daring to share his hopes and dreams. "I just want to be normal again," he would tell me, embarrassed by his loping gait and the awkward position of his right arm. He believed that further surgery might bring about the normalcy he coveted. He obsessed over his damaged limbs and talked about them often, yet he never let his disabilities stop him from going full steam ahead.

The wheelchair was the first to go. The bulky metal braces he wore on his lower legs went next. Fitted with new plastic braces, disguised by long pants, he began walking laps in the aerobic room with the aid of his cane. On his first day, it took him over five minutes to travel five laps. This introduced a whole new dimension to our sessions. "Today, I'm going to break the record," he would announce upon his arrival at the gym. Thus began *Dan's Record Book*—a journal of his timed efforts and obsession to improve.

Weeks later, Dan discarded his cane; then we had to start a whole new record book without it. We took his laps outside, to the gym parking lot and eventually to a local bike trail. He was thrilled by each challenge the hills provided. Always concerned about Dan's way of pushing himself to the edge, I was less than thrilled when he overdid it one day and I had to buddy-carry him back to the car. After one spectacular spill on the trail, as I hauled him up and brushed him off, his only comment was, "Don't tell my wife I fell again."

Now the father of two young children, Dan tries to be more careful.

Dan's recovery amazes everyone who knows him, including his brain surgeon. He still falls on the trail and occasionally stumbles on the treadmill. And despite further corrective surgeries, he still walks with a limping gait, and his arm remains slightly crooked. He rarely talks about his desire to be normal anymore. Instead, Dan has redefined "normal." He still yearns to break records, but has clearly made peace with his limitations.

Dan is now working part-time at the gym where he is looking for a full-time job. He offers encouragement and hope to others whenever and wherever he can, and he recently visited an ailing police officer who had been hit by a car and suffered brain injury. Dan may not realize it, but he's been inspiring others for a long time now.

I still glare at Dan when he commands me to increase the speed and elevation on the treadmill, but I hope he will never stop asking to go faster and higher. Because in reinventing his life, he has transformed mine.

Mark Grevelding

FRANK & ERNEST *reprinted by permission of Newspaper Enterprise Association, Inc.*

Living His Dream

Do not let what you cannot do interfere with what you can do.

John Wooden

Bob Bennett's frustration and dour outlook on life was understandable. With the right side of his body partly paralyzed from cerebral palsy, he struggled with such basic skills as cutting food and counting money. Sometimes he sounded like a broken record as he repeated the phrase, "I keep trying and trying, but I can never get it right." High school teachers and aides like me continually tried to reinforce a more positive attitude, but we had an uphill struggle.

After graduation, Bob entered a Supermarket Careers program at a local vocational school and began to work at a nearby food store. His days were spent returning shopping carts to their proper places, and he greeted each customer with a friendly "Hello." To help with training and any work-related problems, he was assigned a job coach, Mary Di Napoli, who worked for an organization that assists disabled people. She listened compassionately to Bob, and began to care deeply about the struggling boy. During one of her visits, he confided, "I've always dreamed of practicing martial arts, but I can't because of my disability."

Mary said, "I'll see what I can do." After some research, she discovered that a local martial arts instructor would accept Bob into his Tae Kwon Do classes. He arrived early for his twice-a-week sessions, and although he had already spent many hours at his supermarket job, he still averaged nearly five hours a day stretching and practicing martial arts' moves.

As the months went on, "C'mon Bob, you can do it!" was heard often in Master Joe's class, because Bob had to work harder at perfecting his form than any of his classmates. He started classes with a white belt and then slowly progressed through the colored belts. Bob earned his green belt through months of rigorous exercise, discipline and determination—and he lost over forty pounds in the process. "I did it not from dieting," he says, "but from hours and hours of practice." Through the loving guidance and patient coaching of his instructors, he worked hard to reach his ultimate goal—the revered black belt. Any negative attitudes left over from his high school days disappeared.

His cerebral palsy became less noticeable as his sense of balance improved. He even regained motion in four fingers of his right hand, which he previously couldn't move at all, even after corrective surgery.

Tae Kwon Do has a simple, beautiful philosophy: to build a more peaceful world, one person at a time. The character and spirit of each individual are developed through physical training. "We train the body to polish the soul," Bob has said. He inspires everyone around him, because he is living proof that sweat brings transformation.

Bob recently traveled to his first Tae Kwon Do tournament. Initially, he was going to attend only as a spectator, which would have been a thrill, but he was allowed to participate in one event: the board-breaking portion of the competition. The crowd was large, and Master Joe's assistant helped him with preparations because Bob seemed overwhelmed and a little confused at first. She gently reassured him, "Don't be nervous—all your hard work will guide you."

He broke all his boards on the first try.

The awards table was filled with trophies of all sizes and colors. When the trophies were awarded, Bob's name was called, but, caught up in the sights and sounds of the tournament, he didn't hear. The thought that he might have a chance to win a trophy hadn't crossed his mind. When Bob realized they were calling his name, he was overwhelmed. The crowd erupted in cheers and there were many wet eyes. He had won fairly; his board-breaking skills *were* superior. At twenty-six, Bob won the first award in his life—third place. It might as well have been crafted from solid gold.

Bob clung to his trophy throughout the rest of the tournament. Over and over he repeated the words, "Wow, I really won this!" What a remarkable change from the same young man who used to say, "I keep trying and trying, but I can never get it right."

Another awards ceremony is still to come: Bob will soon receive the coveted black belt. On that day, Bob's family and many friends will attend to honor the courage he has shown.

Susan J. Siersma

There's a Lot Going on up There

Great works are performed, not by speed or strength, but by perseverance.

Samuel Johnson

Lon is nine years old. His body is controlled by cerebral palsy, robbing him of the ability to walk, talk or use his hands. But without ever being able to say a single word to me, this brown-haired boy taught me to look at life differently.

I first met Lon when I was walking my six-year-old daughter, Nikki, into school. He was parked in front of the building, strapped in his wheelchair. Nikki yelled, "There's Lon!" and ran to him.

"Hi, Lon," she cooed at him. His head was slumped down, but as she grabbed his hand he looked up and a huge grin appeared.

Nikki talked to him a few moments before she noticed the driver taking more kids off the bus. She dropped Lon's hand and ran over to them. I watched as he struggled to turn his head to see where she had gone, but he wasn't able to do this simple movement, so I went over and took Nikki's place, holding his hand.

"Hi," I said. "I'm Nikki's mom. She just went to say hi to some other kids." But his head dropped and he slumped again. I could feel his soft hand in mine the rest of the day. I found myself wanting to know more about him.

He was a student in a physical support class at Nikki's school that was comprised of physically disabled children, all nonverbal. Their language consisted mostly of grunts and groans. And smiles—big, wide smiles. Once I asked my daughter if Lon ever spoke to her, and she said, "Yes, one time he talked to me."

"What did he say?" I asked.

"When I said 'hi' to him, he smiled at me," she replied.

It was clear that Lon was one of Nikki's favorite friends and his name was at the top of the list when her birthday rolled around. We planned a pool party at a hotel, and I was nervous about how much he could enjoy it. His mother, Amy, wheeled him in and began to unstrap him. I made eye contact with my husband, signaling that he should make his way over to them. Jack knew he'd have to carry the boy. Amy gently placed her son into my husband's arms, and Jack walked around, dipping him in and out of the water.

She mentioned this was the first party Lon had ever been invited to, at least the first party hosted by a non-disabled child. I was so proud my daughter had invited him.

I spotted my husband and Lon at the end of the pool where three boys Nikki had invited were lined up, taking turns doing "cannonballs" in front of them. At the last second, Jack would hold Lon out in front of him when the others jumped in, then he'd pull him back. A splash of water would douse Lon, and he laughed and laughed and laughed, having the time of his life. I looked over at his mother as she beamed at her son's pleasure.

Then Jack put his arms under Lon's and pulled him through the water, chasing Nikki and her girlfriend. There was screaming and laughing as Lon tried to catch them like any other nine-year-old boy would have. I wondered if he had ever had the opportunity to laugh and play like this before.

I was so grateful Amy had brought him. It would have been easy for her to skip the party, and I watched with admiration as she changed him into dry clothes. She had to do this in the pool area, where the others were still swimming. She laid Lon on a lawn chair, covered him with towels and expertly, quickly, got him out of his wet suit and into dry clothes, maintaining his pride and dignity.

Since Lon can't speak, his mother and teachers aren't entirely sure of his intelligence level. But his mother told me, "We think there's a lot going on up there." The challenge was figuring out how to get him to communicate.

It became obvious that he had a great sense of humor. One day Nikki was wheeling him to her math class, but barely able to see over the top of him, she pushed him right into a fire extinguisher, shattering the plastic covering. She was so upset about it, her teacher had to call me, but before she handed the phone to my daughter, I asked her how Lon was. "Oh, he's fine, not hurt at all," she said. "He laughed his butt off. In fact, I think he's still laughing."

As endearing as Lon is, his mother, Amy, is even more inspiring. Her life is obviously centered around him—not only as mother and caregiver, but also as playmate. Lon was on a baseball team with other disabled kids, and played in a game every week. Amy stood at the plate with him, put the bat in his hands and swung for him. If he hit it, she'd push his wheelchair around the bases. Lon played left field, and Amy stood next to his chair. She laughed when she told me that no one had hit a ball out there yet. "I don't know what I'll do if the ball ever comes out here," she said. "I guess I'll have to throw my body in front of him since I'm not a good catcher."

Lon also belongs to "Steve's Club," where able-bodied children, like Nikki, are paired with disabled kids, in the hopes they'll learn from each other. Lon is the only member who has never missed a meeting.

A friend of mine attends the same church Lon and Amy go to every week. At the church Easter egg hunt, Amy pushed Lon around, picking up each one she found and placing it in his basket, the two of them having a joyous time.

I admire Amy more than anyone I've ever met. She's missed

so much because of Lon, but at the same time, she has gained more than most of us ever will. She appreciates every small sign of progress he makes, even as many of us only continue to want our children to excel. It's inspiring that she isn't even certain how much he can understand, yet makes sure he has all the same opportunities available to other kids.

Amy and Lon have changed the way I look at life. If a boy trapped inside his own body can still laugh and find reasons to enjoy life, with a mind that must be yearning to express itself, then I can also do more of that.

I will not groan when Nikki is invited to yet another birthday party. I'll be grateful.

Nor will I complain when my children have a temperature, and I have to stay home from work to take care of them. I will thank God that's all it is.

I will not nag when Nikki pokes around on her way to the bus stop, picking up every stone and leaf. I'll be grateful that she can.

I will not become impatient when it takes forever for my kids to tell a story. I will relish their ability to speak.

I will do my very best, every day, to be grateful for all that life gives me, because it's what Amy and Lon must do every moment of their lives.

I believe that God placed Amy and Lon on this Earth together for a reason. And so, in more ways than one, I too believe that "there's a lot going on up there."

Cheryl M. Kremer

Phoenix Rising

I was five years old and had no idea what had just happened to me. The last thing I remembered was being held in my mom's arms and hearing her scream for help. The night sky turned orange as flames rose above the treetops.

By the time we made the four-hour journey to Children's Hospital in Los Angeles, my now-blackened face—what was left of it—had swollen to the size of a watermelon. Two days passed before the doctors would say that I had a good chance of surviving. After weeks of intensive critical care, I regained consciousness, breathing through a tracheotomy tube. I thought I was blind, until I learned that my eyes had been bandaged shut.

When the day finally came to remove the bandages, it was nothing like the movies, where the injured person opens his or her eyes to see the vision of a loved one or a beautiful woman. My first vision was of a nurse, whose wrinkled face frightened me. Looking back, I'm amazed that she wasn't terrified of *my* face. As time passed, I came to know her as one of the most caring people I would ever meet.

After more weeks of surgeries, skin scrapings and nurses waking me constantly to probe me or give me shots, I finally had the strength and desire to get up and slowly make my way to the bathroom without assistance. After using the toilet, I noticed a reflection on the stainless-steel towel dispenser and saw my reflection. I hobbled back to my bed and lay down.

Everyone was quiet, but Mom knew what I had seen.

"It's pretty bad isn't it?" I asked her.

"Yes, Mike. It's bad," she said. "But you're going to be just fine." She hugged me gently and kissed my forehead, then repeated, "Everything is going to be just fine."

Lessons came hard and fast in the years that followed. When I was ready to return to school, my parents had to fight countless battles with public school policy about kids who were "different." They eventually had to put me into a school for the mentally and physically handicapped.

The following year, however, they won their battle with the school system, and I was accepted into public school. I didn't realize how much harder it was going to be. Before I arrived, announcements were made over the PA system, asking students to be kind and not to stare. But everyone did. It took most of the year before the "Hey, Frankenstein!" calls subsided, and I was finally accepted.

In the next twelve years, I had twenty-four plastic surgeries to repair my "melted" face and hands in order to provide mobility in my neck and replace the damaged skin on my face. My legs and backside read like a historical map of the technology; with each new improvement, the graft scars (where they took skin from one part of me and sewed it onto my face) shrank, until later grafts no longer added scars.

By the time I was in my late teens, experience had provided me with excellent skills when it came to dealing with people. I had become a chameleon, always changing to fit the situation. I had also achieved a measure of success in school and sports, but had few genuine accomplishments. As I entered my early twenties I felt restless—I couldn't understand why a smart guy like me couldn't seem to find the right woman and the right job to give my life meaning. After some months browsing through self-help and spiritual books, I was *almost* ready to admit that the problem might be me, rather than the world.

Soon after I completed high school, I moved to a town in the mountains of California where there were fewer people to face, and I could live in peace. One weekend, my mom came up to visit me. It was raining, so we sat inside and played cards and watched movies, just like the old days back in the hospital.

She asked me what I was going to do with my life. "Why aren't you in school anymore? Mike, I'm disappointed in you. So many people gave so much of their time, their energy, their lives to you. And what have you done with *your* life? I thought you would wind up a doctor or something like that."

I didn't know what to say.

Later we went to a local hole-in-the-wall diner to eat. The waitress greeted us. Her boy had recently been in a serious car accident, and she had confided her fears and sorrows to me. When she came to our table she said, "He's coming home tomorrow. I want to thank you for listening, Mike—I don't know what I would have done without you." Then, to my mother, "Your son is a good man; I expect that you're very proud of him."

She took our orders and we sat in silence for a while. Then I spoke without even thinking about it—the words just tumbled out: "One thing I've learned is that I have an opportunity to make a positive impact on every person I meet. I try to help; I want to make a difference. I'm like the phoenix, Mom—that bird that rises from its own ashes. Just by being myself, I show people that no matter what life throws at you, you can make the best of it."

Mom smiled, and I thought things were okay. After she left, though, I really started to question if it *was* enough and when I would truly make something of my life. The next few weeks found me restless and discontented—as if I were standing on the edge of a great chasm. After the fire, not much frightened me anymore, but now I was scared: I picked up the telephone and called my father. "Remember that offer you made a while back? I'm ready to come down from the mountains."

I packed my belongings and hit the road. Soon, my beloved mountains—my safe refuge—were behind, and ahead was a long road into the unknown. At a rest stop, I climbed up to a rock overlooking a lake and pine trees as far as the eye could see, and cried.

From my first day at the office, I worked hard, meeting new people and learning the latest technologies. And a funny thing—because I didn't think about the scars on my face, people didn't seem to pay much attention to them, either. As the years passed, I climbed the corporate ladder and eventually was promoted to manager. That's when I met my wife, Debbie.

From the start, it was like "Beauty and the Beast." Well, she's not really a beast—she's actually quite pretty. That's my little joke, of course. Who would have guessed that a guy with a mug like mine would love and be loved by such a gorgeous woman? But she saw more than skin deep because she *is* more than skin deep. Our romance is a story for another time—the short of it is that we married and moved to Austin, Texas, where we live today.

On a recent Labor Day weekend, my mom came to visit. "Mike," she told me, "your business must be doing pretty well—I'm so proud of you." Then tears filled her eyes as she asked, "Do you remember that day in Tahoe when I said—"

"Yes, Mom, I do."

We sat quietly for a time, remembering. And when the words finally came, I knew what I had wanted to share all these years, but couldn't find a way to express until now: "You know, Mom, when I got burned it wasn't a tragedy—it was a gift."

"What do you mean?" she asked, surprised.

"I've learned not only to watch people, but to *see* them, inside and out. And I've come to appreciate how fortunate I am, because my scars are only on the outside.

"Now let's go eat, shall we? I know a great little hole-in-the-wall restaurant."

Mike Gold

Mike and Debbie Gold

A Matter of Perspective

I am not bound to win but I am bound to be true. I am not bound to succeed but I am bound to live up to what light I have.

Abraham Lincoln

I am surrounded by a family of athletes. My husband, Thom, cycles regularly and thinks nothing of racing fifty miles at a stretch. He has the sleek, spare body of a human greyhound. He frequently rides with U.S. Cycling Federation Category-2 riders—men with a shot at professional cycling—who help him hone his skills and focus his training regimens. He calls them "the big boys," but he's as big at heart as any one of them.

My sister, Nancy, who in high school regaled us with gymnastic prowess, recently taught herself inline skating and completed the grueling course of study at the National Fire Academy.

My "adopted brother," Will, affectionately known as "Willful," was slated for the U.S. Olympic Swim Team prequalifier before a serious knee injury sidelined his swimming career.

I, however, never made the team—any team. I'm short in stature and was obese as a child. For as long as I can remember, I've struggled to keep my weight under control. I've undergone several medical procedures to correct congenital organ abnormalities, and I also suffer from a localized autoimmune disorder that is causing my left eye to deteriorate. At age thirty-nine I had a cataract operation.

Then, a few years ago, I took up jogging under the watchful eye of Will—friend, trainer and past-swimming whiz—to help me cope with the stress of losing part of my vision, and to provide a measure of healthful exercise. I have consistently risen at 5:30 A.M., donned my sneakers and hit the pavement, making a mile-long circle of my city neighborhood. At first, I could only run a short distance, so I walked most of the way. Gradually, I built my endurance and was able to run longer and longer distances, in rain or shine, on rosy summer mornings, or in the predawn darkness of a New England autumn when the morning stars still shone. Finally, I reached my goal—I could run a whole mile.

On each of my early morning runs, I encountered a gentleman walking a German shepherd in the opposite direction. As I passed, he would nod, and I would nod in turn. It became a regular ritual. I never knew exactly where I would come upon him. Sometimes I could see him coming from a long way off. At other times he seemed to appear unexpectedly out of my moving reverie, from somewhere in the morning mist.

Over time, life intruded on my running, and my schedule fragmented. We bought an older home in a different neighborhood, and my time was filled with renovation work, then graduate school. By then I wasn't feeling well and could no longer run a full mile. My weight, though stabilized, refused to budge lower despite great effort on my part, and the reflection in my mirror was always nagging me to work harder. Prescribed steroids complicated the picture; I felt a fatigue as frustrating as it was mysterious, along with the loss of muscle mass I'd worked so hard to gain.

Around the same time, Thom informed me of his goal to lower his body fat to an even smaller percentage than it already was. Something about his confidence, his naturally lean physique and his endurance brought a stab of jealousy and burning hot tears to my eyes.

"What's wrong?" he asked, surprised by my reaction.

"You don't understand," I replied. "Your goals are things I can't even dream about. You're an athlete; I have to struggle just to be normal." Humiliated, I fled up the stairs.

The next morning, I ran hard. It hurt, but I felt wonderful afterward—though somewhat disheartened that I couldn't run as long and as far as I used to.

About a week later, preoccupied by my own difficulties, I stepped into an elevator at my workplace and noticed a man standing next to the buttons. "I haven't seen you for a while," he said.

Startled, and trying to maintain decorum, I replied noncommittally, "Oh?"

He smiled. "You don't recognize me. I used to see you running every morning. You must be an athlete. Right?" The moment seemed to slip out of time, became numinous, as if we were the only two people in the universe. It was the man with the German shepherd. Openmouthed, I couldn't find my voice. I kept hearing the words, "You must be an athlete, right?"

I managed to stammer, "Uh, right."

"Are you still running?" he inquired politely.

"Um, yeah," I responded, as if I owed him an explanation for why we no longer crossed paths. "We moved," I added.

He nodded, the elevator pinged, the doors opened and I stepped off.

His parting words were, "Have a nice day." Some people say it just to say it—this gentleman meant it, and his words warmed me like a soft old blanket.

When the doors slid shut, I had to lean against the wall for a moment. I was weak in the knees. "You must be an athlete."

What is an athlete, anyway? Maybe it's someone who views the world in a positive light; someone who is in training, who pushes the limits of endurance, who sets goals and then wills herself toward her own personal finish line. Athletes suffer setbacks, and in tough times they use their intellect to plan for the future. Above all, athletes never give up, because whatever their bodies look like, they have the heart and spirit of a warrior.

No matter how positive I am or hard I train, I will never win Olympic gold. You will never see my name in the national, regional or even local newspaper. I may never run the Boston Marathon. But that man, whose words brought new light into my life, was right: In all the ways that count, I *am* an athlete. Because no matter what happens, I refuse to give up.

Donna Beales

The Canyons of My Heart

The fullness of life is in the hazards of life.

Edith Hamilton

I've wanted to hike to the bottom of the Grand Canyon for some years now. Most of my friends and family were incredulous when I first told them. I could guess what they were thinking, and I don't blame them. At fifty-one, with as many extra pounds on my body as years in my life, I'm not exactly the poster girl for a hike that's been compared to running a marathon. But I possess something that few aspiring runners or hikers have—a reservation for two nights at the Phantom Ranch, at the bottom of the Grand Canyon. It's dated October, two years from now.

Last Christmas, I asked for and received a couple of movies about hiking the Grand Canyon. When my husband watched them with me, he kept repeating how this was the last thing on Earth he would want to do. He said he would drop me off at the South Rim for my canyon odyssey, while he headed for Las Vegas.

I smile every time I watch my Grand Canyon hiking

movies. I smile because I envision myself there in that unfamiliar terrain. I see a version of myself that I long to meet, climbing among the aged rock faces and cliffs that match the amber of my hair.

I don't know what I'll find of myself on that hike, but I guess it will show the bitter and the sweet. That's what I've found when I've faced other challenges, like giving birth. Only the birthing in the canyon will take longer, with deeper highs and lows. And the one born, or reborn, will be me.

Maybe it will feel like watching my only daughter, Gina, live a gloriously full but short life. I can imagine my labored breaths as I hike, similar to how I breathe when I try to run too fast or when my asthma catches up with me. Similar to my daughter's labored breathing when she needed a tracheotomy to get more air. I'll have to help myself, too, as I had to help her breathe.

I can almost feel my legs burning with exhaustion, pushing for each step, like Gina's struggles to walk unaided. Maybe I'll feel pride like hers, and mine, when she finally was able to walk at three years old.

I may wonder what the hell I'm doing there, or how in the world I thought I'd be able to do something so strenuous. Maybe Gina wondered the same thing in her child's mind. Or maybe she was too busy celebrating the life she had.

One thing's for sure: I'm no athlete. So I expect I'll want to turn back. But wanting to turn back and turning back are two different things.

On my hike into the canyon I may remember again how it felt to learn my beautiful baby daughter had Down's syndrome and a congenital heart defect—and how I wondered, only for a moment, what it would be like to turn back from having had that baby. I'll also remember how very much I wanted to get a chance to know her, and how glad I am that I did.

I imagine I'll see, hear and smell things I never knew existed, down there in that Grand Canyon in Arizona. Just like the three-year journey of Gina's life.

I know I'll be proud of myself when I reach the bottom, but also anxious because I will still have to climb out. Just like I was proud when I helped Gina, but anxious, too, because I knew in the deepest part of my soul that after her passing, the hardest part was yet to come: climbing out of the hole she forever in the Grand Canyon of my heart. I always knew I'd lose her someday; still, it was the biggest fear I've ever had to face. Compared to that, all things are easy.

After my ascent from Phantom Ranch, will I have learned anything new? Will I be more fit in ways that stretch beyond physical strength or toned muscles? How will I know unless I try? I need to know, so I need to try. Even if I don't make it all the way, I'll have one hell of a story. And toned muscles would also be grand.

I hope that the lesson of the canyon is to go with the flow of the river of life. A canyon is formed because it allowed part of itself to be carried out to sea; in letting go of its sediments, it found its beauty. Maybe it will be the same with me.

* * *

I faced every fear I own on those trails, and uncovered a few new ones as well, like physical pain in knee joints unaccustomed to such steep terrain; the pain of separation from loved ones; apprehension about slipping on wet, mud-coated rocks; not to mention cold, achy muscles. But I also found that although I wasn't the most graceful hiker on the trail, I could do it. With my hiking poles in hand for support, trail mix spilling from my pockets, the footsteps of my friends to follow and my inhaler in hand, I did it.

I went to Arizona to conquer fear. I went to find my spirit.

I sang and laughed and cried and saw and felt the beauty of Joshua trees and soaring condors and a deep green river cradled by strong marbled walls—so many things this Louisiana gal had never seen before. I also found that love and a little courage will take you anywhere and back again, and that your body will follow—if you just stay open to each step in a new direction.

Rose Marie Sand

6

SHARING OUR BEST

Fragrance always remains in the hand that gives the rose.

Heda Bejar

Jessica's Story

Life is uncharted territory. It reveals its story one moment at a time.

Leo Buscaglia

Once upon a time, in a not so far away kingdom, a little girl with a true and loving heart was about to celebrate her sixth birthday. Somehow, she knew it would be her last. She had been ill for a very long time with a disease that did not improve no matter how many physicians attended her. So one night, the child searched the sky for a shining star to wish upon, placed her tiny hand over her heart and said, "I wish I could become a fairy-tale princess in a magical kingdom where all my dreams would come true."

On a Monday at 9 A.M. my phone rang. It was the director of the local Starlight Foundation with a request to help plan a birthday party and perform a storytelling program for Jessica Hageman, a terminally ill cancer patient. Jessica had been diagnosed with leukemia when she was eighteen months old. Her treatments had included chemotherapy, radiation and a bone marrow transplant. The current prognosis gave her only several weeks to live, and we had six days to plan the memorable party her family wanted to give her.

Jessica's mother, Denise, was convinced that Jessie's love of fairy tales had helped sustain her—especially her favorite, "Beauty and the Beast." She had announced one day that when she grew up she was going to be Belle (Beauty).

I began to create a real-life, royal setting for Princess Jessica. The Rosalie Whyel Museum of Doll Art's internationally acclaimed doll collection would provide a magical background. The museum's founder donated the museum itself for Jessie's party and even agreed to dress up as the "queen of the palace." Her staff would be ladies-in-waiting.

Another friend agreed to transform Jessica and her sixteen playmates into princesses and princes. The girls would be dressed in shimmering satin, sequined tiaras, feather boas and sparkling jewelry; the boys would be decked out in capes and crowns. We decided to create a processional so the children could be admired in their finery by all. Leading the way would be Princess Jessie, riding in a "gilded carriage"—a well-disguised wheelchair covered with yards and yards of gold brocade. Her crown would become an interactive part of the story: As Jessie's fairy tale was told, friends and family would come forward one by one, decorate the crown with jewels and share their good wishes with her.

Everyone was delighted to participate in Jessie's magical day. The Seattle Repertory Theater donated a royal throne, a local market provided the three-tiered cake and neighborhood stores supplied bouquets of balloons. The local cable television station offered video coverage of the entire party so the family would have a keepsake of the day. With each gift, I called the family to tell them about the wonderful new developments. Each generous person became a light in the darkness of their ever-present reality. We were all enmeshed in their lives—and willingly so.

Most of all, I wanted to create an enchanted, healing story for Jessie—one that would help her face her death with courage. She would be the heroine of her fairy tale. *But what is Princess Belle searching for?* I asked myself. *What is the conflict? What are her resources, strengths and gifts?* I began to imagine a giant beast, a hairy, misshapen creature living in a cave, who weeps each night. The giant needs to be understood by the princess, and she must overcome her fear of this creature and go to him.

In my story, when the king asks the princess what gift she wants for her birthday, the princess thinks a long time and finally says, "I want to go into the woods and make friends with the lonely giant who lives there."

"Impossible!" say the king and queen, but the princess insists—and the members of the kingdom walk her to the edge of the dark woods. She finds the giant and asks him to come out and play with her. He doesn't know how to play, but she teaches him to sing and dance the "Hokey Pokey."

The giant says, "I love this 'Hokey Pokey!' When I sing and dance, I don't feel like crying!" He holds Jessie's tiny hands, and says, "Dear princess, what a brave and courageous little girl you are to come all this way to be my friend on *your* birthday. You've given *me* a present! Now, I'm going to give you a present in return. Should you ever return to this dark place, I want you to remember this: I will be here waiting for you, and I will protect you, keep you safe and be your friend forever."

The next morning—the day of the party—a phone call shattered the stillness. At 10:30 A.M., Jessie had suffered a stroke. She could not focus her eyes, sit up or speak without stuttering. Her left side was no longer functioning. She was in the hospital, and there would be no party that night.

At 9 A.M. Monday, there was a new report: Jessie was home from the hospital and had slept peacefully. She had awakened and said, "Can I still have my party?"

Could we modify our plans to accommodate her condition? Secure the castle on the new day? Salvage the cake? Refill the balloons? Re-enlist all the volunteers? Call all the guests? Create the enchantment? "Absolutely!" we all said, and began to rally the troops.

A portable daybed was secured from Children's Hospital, and we plumped it with soft pillows and wrapped it in yards of purple silk. Jessie was crying in pain as the Hagemans left their home. They almost turned back. Once they arrived at the palace, however, and were greeted by the queen, her friends and Jessie's playmates—all dressed up for her party—Jessie stepped into the pages of her very own fairy tale and her pain was left behind.

As excited as they were, when the children approached Jessie's purple silk bed, they spoke in hushed, lullaby tones as their hands reached out to gently touch hers. The Pied Piper sounds of a flute beckoned everyone to travel down the marble corridor into the wings of the palace where the dolls were housed, waiting to celebrate, too. The procession of children, parents and family fell into place behind Jessie.

Her fairy-tale story unfolded like a flower, petal by petal, adjusted in each moment to meet her needs. When the royal cook presented the birthday cake all aglow with six pink birthday candles, Jessie was able to sing "Happy Birthday" to herself in a tiny voice, and—with the help of her family—blow out the candles. With the queen's help, Jessica was able to tear the paper from each gift package, but she also let everyone know she could open the present herself. Later, she was lifted onto the royal throne, on her mother's lap, and ate a piece of birthday cake.

Her doctor said, "Never would I have believed that this little girl, who couldn't even take her medication yesterday, could be opening presents and eating birthday cake. It is truly a miracle."

It was a miracle for each of us as well. Through the language of the human heart, we had come to know her story. By stepping into Jessica's life, we had looked into the window of her soul and she had touched us deeply with her magic.

Three weeks after the party, Jessica Hageman died at home, cradled in the arms of her parents.

They asked me to tell her life story at the funeral. To my right was a table filled with her favorite books and toys, and on the lectern were her princess ball gown and a single red rose. I chronicled Jessie's life, weaving stories from her family, friends and health-care providers of how she touched lives through the power of her love. It was no wonder "Beauty and the Beast" was her favorite fairy tale: In her own personal mythology, Jessie's pure heart, steadfast love and extraordinary courage transformed everyone who came to know her. My message celebrated her return to heaven, where the heavenly host escorted her before the throne of God. He told her how she had touched everyone, and allowed them to discover their very own gifts.

And God said, "Your return here calls for a great celebration. How would you like to mark your return to heaven?"

"Well, dear Lord," Jessie said, "While I was on Earth, I celebrated my sixth birthday, but I wasn't feeling very well. Now that I'm feeling wonderfully well, may I celebrate it again, all dressed up like a princess, and can the angels dress up, too, and bow and curtsey to each other?"

God said, "So be it."

I invited the congregation to imagine themselves at Jessie's party, and asked them to rise, and bow and curtsey to each other. They did.

"Then the storyteller told my very own story about making friends with the giant in the woods," continued Jessie, "and everyone danced and sang the 'Hokey Pokey.' But I wasn't feeling very well, so I didn't get to join in. Now that I'm feeling wonderfully well, I'd like to do it here, in heaven."

God said, "So be it."

Then the whole congregation joined me in singing and dancing the "Hokey Pokey."

". . . And that is the story of angel princess Jessica Belle, who is now living happily ever after—in the Ever After."

Michale Gabriel

A Surprise Wedding

Love alone matters.

St. Thérèse of Lisieux

Over the years, my wife, Sue, expressed interest in renewing our wedding vows. It was not something she talked about frequently, but she brought it up on such special occasions as weddings or anniversaries.

Like most macho men, I believed that once was enough. But as time passed, since it still seemed important to her, I began to relent: "Honey, I might consider it someday, but only if it's just you and me—maybe on vacation somewhere." (I really didn't need an audience for something like this.)

Then, four years ago, Sue had a cancerous mole removed from her leg. The diagnosis: malignant melanoma.

My attitude at that time was that the mole wasn't so bad. After all, it was removed and the cancer was gone. I knew little, however, about this cancer's ability to resurface.

In November, Sue found a new lump on the same leg as before—it turned out to be a swollen lymph gland—and the biopsy again revealed malignant melanoma. Sue went in for surgery and had numerous lymph glands removed from her leg and abdomen. The doctors had good news: The cancer had not spread beyond the two lymph glands—the one that was swollen and one next to it.

One week after Sue's diagnosis, however, her father was diagnosed with cancer—not the best week my wife has ever had.

In December of that year, like every year, I struggled with what to get my wife for Christmas, but even more than usual. Sue always said that she wanted "something personal." When the cancer returned, it made me think long and hard about what our future might be like. I wondered about what I might get her for Christmas that would be personal, show her how much I loved her and express what she means to me and to our family.

I'm the kind of guy that thinks of grand things I would like to do for my wife but rarely gets around to doing them. That year I really searched my soul—and the thought of renewing our wedding vows suddenly took on more meaning. This was a way to show her I truly wanted to do it all over again.

Then I thought of the verse "In sickness and in health" and began to cry. I'm glad I was alone.

Even with all Sue had been through—and maybe because of it—she wanted to host Christmas Eve at our house this year. It was only going to be a small group of relatives. It seemed to me that this would be the perfect time to renew our vows, so I recruited Karen, my sister-in-law, to help me. I called everyone and told them to come two hours early. I said I had a surprise for Sue but didn't tell anyone what it was. I didn't want this gift to be spoiled.

I called on our neighbor, Jean Partridge, a justice of the peace. We had never really stopped and talked or gotten to know one another, and I hoped she would be willing to come over on Christmas Eve. She said she was busy that night and had to arrive at her daughter's house by six o'clock. My heart sank. As I turned to walk away, Jean asked, "Why do you need a justice of the peace on Christmas Eve, Don?"

"I want to get married to my wife again," I answered. "It's a surprise wedding." I hesitated, then asked, "Do you think you could marry us at four o'clock and still be on time for your daughter's Christmas Eve celebration?" I told Jean what the ceremony meant to me and would mean to my wife at this particular time. I told her about Sue's health problem. I explained all this so in case I started to cry, she'd understand why. After that, she said that she might have to toss down a shot to calm her nerves before the wedding, too.

"I'll be there at four," she smiled.

A great wave of joy swept over me. I had found a way to show how much I loved Sue—and this time, instead of just thinking about it, I was going to make it happen.

I finally found something unique and meaningful to give my wife on Christmas. The only other people I told were Sue's parents, since I really wanted them to be there. When they heard the plan, there was only silence on the phone for a few long moments. Then Sue's dad, who had his good and bad days due to his own illness, declared in an emotional voice that he would be there no matter how he was feeling.

I realized that I also needed fluff—or should I say, some *schmaltz*—all the details that women think of and men usually don't consider. I had my youngest son, Shaun, get a song off the Internet—the same song that was played in church when we were married twenty-three years earlier. Sean made a CD for me so I could play it when she walked in the door. Oh, and flowers—I got a wristlet for Sue, a flower for my lapel and two poinsettias for the mantel. And I got a cake, champagne, glasses, boxes and boxes of Kleenex, and disposable cameras. I even bought some special rings.

In the flower shop, a small snowman statue caught my eye. I picked it up and saw that it was some sort of jewelry holder. This snowman had a small sign he was holding and on that sign was the word "hope." I thought how perfect it was, and my eyes welled up with tears again. I've been crying a lot, lately, for a macho man.

That afternoon, everything was in place. Karen, my sister-in-law, took Sue out to visit a sick relative. When she returned, she looked puzzled to see everyone at our home two hours early. After all, she had to get the food ready for our guests.

"What's going on?" she asked, a little upset.

The rest I'm going to leave to your imagination.

Just picture this: Our wedding song begins to play, people are taking pictures of Sue and me, and the tears and champagne are beginning to flow.

And I said, "Honey, Merry Christmas. I love you. Will you marry me again tonight?"

Don Flynn

Life Lessons

Happiness begins where selfishness ends.

John Wooden's favorite maxim

He speaks softly and sometimes carries a big stick, but that's only to help him walk when his knees are aching.

Ninety-one-year-old John Wooden is speaking to a large group of young, brash, information technology experts in Monterey, California; the men and women in the audience are vying for advancement in a highly competitive industry. For the next twenty-five minutes, his message is about humility, teamwork and achieving success by helping others. His timeless words of wisdom—entitled the "Pyramid of Success"—are a collection of life principles for which Wooden has become well-known. They are considered by many to be the building blocks of personal and professional achievement.

The building blocks include attributes such as friendship and loyalty at the base of the pyramid, and ascend to values such as self-control, initiative, team spirit, poise and confidence. At the apex is competitive greatness. In the process, Wooden coined his own definition of success: "Peace of mind obtained only through self-satisfaction in knowing you made the effort to do the best of which you're capable. It doesn't matter if it's in business or in the classroom or on the athletic field."

Wooden knows a bit about ascending to incredible heights. He is known throughout college basketball as "The Wizard of Westwood" for guiding his UCLA teams to unparalleled feats and making basketball history. His teams won an unprecedented ten national titles—seven of those in a row, from 1967 through 1973, including four perfect seasons, an eighty-eight game winning streak and thirty-eight consecutive NCAA tournament victories.

Wooden retired suddenly, at the top of his game, but has few regrets. He misses the practice sessions most of all. "I love to teach, and that's what the practice sessions were," he says. He didn't resort to verbal or physical intimidation techniques—in fact, he rarely raised his voice. He was—then and now—a teacher, a gentle man whose lessons remain timeless.

Swen Nater, a former player, says, "He rarely talked to us about basketball. He spoke about human values and characteristics we'd need to be successful. He taught us how to create fun and enjoyment in our lives." Wooden's students listened because they knew they'd win if they learned their lessons. The fundamentals came with useful proverbs attached:

> *Be quick, but don't be in a hurry.*
> *Failure to prepare is preparing to fail.*
> *The purpose of discipline isn't to punish, but to be correct.*
> *Do not mistake activity for achievement.*
> *If I am through learning, I am through.*
> *Make each day your masterpiece.*

"We thought we were the coolest things, living the life of collegiate athletes," former UCLA and NBA great and Hall-of-Famer Bill Walton remembers. "Coach Wooden came out with all these sayings. We thought he was a walking antique—little did we know then that all the life lessons he gave us would ring perfectly true."

Wooden says, "We're not all equal in talent. All we can do is make the most of what we have and try to improve at all times.

That was the idea I've always tried to get across, whether I was teaching English, coaching my basketball teams or talking to a group of business people."

He never mentions that he is one of only two men (along with Lenny Wilkins) to be honored in the Naismith Memorial Basketball Hall of Fame as both player and coach. He never needs to mention that he's still mentally sharp—although moving a little slower—at an improbable age. He is what he has taught: a highly moral, successful person who has made a difference in the lives of many. He is truly a legend in his own time, and a beloved one.

Mark Stroder

What Did You Do for Someone Today?

When I was a child, we observed Father's Day by walking to the local Methodist church and listening to my father preach. We didn't have a car—my dad believed he could not "support Mr. Ford" on a minister's salary and see that all of his seven children went to college. While we understood it was a special day—my mother would have something exceptional like a roast or a turkey cooking in the oven—in many ways it was not all that different from any other day. As soon as my brothers and sisters and I got home, we'd all gather around the dining room table, where we took turns answering our father's daily question: "And what did you do for someone today?"

While that voice and those words always stuck in my mind, they often got pushed aside later by more immediate concerns: long hours in medical school, building a career in medical research, getting married, raising children and acquiring the material accoutrements every father wants for his family—all the hallmarks of a "successful" life, according to today's standards. When these goals were met and that busy time of life was over, retirement followed on Hilton Head Island, South Carolina.

My wife and I built our home in a gated community surrounded by yacht clubs and golf courses, but when I left the compound and its luxurious buffer zone for the other side of

the island, I was traveling on unpaved roads lined with leaky
bungalows. The "lifestyle" of many of the native islanders stood
in jarring contrast to my cozy existence. I was stunned by the
disparity.

By means of a lifelong habit of mine of giving rides to hitch-
hikers—remember, I grew up without a car—I got to talking to
some of these local folks. And I discovered that the vast major-
ity of the island's maids, gardeners, waitresses and construction
workers who make this island work had little or no access to
medical care. It seemed outrageous to me. I wondered why
someone didn't do something about that. Then my father's
words, which had at times receded to a whisper, rang in my
head again: "What did you do for someone today?"

Even though my father had died several years before, I guess
I still didn't want to disappoint him. So I started working on a
solution. The island was full of retired doctors. If I could per-
suade them to spend a few hours a week volunteering their services, we could provide free primary health care to those who
were so desperately in need of it. Most of the doctors I
approached liked the idea, so long as their life savings wouldn't
be put at risk if there were any malpractice suits. They also
wanted to be licensed without a long, bureaucratic tangle. It
took one year and plenty of persistence, but I was able to per-
suade the state legislature to create a special license for doctors
volunteering in not-for-profit clinics, and got full malpractice
coverage for everyone from South Carolina's Joint
Underwriting Association for only $5,000 a year.

The town donated land, local residents contributed office
and medical equipment, and some of the potential patients volunteered their weekends stuccoing the building that would
become the clinic. We named it Volunteers in Medicine (VIM)
and we opened its doors in 1994, fully staffed by retired physicians, nurses, dentists and chiropractors, as well as nearly 150
lay volunteers. That year we had 5,000 patients; last year we
had 16,000.

Somehow word of what we were doing got around. Soon we
were fielding phone calls from retired physicians all over the

country, asking for help in starting VIM clinics in their communities. We did the best we could—there are now fifteen
other clinics operating, but we couldn't keep up with the need.
Yet last month I think my father's words found their way up
north, to McNeil Consumer Healthcare, the maker of Tylenol. A
major grant from McNeil will allow us to respond to those
requests and help establish other free clinics in communities
around the country.

According to statistics, there are 150,000 retired doctors and
400,000 retired nurses somewhere out there, many of them
itching to practice medicine again. Since I heeded my dad's
words, my golf handicap has risen from a 16 to a 26 and my
leisure time has evaporated into sixty-hour weeks of unpaid
work, but my energy level increased and there is a satisfaction
in my life that wasn't there before. In one of those paradoxes of
life, I have benefited more from Volunteers in Medicine than
my patients have.

This Father's Day, of course, my dad is not around. And my
children are all grown and out on their own. But now I remind
them the best way to celebrate this holiday is by listening and
responding to their grandfather's question: "What did you do
for someone today?" That's my father's most valuable legacy—
to me and my children.

Jack McConnell, M.D.

The Beautiful Girl in the Mirror

All children are beautiful when they are loved.

Bertha Holt

I fell in love with her image even before we met. Other children were pictured on the same page of the *Children's Hope International* newsletter—but I was drawn to her. Tears streamed down my face and fell on the page, blurring the caption under her photo: "Child #151. Zheng Kang. Girl. DOB: 1/17/94. This little girl has no vision in her right eye. She needs a 'Forever Family' to help her overcome her disability."

My heart longed for her to be our daughter. In the margin of the newsletter beside her picture I wrote: "This is Sarah Norwood. 2/13/99."

I prayed. I hoped. I planned . . . and waited. *We* waited—my husband Ed and I.

We were both over fifty years old with two adult, homemade children and two precious grandchildren, yet through the miracle of adoption we were expectant parents again. Our "sonogram" was the copy of her image. We placed other copies of her photograph on our refrigerator, in other prominent places around our home and in our billfolds. We sent our photographs in a picture book to Zheng Kang, who lived at an orphanage in southern China.

When our package with the picture book arrived at the orphanage, a caregiver told us the other children knew it meant Zheng Kang was getting parents. They said, "Zheng Kang's parents have sent something. What about my parents? Do I have parents?"

Her "Abandonment Certificate" stated (in part): "Zheng Kang, female, born on January 17, 1994, was abandoned. She was sent to the Changsha First Social Welfare Center. Her birth parents and other relatives have not been found up to now."

Additional reports noted: "Zheng Kang is kind to others and obedient to adults."

We learned later what the reports didn't mention: She was ridiculed and abused for looking different. Her blind eye was enlarged and covered with protruding scars. In order to survive, she tried to be the best little girl she could be, but withdrew when things were too painful and tried to make herself invisible. Her eyes locked in a fixed stare—almost like a trance. At night, some of the other children cried because they were afraid of the dark, or of the thunder and lightning. Zheng Kang did not cry, except when her life was threatened. She hid under the covers.

We labored through nine months of domestic and international paperwork. We were weighed, measured and fingerprinted. Each document for our dossier was notarized, certified by the Missouri Secretary of State, authenticated by the Chinese Embassy/Consulate and finally translated into Chinese before being sent to China.

On November 28, 1999, our twenty-ninth wedding anniversary, Ed and I flew to China. We were excited walking up the Great Wall of China, but we were nearly breathless with anticipation waiting to meet one little Chinese girl.

Hotel room doors were flung wide open on the nineteenth floor of the Grand Sun Hotel in Changsha City, as expectant parents waited for their children to be brought to their hotel rooms. Ed paced up and down the hallway. I rearranged things inside our room.

"Marcia—come quick! It's Zheng Kang!" Ed recognized her—

her image was already written on his heart. I ran into the hall-way, and fell down on my knees. Face to face at last, I opened my arms to Zheng Kang. She was almost six years old, but looked much younger, partly because she weighed only thirty-seven pounds. I hardly noticed her bulging eye as I looked into the soul of a terrified child who had no one to wipe away her tears. Her silky, black hair was cropped close to her head—nearly shaved—in a pixie cut. Her two black eyes filled with tears. She was dressed in seven layers of tattered, handmade clothing, and the backpack held her only possessions: a bottle of milk and a small framed photo of herself. Her arms clutched the picture book with images of Ed, me and our family that we had mailed to her weeks before our arrival.

The "auntie" who brought her to us pointed to Ed and me and said, "Zheng Kang's Mama and Ba Ba (Chinese for Daddy)!" Zheng Kang began to cry.

"Tell her I will cry when she cries," I said to the interpreter, but I looked directly into Zheng Kang's eyes.

I encouraged her into our room with toys and bubbles. I offered her Cheerios. She accepted our gifts and stuffed them in her hands or in her old, red backpack. When she realized that she would have to stay with us, she gave back all the toys and began to shake her head "No!" She kept the food, especially the Cheerios, but was inconsolable when our interpreter and the "auntie" from the orphanage left.

The room was stifling, so I wiped her face with a cool wash-cloth. Zheng Kang refused to take off her raggedy coat until I gave her new clothes. As she handed me the ones she had on, we slowly exchanged the old for the new.

Reluctantly, she got in the warm bath water, but actually smiled when she smelled the shampoo and conditioner. She played with the fishy washcloth amid the bath bubbles. When I lifted her out of the tub and wrapped her up in a towel, I hugged and hugged her. I thought my heart would burst with joy as I gently massaged her with lotion. After nine months and thousands of miles, I embraced our new baby in my arms and she let me.

Zheng Kang looked curiously at her reflection in the mirror as I combed her hair, and she grinned when I added barrettes and butterfly clips. She put some in my hair, too. Then she pointed to all the new toys and Cheerios and wanted them in bed with her.

I stroked her hair and sang: "Jesus loves the little children of the world."

Ed put his arm around her. She clutched our picture book and as many things as she could in one of her little hands, then reached out to him with her other hand. They fell asleep, but I stayed up most of the night watching them. Sometime in the middle of the night she reached out to me, and soon we drifted back to sleep—our first day together.

At home in the United States, people pointed and stared at her blind eye. Sarah (her new first name) Zheng Kang endured six months of multiple doctor visits with a team of pediatricians and pediatric ophthalmologists. Finally, her blind right eye was removed by a plastic surgeon. He gave her patches for her dolls to wear to match the patch she wore over the cavity where her eye had been.

An ocularist created an artificial eye just for her. Sarah Zheng Kang watched as he completed painting the details. After it was dry he gently inserted it into her socket.

She examined her reflection and whispered to the girl in the mirror: "You are so beautiful." Then she gently kissed the image. That was the first day *she* believed she was beautiful.

"No one in China say I'm beautiful," Sarah said to me.

"You have always been beautiful to me." I answered.

In the two years since she has become our daughter, we have sent photographs back to her orphanage. Most people there do not recognize Sarah Zheng Kang's image. Many had only seen her as her disability.

Mary Marcia Lee Norwood

"I wonder if people had to walk this much
before the age of jet travel."

Style

*God made the human body, the most exquisite
and wonderful organization which has come to
us from the divine hand.*

Henry Ward Beecher

While an impulse toward wholeness is natural and exists in
everyone, each of us heals in our own way. Some people heal
because they have work to do. Others heal because they have
been released from their work and the pressures and expectations that others place on them. Some people need music, others
need silence, some need people around them, others heal alone.
Many different things can activate and strengthen the life force
in us. For each of us there are conditions of healing that are as
unique as a fingerprint. Often I just remind people of the possibility of healing and study their own way of healing with them.

Some time ago a young man was referred to me by an
imagery-training program for people with cancer. Despite a diagnosis of malignant melanoma, he had been so poorly motivated
that only a month after completing the intensive training, he
could not remember to do his daily imagery meditation. The
referral had been clear; perhaps I could turn around his self-
destructive tendencies and encourage him to fight for his life.

Jim was an air-traffic controller at a major airport. He was a reserved and quiet man who might have been thought shy until you noticed the steadiness in his eyes. He told me with embarrassment that he was the only one in the imagery class who couldn't stick to the program. He didn't understand why. We talked for a while about his plans for life and his reaction to his diagnosis. He certainly cared a great deal about getting well. He enjoyed his work, loved his family, looked forward to raising his little boy. Not much self-destruction there. So I asked him to tell me about his imagery.

By way of an answer he unfolded a drawing of a shark. The shark's mouth was huge and open and filled with sharp, pointed teeth. For fifteen minutes three times a day he was to imagine thousands of tiny sharks hunting through his body, savagely attacking and destroying any cancer cells they found. It was a fairly traditional pattern of immune system imagery, recommended by many self-help books and used by countless people. I asked him what seemed to prevent him from doing the meditation. With a sigh, he said he had found it boring.

The training had gone badly from the start. On the first day, the class had been asked to find an image for the immune system. In the subsequent discussion, he had discovered that he had not gotten the "right" sort of image. The whole class and the psychologist/leader had worked with him until he came up with this shark. I looked at the drawing on his lap. The contrast between it and this reserved man was striking.

Curious, I asked what his first image had been. Looking away, he mumbled, "not vicious enough." It was a catfish. I was intrigued. I knew nothing about catfish, had never even seen one, and no one had ever talked about them in this healing role before. With growing enthusiasm he described what catfish do in an aquarium. Unlike more aggressive and competitive fish, they are bottom feeders, sifting the sand through their gills, evaluating constantly, sorting waste from what is not waste, eating what no longer supports the life of the aquarium. They never sleep. They are able to make many rapid and accurate decisions. As an air-traffic controller, he admired their ability to do this.

I asked him to describe catfish to me in a few words. He came up with such words as "discerning, vigilant, impeccable, thorough, steadfast. And trustworthy."

Not bad, I thought.

We talked a while about the immune system. He had not known that the DNA of each of our billions of cells carries a highly individual signature, a sort of personal designer logo. Our immune cells can recognize our own DNA logo and will consume any cell that does not carry it. The immune system is the defender of our identity on the cellular level, patrolling the Self/Not Self boundary constantly, discerning what is self from what is other, never sleeping. Cancer cells have lost their DNA logo. The healthy immune system attacks them and destroys them. In fact, his unconscious mind had offered him a particularly accurate image for the immune system.

As a medical student I had been involved in a study in which a micrograft, a tiny group of skin cells, was taken from one person and grafted onto the skin of a second person, and I told him of these experiments. In seventy-two hours, the second person's immune system, searching the billions of cells that carried his own DNA signature, would find this tiny group of cells and destroy them. I described the many ingenious things we did to hide or conceal the micrograft. Try as we might, we could not outwit the immune system. It found those cells and destroyed them every time.

He still seemed doubtful. The teacher and the class had talked of the importance of an aggressive "fighting spirit" and of the "killer motivation" of effective cancer-fighting imagery. He flushed again.

"Is there something else?" I asked.

Nodding, he told me that catfish grew big where he had been raised, and at certain times of the year they would "walk" across the roads. When he was a child this had struck him as a sort of miracle and he never tired of watching them. He had kept several as pets.

"Jim," I said, "what is a pet?" He looked surprised.

"Why, a pet is something that loves you, no matter what," he replied.

So I asked him to summarize his own imagery. Closing his eyes, he spoke of millions of catfish that never slept, moving through his body, vigilant, untiring, dedicated and discriminating, patiently examining every cell, passing by the ones that were healthy, eating the ones that were cancerous, motivated by a pet's unconditional love and devotion. They cared whether he lived or died. He was as special and unique to them as he was to his dog. He opened his eyes. "This may sound silly but I feel sort of grateful to them for their care," he said.

This imagery touched him deeply and it was not hard for him to remember it. Nor was it boring. He did his meditation daily for a year.

Years later, after a full recovery, he continues this practice a few times a week. He says it reminds him that, on the deepest level, his body is on his side.

People can learn to study their life force in the same way that a master gardener studies a rosebush. No gardener ever made a rose. When its needs are met, a rosebush will make roses. Gardeners collaborate and provide conditions that favor this outcome. And as anyone who has ever pruned a rosebush knows, life flows through every rosebush in a slightly different way.

Rachel Naomi Remen, M.D.

If You Think You Can, You Can

If you think you can, you can. And if you think you can't, you're right.

Mary Kay Ash

"Tumbling time!" I called out. My group of giggling children lined up before the sea of blue mats. Megan trailed behind and stepped quietly into the back of the line. She was eight years old, the same age I was when I began sports acrobatics.

I started the class with forward and backward rolls, cartwheels and handstand forward rolls. The children had mastered this series months ago. Two girls and a boy had even achieved back handsprings on their own. But Megan was still working on handstand forward rolls. It simply took her a little longer to learn the tumbling moves.

I caught her ankles as she kicked into a handstand. While checking her body alignment, I reminded her to straighten her legs, to push against the floor and to tuck in her chin. I guided her as she rolled over, then we started the process again. Each time she stood up I made a special effort to find something to compliment. "What beautiful pointed toes you have," or "Your legs were much straighter than last time," or "That was the strongest handstand I've seen you do yet."

One day before class, Megan's father asked to talk to me. By his somber expression I didn't know what to expect.

"I'm thinking of taking Megan out of class," he said.

"Why?" I asked. *Had I done something wrong?* I wondered.

His arm draped protectively over Megan's shoulders, he said, "She isn't catching on like the other kids are. I don't want her to hold them back." I could see his pained expression as he said this. Megan's eyes were downcast as if she wanted to disappear.

"I think you're making a mistake," I said. "Megan needs this class, possibly more than the other children need it. I didn't start out as a seven-time national champion. I started out as an eight-year-old girl, just like Megan. My coach Igor used to say, 'There are children with talent, then there is Christine. She just works hard.' When I look at Megan I see myself. She works hard.

"Sir, your daughter may never win a competition. She may never even compete, but I promise you that if she keeps trying and believing in herself, her self-esteem will be more important than any gold medal ever won. I believe in Megan. I believe that she can accomplish anything she sets out to do, in her own time."

As I said these words Megan looked up at me. Her eyes were filled with tears, and she was smiling like a bud flowering into bloom.

Her father hugged me and whispered, "Thank you. Thank you so much." He turned to Megan and said, "Honey, go and put on your leotard. It's time for your class."

Megan eventually did learn handstand forward rolls as well as many other skills—in her own time. More importantly, she never again stood at the back of the line. From that day forward, whenever I asked the children to line up for tumbling, Megan ran to stand in the front.

Christine Van Loo

Open Eyes and the Human Spirit

I feel what you feel, but you name it fear and I name it a call to action.

Master Morehei Ueshiba

Tom Sullivan is a sight to behold, standing on the driving range at the Palos Verdes Country Club, hitting 260-yard drives, one after another, each as straight as a Kansas highway. Such shots are routine compared to the time Tom was paired with PGA (Professional Golfers' Association) pro Fuzzy Zoeller. Tom was faced with a deep bunker shot to a hidden green that Zoeller himself called "impossible." With 5,000 fans watching, Sullivan made an impossible birdie with the prettiest shot you will ever see.

Tom didn't get to see his pretty bunker shot, however—not because he had a blast of sand in his eyes, but for the same reason he didn't see his beautiful drives on the practice range or the glorious sunset the night before.

Tom Sullivan is blind.

He is not the best golfer ever born, but Tom is arguably the greatest golfer ever born blind. "All other top blind golfers were five-handicaps or better before they lost their sight," says PVCC pro Ross Kroeker. "Tom is a rare exception."

In fact, Tom has had an exceptional life filled with ironies and contradictions: He was born in 1947, three months premature. The doctors pumped extra oxygen into baby Sullivan's incubator because his lungs needed it. The same rich oxygen that saved his life also destroyed his eyesight. Tom weighed just over three pounds at birth, but grew to be over six feet, two inches and 205 athletic pounds. He lettered in track, won a high school national wrestling championship and rowed on Harvard's eight-man crew.

Tom learned many valuable lessons in his life, but he never learned the meaning of "can't." He has run marathons (three hours, fifteen minutes is his personal record), completed triathlons, climbed mountains and even skydived. "I refuse to let my blindness stop me," Tom says.

Stop him? In truth, his blindness pushed, motivated and even angered Tom. And that anger carried him to the top of mountains, to the finish line of races, to Harvard and to Hollywood. "I needed that anger," he says, reflecting on his past.

Contradictions. Many people see a blind person and look away, yet Tom has spent his lifetime being watched. "Stevie Wonder told me once that sports and music were my ticket out of darkness," says Tom, who sang the national anthem at the 1976 Super Bowl. He has made more than forty guest appearances on *The Tonight Show*, as well as appeared in sixty TV shows and numerous movies. "Stevie was right."

Contradictions. Tom has never seen the colors of a rainbow, but neither has he judged anyone by the color of his skin. "I see people as they really are," Tom remarks.

Contradictions. Being blind is one of the worst fates most of us can imagine, yet Sullivan sees it as a gift. He has found sunlight in total darkness.

Contradictions. Tom has spent much of his life fighting for independence, but sitting by his feet during this interview was Partner, his German shepherd guide dog of five years. "All my life I've struggled to be independent while the world was telling me to be dependent." His voice is tinged with sadness for the first time all afternoon: "I railed against the windmills for a long time. Then I began playing golf and met Ross Kroeker, my current golf teacher, and Laird Small, my first golf pro. That's when I came to understand interdependence. I needed their help, but they also benefited from our relationship. This concept changed my life. It made my marriage, a good one, even better. Understanding interdependence also enhanced my professional life—in fact, it impacted everything, as I realized that sighted or not, we all need help from each other."

Tom likens his relationship with Ross to the mythological Damon and Pythias, but they may actually relate to one another more like Bill Walsh and Joe Montana. Coach Kroeker calls the play, and it's up to quarterback Sullivan to execute it. "If Ross tells me the shot has to fly forty-five yards over water, I have to trust him."

"Sometimes I don't mention the water until afterward," laughs Kroeker, thirty-five, who lines up Tom's stance and sets the clubface squarely behind the ball before Tom takes each shot.

"Actually," he continues, "there isn't much he doesn't 'see' on the golf course. Like a bat, he seems to have sonar. Tom can tell how far the ball goes accurately, within five yards."

How?

"I can hear the ball land," Tom adds. "And on putts I can hear the roll." He listens to other players' putts to learn the speed of the green. He then "reads" the greens by pacing off a putt, feeling the contour and slope with feet as sensitive as a safe-cracker's fingertips. "I can feel the cushion—feel if it's hard, feel if it's wet. I can even feel the grain of the grass with my feet. I have no doubt I can pick the line of a putt better than most sighted people." No, he doesn't play barefoot; he has developed a keen sensitivity to vibrations of all kinds.

Kroeker, who has been Sullivan's eyes in the Blind World Golf Championships in England at St. Andrews, agrees: "He's absolutely amazing with his reads."

Speaking of reading—one of the seven books Tom Sullivan has authored is aptly titled, *If You Could See What I Hear*. He comments, "I've never seen my wife in a beautiful dress, but I've heard the sound of Patty's smile." Imagine that—hearing your spouse smile, hearing a putt roll, hearing the footwork of Los Angeles Lakers' superstar Kobe Bryant driving for a slam dunk.

Had he been born today instead of fifty-three years ago, Tom's ears might not be as sharp, but because doctors now understand the dangers of too much oxygen to premature infants' eyes, Tom would likely have 20/20 vision. That's not to say blindness in preemies has been eradicated. Science today saves babies who are younger and younger, smaller and smaller, but with that comes more complications. And more blind babies.

Unfortunately, the Blind Children's Center of Los Angeles is not in danger of going out of business for lack of patients. Fortunately, Sullivan continues to see to it that it doesn't go out of business for lack of funds. In the past twelve years, he has raised $3 million for the center by holding annual celebrity golf tournaments and 5K runs. "Helping others is the best use of celebrity there can be," he says, "I believe anyone can take a disadvantage and turn it into an advantage."

A final contradiction: Instead of having your mood depressed by Tom's blindness, you feel uplifted in his presence, because he opens people's eyes to the strength of the human spirit.

Woody Woodburn

7

OVERCOMING ADVERSITY

Miracles do not happen in contradiction to nature, but only in contradiction to that which is known to us of it.

St. Augustine

Little Angel in Heaven

Like a bird out of our hand, like a light out of our heart, you are gone.

Hilda Doolittle

Two years ago, I met the most precious five-year-old in Hawaii, the only daughter of Keola and Lani. When I stood in the doorway to her room, her parents introduced me as their special friend.

Maile was on her bed, coloring pictures in a coloring book. Her eyes, rich with warmth and innocence, looked at me, and my heart melted as we exchanged greetings. She invited me to sit on her bed and color with her, and I accepted.

Maile had been battling leukemia for the past two years, and it had progressed beyond help three weeks before I was contacted by Hospice of Hilo, Hawaii.

We were silent, except for an occasional, "Please pass another crayon." I finished my masterpiece and watched Maile completing hers. As she finished, she sighed deeply and asked, "Are you here to help me die?"

Our eyes linked, and I asked, "Do you want help?"

She shook her head, "no," and began looking for two more blank pages for us to color, found the ones she liked and we began again. Coloring the trees green, Maile said, her eyes down, "Mommy and Daddy need help, though."

I continued coloring along with her and said, "Do you want me to help you help them?"

No words came back, but as a tear hit the page she was nodding her head, "yes."

I found her mother crying in the kitchen as she sipped a cup of tea. She said, "I can't let Maile go." As I hugged Lani, I reassured her that I would help her and her family through this hard time in their lives. She walked me out to my car and we found Keola aggressively sanding wood in his backyard with an almost uncontrollable runny nose. Having lost a daughter of my own, I recognized the silent pain held within their hearts.

Much of the time in my following visits to their home was spent with Maile, listening to her understanding of what was happening. She understood the doctors and nurses were no longer going to be poking her with needles or giving her medicine that made her sick. "One day I will go to sleep and never wake up, and the pain will go away then." That was the most important part—no more pain.

"Do you know God?" I asked her.

She began singing, "Jesus loves me this I know . . ."

I asked her what she thought heaven would be like, and she said, "My uncle and my friend Tommy from the hospital are there already, and I'm excited to be with them again."

But Maile had a very worrisome problem: "Mommy and Daddy cry a lot, and I don't want them to be sad anymore," she told me. We began to think of gifts she could leave them. She came up with the idea of taking out her first loose tooth.

"That's a special gift that I think they would really like," I said. "But we need to come up with something else your family can remember you by all their lives—not just Mommy and Daddy, but the grandmas, grandpas, uncles and aunties as well." She agreed.

With Maile's childlike connection with God in its purest form, I knew that her final gift to her family—which was for her to discover without my help—would be unique and special.

Knowing she was okay, I spent many of my final visits with the family.

I posed the same question to Maile's family that I had asked her: "What will be your final gifts to her?" I wanted to involve all the family members and establish family rapport, too.

Their grief hindered their creative thoughts, so I mustered up the only idea God placed in my heart. "Suppose you men gather together and carve a casket out of koa wood with your loving hands." Koa wood is sacred to Hawaiians, and I knew it would have multiple meanings for them. The project would also unite them and give them strength. They jumped at the thought and agreed that the project would begin at Grandpa's house.

The women also struggled to think clearly about what they could give Maile. I saw a vision of a quilt made of all the special clothing pieces that had been worn and imbued with love by family members. I saw this colorful quilt surrounding and com-forting Maile's little body in the koa casket. After many tears and hugs, the women agreed to begin the project at the other grandma's house.

With the projects assigned and support established among family members, I spent much of Maile's final few days with her while her parents and relatives were making their gifts.

Her days became quieter as she rested more. Her coloring book sat on the shelf with the crayons, never to be used again. As her breath became shallower, I had Lani and Keola take turns rocking their fragile child in their laps.

On my final visit, before I left Maile in the laps of her parents, I asked, "Have you thought of any special gift you want for your family?" Her big brown eyes looked up at me, then at her mommy and daddy. She said, "I want a baby brother or sister."

Both her parents were crying. Keola knelt beside Lani, who was holding Maile in her lap, and said, "Honey, we can't give you that gift."

She looked at them with a labored smile and said, "Not right now, but later. Then I can be the baby's angel, and watch over it and protect it."

I left the family alone that night. When I returned the next morning, Maile was in her bed, peaceful and with God, as family members surrounded her. Keola and Lani hugged me, and Keola opened his fisted hand, showing me his baby's first missing tooth. It fell out as they put her lifeless body back into her bed.

Her funeral was more special than I could have imagined. The quilt surrounding her little body was comforting and smelled like love. Loving hands also created the beautiful koa casket in which she rested. God had blessed this little family with a union that could not be torn apart.

And Maile's final gift? I got a call from Lani recently. They are expecting Maile's little angelic wings to go to work in June.

Gail Eynon

On My Own

It was tough breaking into the L.A. film business as a stunt performer, even though I was a world-class trampoline champion and acrobat. So, when my boyfriend asked me to move away with him, I agreed. After three weeks, one beautiful morning I found myself sitting in front of our duplex, crying my eyes out and gathering my belongings off the ground.

Looking back, I wonder how I, a skilled athlete with a wealth of academic achievements and confidence in my physical skills, could have tolerated an abusive relationship that ended after an escalating pattern of scorn. For a fleeting moment—before I started wondering what I was going to do with the rest of my life—I felt an affinity with so many other women who had let someone else control their lives with a promise of security and safety. So what had begun so lovingly ended abruptly. In retrospect—a blessing and a grace.

I was out on the streets with no home, no local acquaintances, no transportation and no bank account. All I had was three hundred dollars I had saved from my work at a temporary employment agency. I wandered aimlessly, with two questions echoing in my mind: *How did I get here? Where did my hopes and dreams go?*

I took stock of my situation. I was still young—in my early thirties. I had my health, a master's degree (magna cum laude),

Capitol Hill work experience for a congressman and my world travels while competing in sports. I had won the World Trampoline Championship. What had happened? I realized nothing had happened that I hadn't chosen. So I could choose differently now and by God, I would.

I had some more crying still to do as I carried my belongings toward a bus stop up the street, dropping socks and undies along the way. Then I remembered this was to be my first day of work at a gymnastics club.

After teaching an extremely patient trampoline student who had waited for me, I noticed that doing something for someone else, like teaching, took me out of my own self-absorbed reveries—a relief and a joy!

I needed money to pay the rent. My temp agency found jobs, and I was offered more classes to teach. I also got a job doing a national R.C. Cola commercial. I had the feeling that God was looking after me.

Many months before, I had indulged dreams of qualifing for the U.S. National Trampoline Team, eleven years after my retirement. It seemed that focused training toward a challenging goal might reawaken the sense of confidence I had once felt.

I trained during off hours—late at night and early in the morning. Ultimately, every athlete is alone—no one is going to train for her, but without companions to pace and push you, it's a much bigger challenge.

Strange as it may seem, during the following weeks a new relationship began to blossom in that gym—a relationship with myself—and with life on its terms. What had begun as training toward a competition was evolving into a kind of spiritual journey. I became my own coach—sometimes tough, sometimes kind, and always showing respect for my student.

New practices included meditation, visualization, yoga, inspiring music and conditioning exercises of my own design. Another change involved rewards. I no longer felt compelled to win, to beat others, earn medals or recognition—not even to travel overseas or attend social occasions to motivate myself. I simply *was*. I existed in the moment—moving, flying, defying gravity, dancing in the air.

I had a goal. I was, after all, training to make the U.S. National Team. I questioned *why* I was training and this became the subject of contemplation. I came across a phrase written by Marianne Williamson: "The miracle is to think of our career as our contribution, however small, to the healing of the universe." I saw my training as a career, so I asked myself, *How might my training help heal the universe?* An answer soon appeared: I could demonstrate to women that we are as strong in our thirties as when we were younger—stronger than we believe, more powerful than we can imagine and something I always knew I wanted to prove.

But it would not be easy. To those who are forty, or fifty or older, someone in her thirties may seem young, yet anyone who has trained for world-class competition knows that after a decade away from the sport, with many enthusiastic youngsters as competitors—well, it was a distant dream, not a done deal.

Still, my mantra and mission statement became: "My contribution, however small, will show women of all ages their possibilities." This mission gave me strength and spirit—it helped me jump higher and move quicker. I started to feel the old magic, and my routines became more polished. Over and over I somersaulted over twenty feet in the air, performing advanced routines in the still of night, with no one to witness these acts of power. I took tremendous risks, and learned to trust God manifesting through the forces of nature, and through my own body.

I had never before performed for myself, by myself, at this level. Now I was coach, judge and jury. No external rewards or encouragement. It had to come from me.

But I confess, I hoped God was watching.

My routines began to feel like rhythmic flight, the way one feels in a flying dream. Every small movement was in focus; each skill seemed to last forever. I suspended time as I floated in the air. I combined dynamic activity with inner stillness. I experienced effortless effort. I was meditating in midair.

A little later, I met a man who understood acrobatic movement, so I asked him to critique my form; the one thing I
couldn't do was watch myself jump. He told me what he saw;
in return, I taught him some basic trampoline routines. We
formed a solid friendship, and from this kind man I learned to
surround myself with people who would enrich my life.

To qualify for the U.S. Trampoline Team, I would need to do
my best work at three trial competitions. I found sponsorships
and booked plane tickets.

At the first trial, I didn't perform well. The trampoline equipment was different from mine and I had trouble adjusting—a
good lesson. For the second trial, I arrived a week early to get
comfortable with the equipment. In the second trial, I placed
second—only a hair behind first place. That's when I knew I
might have a chance despite my poor showing at the first. It
would all depend on the final team trial—I had to finish in the
top three.

Two weeks before the third team trial, a car pulled in front of
my scooter and I crashed, sliding across the asphalt and badly
scraping my right side. Despite the potential end of my quest
to make the U.S. Team, I felt remarkably calm. My scooter was
wrecked, but my injuries were relatively minor, except for a
huge hematoma, the size of a grapefruit, jutting out of my
thigh. It would take two weeks to drain.

That ball of blood prevented me from training at all before
leaving for the third team trial—the U.S. National Trampoline
Championships in Nashville, Tennessee. For the next two
weeks I relied on training methods that didn't require physical
activity: Over and over I meditated and visualized my routines
that I had done so well.

There was a great deal riding on this third and final team
trial. I was, as I expected, the oldest woman competitor in the
meet. When the time came, I performed my routines just as I
had performed them in my head over the previous two weeks.
And by the end of the day, I had made the team. The other
finalists were fifteen, seventeen and twenty-one years old.

I was the oldest woman *ever* to qualify for the U.S. National

Trampoline Team. I had made my dream happen. And after that, I made other dreams happen, too, because I knew the process. During this time my stunt career took shape as well. Since then you've seen me double for stars like Demi Moore (in *G.I. Jane*), as well as Sela Ward and many others.

But beyond the professional success or athletic laurels, I've experienced an even deeper sense of fulfillment, because while I trained and competed, I didn't know if there were women in their thirties cheering me on and perhaps feeling encouraged or inspired. But I do know that in finding my contribution, however small, I found my own strength. I had stood on the shoulders of those before me, and enjoyed the support of friends and loved ones—yet I had done it on my own, and it felt good. Even if the only person watching was me.

Leigh Hennessy

A Gift of Spirit

Music is our myth of the inner life.

Susanne K. Langer

I was born with a "lazy eye"—at least that's what some people call it. Actually, it was never really lazy; it just floated around my socket, looking this way and that, when I was young, until it finally settled down in the wrong place. I've been plagued with double vision ever since.

As soon as I learned to crawl, I would smack headfirst into walls, tables and chairs. I also enjoyed extreme close-ups of our family dog. As a toddler I walked like a drunken sailor—even more than other toddlers my age. I probably ran into more walls and doorways than the entire Seventh Fleet on liberty in the Philippines.

At the age of five, I began piano lessons. Learning to read all those little black dots, especially two sets of them, posed special challenges. But I persevered, closing one eye at a time. In this way I joyfully learned to play such classics as "Chopsticks," "Polka Dot Polka" and the "Sewing Machine Song." Meanwhile, I ignored the headaches that plagued my practice time.

The first time I ever saw a bass guitar, it was hanging on the wall in the local music store, all shiny and supremely cool, as if waiting there for me. I sat on the amp to thump out a few notes—and my whole body rumbled with its power. It sounded to me like the voice of Spirit. I was in love with music at the tender age of thirteen. I studied guitar like a mad scientist searching for the answer to life. The headaches continued to bother me off and on, but I loved the instrument. I knew that I was born to play the bass, though at the time I wasn't sure why.

In my freshman year of high school, I began working with someone who knew the band leader at a local polka hall and who sat in with the band. He arranged the same privileges for me, and these sessions became a regular part of my musical training.

But that all changed on a breezy Sunday afternoon in the fall of 1973. A neighborhood friend had talked me into joining an impromptu afternoon football game to even up the sides. I did little for most of the game until a teammate tipped the ball as the opposing quarterback attempted to pass. To my surprise, and everyone else's, the ball floated into my outstretched arms. I had never in my life handled the ball in a game and I ran for the sheer joy of it. The smile on my face threatened to split my cheeks in two as everyone stood staring, their mouths agape.

A varsity player who existed for football was livid. His team was behind and he wasn't about to stand for a little goofy-eyed kid running an interception back for a touchdown. I glanced behind me to see this freight train of a man pounding the turf at full speed, gaining fast on me. I ran for my life. If he caught me, I'd end up bleeding in the mud.

Aiming to dance in the end zone, I ran madly, wildly, until I hit a patch of slick mud and fell face first to the ground. I rolled over to my right, just as his careening hulk reached me. Seeing me down, he tried to jump over me but the corner of his left heel met the corner of my left eye. I remember the pain, then blackness.

When I came to, I noticed something weird—no ghost image, no double vision. My sight was blurred and the world was filled with fuzzy shapes. But there was only one of each shape, not two. Carefully, I closed my right eye to see what my left eye's sight was like and the world went dark. That's when I got scared and started yelling.

My friends drove me to the emergency room where a doctor

pried my swollen eye open and pronounced it fine. The eyeball itself was intact—only the socket area was destroyed. He squirted some antiseptic goop on me, taped a huge bandage over half of the left side of my face and sent me home with a stern note to my parents about the dangers of football (especially, I supposed, for a goofy-eyed boy).

I tried to stay home, embarrassed by the bandage, but a friend urged me to play that night, as scheduled, promising that "all the chicks dig war wounds." He figured I was sure to get major sympathy points.

At first I thought I'd actually have an easier time with one eye bandaged. I wouldn't have to alternate eyes to see the music clearly. Then I realized that I couldn't see my bass at all. Without my left eye, I had to turn my head far enough that my right eye could see where my left hand was. But in that position, I couldn't see the music. This terrified me.

The bassist for the band was a kindly old grandfather type. Returning from the buffet line, he saw that something was clearly wrong. Setting his plate on the table next to his wife, he came to the stage. I said, "I can't see what I'm doing. Without my left eye, I can't keep track of the notes and my bass at the same time. What am I going to do?"

"Just play," he replied.

"You don't *understand*," I pleaded. "I can't see!"

He climbed on the bandstand and sat beside me. "Lane, you don't need to see," he promised. "You know these tunes—you've played them a dozen times." Pointing a wrinkled finger at my chest, he continued, "You have the music inside you. It's always been there. You know it and I know it. Tonight, let these people know it, too."

For a moment I just sat there, staring, as if I were a deer in someone's headlights. Then something—I don't know what it was, maybe a mixture of fear and the realization of truth—began to swell inside me. He must have sensed this, because he smiled and went on: "God gave you a gift, Lane. He's given you the ability to make beautiful music that makes people happy. Stop worrying. Accept that gift and share it with them," he said, gesturing to the audience.

"But I can't *see*," I stammered tearfully.

"Close your eyes, Lane. Trust yourself. Do you really think God would give you such a wonderful gift then take it back? I promise you—the music is there."

He left me to ponder his words while he ate his dinner. As the other musicians completed their final preparations, I looked up and said a short prayer. In that moment, it seemed that a warm, loving feeling bathed me, as if a light were shining down, as if God were smiling on me. Taking a deep breath, I brought my gaze back into the room as the bandleader counted us off.

Hesitant at first, I felt my strength start to grow. By the time we hit the second chorus, I was really digging in. The second song was better than the first, and the third continued the upward trend. By that time my eyes were closed but I could see the music all the same. Just as promised, it was inside my heart and I realized that the old musician was right. It had been there all along.

That night I learned a new way of playing on faith. All I had to do was open my heart and let Spirit guide me. It took years of practice, mind you, to do this whenever I chose. I continued to study, but added a meditative form of playing to my regimen and constantly strove to build a bridge of faith between Spirit, myself and the music.

In this, I've experienced a measure of success. Some people tell me that I seem lost in the music when I play; that's the greatest kind of compliment I can receive. And they're half right: I am definitely inside the music, but I'm not lost at all. I've never felt so found. I don't have the words to describe how it feels to be nestled in the arms of Spirit, wrapped in the blanket of the song, completely removed from the physical world.

After one particularly Spirit-connected performance not long ago, a friend came up afterward and said, "Welcome back, Lane. For a minute there, I thought we'd lost you for good. I've never seen someone so consumed by music."

I had to smile. "I guess I was born with the music inside me—with this gift of Spirit."

Lane Baldwin

"Michigan, You Walk a Long Way"

I am persuaded that the greater part of our complaints come from want of exercise.

Marie de Rabutin-Chantal

I was into my first week of training for the Avon Breast Cancer Three-Day Los Angeles 2002 event to raise money to benefit underserved women with breast cancer. The walk is sixty miles long—twenty miles each day.

I nearly skipped my walk that day, thinking that I really should get to work an hour early so I could complete a new business proposal I had started the day before. But I decided to walk first, so that it would help clear my head.

According to the training schedule the walk organizers gave me, I was to walk three miles that day. Each week I would progressively walk farther and farther until I worked up to two, twelve-mile back-to-back sessions in one weekend prior to the big event. To prepare for these, I had spent an afternoon mapping out various locations, to determine how far each one was.

I gathered my things, among them my headphones and a book on tape—*Chicken Soup for the Soul,* tape one, volume one. Because my regular gray sweatshirt was in the wash, I dug out and pulled on a very old sweatshirt, one I hadn't worn in nearly ten years. It was a gift from one of my ex-husband's friends, and it had the Michigan logo across the front of it. Off I went, happily listening to my tape, getting weepy now and again at an especially poignant story, and oh so glad I had decided to walk after all.

About three-quarters of the way into it, I spotted a man about a half-mile ahead of me on the same side of the street. I didn't think much of it. He was going in the same direction, but was way ahead. I didn't think I'd catch up with or pass him before I reached the park and turned around. I continued at my pace, while the words, *Stay alert, stay alive,* went through my head—instructions I had received at a walk orientation meeting a month or two earlier.

I soon realized I was gaining on the man, and briefly considered crossing the street. Then I saw a female jogger approach and pass him as she came up the street toward me. He hadn't even glanced at her, so I decided he was just out exercising like the rest of us, and I needn't be concerned. I kept walking, listening to my tape, getting closer to him.

I could now see he was an older Asian man, on the stairs about halfway up to the park from the street. He was looking at me. I could tell he wanted to say something, so I stopped, looked up at him, took off my headphones and smiled. He said, "Michigan [referring to the blue and gold logo on my white sweatshirt], you walk a long way. I watch you."

I said, "Yes, sir, I have," and kept smiling and waiting. I felt comfortable talking to him.

He said, "When I was thirty-five years old, I was sick. My doctor told me to start walking every day. Doctor said it make me healthier, stronger."

"Good," I said.

The man held up his arms in a strongman pose: "See: strong and healthy now! From that day I have walked one hour every day, and today I am sixty-five!"

I smiled, enjoying his story. He went on: "Every day I walk, then go home to my wife and tell her I love her. That keeps me healthy, too." He added that he tells her he walks for her, because he loves her. Then he said something that made me catch my breath. He simply said, with force and a pointed finger, "You will live a long time if you do the same—walk an hour every day and tell your husband you do it because you love him."

"... you walk a long way." That statement could be a metaphor for the last two years of my life, and for the lives of those around me. I am a thirty-six-year-old breast-cancer survivor.

I thought I was doing the Avon Three-Day walk because I had received so much help from so many people and organizations, and because my sister had a passion to do it. That nice man made me realize that I am also walking for the same reason that I endured two mastectomies, chemotherapy, radiation therapy and the removal of my ovaries—because I love my husband, children, family and friends so much that I want to be around for a lot more years.

I *will* walk every day, and I will go home and tell my husband I walk because I love him.

Donna St. Jean Conti

A New Definition of Health

Illusions surround me, so I listen to the sounds of my heart, and trust the path is below my feet. I believe in the meaning of my journey.

Erica Ross-Krieger

One day this spring, I went to the pool to swim my usual laps. I arrived during off-hours, had a lane all to myself and immersed myself in the rhythm of the swim as I enjoyed memories of a recent vacation. Then I glanced to my side and found myself sharing the lane with an elderly gentleman. There were other free lanes, but I guess he'd just decided to share this one. I didn't mind and continued my laps. As I swam, I noticed my lane-mate walked rather than swam, exercising his legs. At the end of my swim, I rested at the end of the lane.

My aged companion walked over and introduced himself, and mentioned that he was exercising to strengthen his hip before surgery. We traded names, and I told him that I thought he was smart to keep exercising his hip.

"I'm eighty," he said. "I want to live five more years and I'll do whatever I have to do. I also want to be able to go for morning walks with my lovely wife of sixty years." Then he asked, "What are you here for?"

Usually I avoid the multiple sclerosis (MS) label. I don't want it to become a "thing," and I don't want it to become my identity. Too many people start to make assumptions about the eventual prognosis and wind up adding to my own anxiety. I'd rather they create their own reality, not mine, so I don't bother with the MS label. Plus, I think of myself as healthy and like to affirm that. This time, however, I felt like it really didn't matter what anyone else thought. "Well, I have MS and I'm here to maintain good health."

"Oh, you must know Jim," he replied. "Jim has MS."

Another reason not to use the MS label, I thought. People tend to think it's a club where everyone who has the diagnosis knows one another. After indulging this sarcastic reverie, I turned my attention back to the gentleman. His good heart and intention were clear. "No, I don't know him," I said.

"Jim walks with a cane," he said. "Do you?"

"No, I don't, but I've thought about using one during the tough times."

He grew quiet, turned to face me squarely with his blue eyes and blessed me with his eighty years of wisdom. "Life's too short," he said. "Don't be a hero." With a smile, he turned and continued walking his laps.

I've always believed that what we need to hear will come to us if we're listening. Well, I was paying attention, and that moment was magical. "Don't be a hero." I began to consider my notion of being a hero, and my belief that I couldn't advise other people about wellness if I had to use a cane. I began to think about all the ways we think things should look or be—our images of health and wellness. And I realized something that felt profound and important. Now I have my own inner-directed definition of wellness that can also include not being a hero.

I realized that a cane was a tool I needed to assist me in living my life more fully and joyfully. I figured, if I cut my finger, I'd get a Band-Aid to help it heal. A cane is no different.

I found a cane that fit my needs and bought it. I needed no instruction; my body taught me all I needed to know in order to use it. I only needed to touch it to the ground lightly, as a means of feedback from the earth to me—a way of reassuring myself that the ground is there, ground I sometimes can't feel through the numbness and tingling in my feet. The moment I used the cane in this way, I experienced a renewed sense of ease and freedom. *Wow*, I thought, *now I can take my eyes off the ground and see the trees.*

I didn't realize how much I had missed the trees.

Recently, I found another new and visceral understanding of health—in the shower no less. I was washing my body with a scrubbie sponge and foaming soap. As I bent over to lather my right leg, enjoying the sensation of feeling my muscles against the sponge, I also noticed the muscular shape of that leg and how good the lather felt against my skin. When I started lathering my left leg, however, I began comparing it to the right one, thinking, *Oh, it doesn't look as strong. It won't hold as much weight. Oh, this poor leg.*

Then I noticed that I had stopped enjoying the simple experience of lathering my legs—stopped enjoying it at the precise moment when I started judging it. Another thought struck me: *What if I love this leg just as it is? What if I honor its weakness? In fact, what if I don't even label it as "weak"? What if I just love the muscles in this leg as they are? What if I love the sensation of scrubbing this leg? What if I love this leg right now? What if I stop waiting until it gets stronger, gets better, gets different? And what if I live my whole life like this—what if I love myself just as I am? What might my life become?*

As I experienced this epiphany in the shower, I found myself standing more balanced on both legs than I had in a long time. This new definition of health and of unconditional acceptance has forever changed my life. And whatever challenges or joys I may meet in the future, lessons like these make the journey worthwhile.

Erica Ross-Krieger

My First Miracle

I *stand in awe of my body . . .*

Henry David Thoreau

I believe in miracles because I've seen so many of them.

A patient was referred to me who was one hundred and two years old. "There's a sore under my denture," she said. "I told my own dentist it's nothing, but he insisted I come see you."

Her eighty-year-old son accompanied her. He would occasionally attempt to add something to her story but she would say, "Hush up, son!" She wanted to tell it herself. I found a large cancer that extended over much of the roof of her mouth. A biopsy later confirmed the diagnosis—a particularly bad sort of cancer.

During her next appointment, I explained to her the seriousness of the problem. She reached down, clasped my hand in hers and said, "I know you're worried about me, but I'm just fine."

I knew differently. After considerable effort on my part, and kindness on her part because she wanted to please me, she consented to have me refer her to a cancer surgeon. She saw him, but as I expected, declined treatment.

About six months later she returned to my office.

"How are you?" I asked. Her son started to speak, but she told him to hush once again.

"I'm just fine, honey," she said to me. "When can I get started on fixing my denture?"

Surprised to see her at all, I sputtered, "Let me take a look in your mouth and we'll see about it." I was thinking, *no way.*

I couldn't believe my eyes. The cancer that had covered nearly the entire roof of her mouth was gone—only one small area of redness remained.

I had read of such things happening, but had never actually seen them with my own eyes. I was dumbfounded.

"You see, honey? Like I told you, I'm fine," she said, patting my antiseptically gloved hand.

Now I believed her.

That was my first miracle. Since then I've seen many others, because they keep getting easier to see. In fact, miracles are daily events for me now. Every time I remember to take a slow, deep breath, I think about the miracle of being alive—how the sun rises and the Earth turns, all the while shooting through space at thousands of miles an hour. And *people* are a miracle, for through them we have a chance to know ourselves, to know God and to love beyond ourselves. We have a chance to show kindness, to provide service, and to see the miracles of one another.

Since my first miracle, I've come to understand that the time and place for a miracle is wherever we choose to find it.

Dane E. Smith

The Fawn

O to confront night, storms, hunger, ridicule,
accidents and rebuffs as animals do!

Walt Whitman

My world had come apart and I thought, *nothing or no one can ever repair it.* I was fresh from eight weeks in the hospital after a wretched accident in which I had lost my right arm and a few other mundane parts and pieces at the age of sixty-three. My blessed family was there through every grueling surgery. With each awakening I was ecstatic to be alive, until ghastly thoughts would take hold of my mind and force reality to creep back in. Self-pity was eating me up, and homesickness often overwhelmed me. (I still find myself a cranky old fussbudget if away from my home for more than two days.)

I was released from the hospital after two months. When at last I looked up to behold the big curved log gateway over my drive, my carefully burned lettering on the ranch sign hanging beneath the gate, and my beloved kids and grandkids running to greet me, I felt renewed, reborn. A small blackish cloud passed beneath the sun releasing a short July drencher as the youngsters helped their bedraggled Granny up toward the deck where our Molly and her Mike were shish-kabobbing.

"The kids need you, Granny," pleaded Mol, as she planted a kiss on my cheek and announced she was pregnant again. "They need to touch their Gran." My littlest babes grabbed onto my left arm lest I should topple over. We lifted our legs high and waded barefoot through the glistening wet grass where a sea of blossoms had raised their heads to drink. It smelled delicious.

"Are you okay, Gran? Do you want a glass of juice?" queried my sweet Mikal.

"No, my darlin', not now," I whispered. As we picked dandelions and wild flowers for the dinner table, I was acutely aware of my surroundings—more than ever before. Suddenly Jamie stared down at her bouquet and mumbled, "You're not going to die, are you Granny?"

The next morning I arose and slipped out into the sunshine in my shorty jammies to look and listen to God's miracles embracing me. The mallards were completely engrossed in caring for their eggs—nested warmly under carefully fashioned bits of grass and straw. The hens took turns scurrying into Duck Soup Waterfowl Refuge to flap their wings and drown their feathers before returning to the nest for a few more hours of incubating. "Only a few more days, ladies," I reminded them out loud. "Then all your worries begin." Our beautiful donkey family had finally shed their scruffy winter coats and looked so fine, all decked out in silky coats with their crosses emblazoned down their backs and across their shoulders. "And what did Mary ride to Bethlehem on?" I called out. As she sensed my frailties, one of the donkeys, Sweet Pea, whimpered ever so softly instead of her usual full-blown hee-haw. She lifted her head and sniffed the air as I walked toward her, then all five suddenly jumped and fled.

I knew I looked and smelled different, but that was okay. I had lots of time and so did they. I could hardly wait to walk the earth . . . to breathe in the scent of lodge pole pine . . . to feel the sweet breezes that made the pond ripple . . . to listen to the piercing sounds of Rocky Mountain birds whose melodies are heard only by those who bother to listen. The cottontails sat up to ogle while their wee ones scurried out of the grass before me.

Our big forested mountain was still there, and I knew this was the place I would feed my soul—forever. As I meandered over the uneven pasture toward the woods, in hopes the shooting stars or Indian paintbrush had bloomed, I thought I heard a cry.

Our dog, Keesha, stopped to listen and sniff—it was probably only a bird. We had taken only a few more steps, however, and there before us hung a spotted fawn caught up on the farm fence. I quietly ordered Keesha to stay while I drew closer, trying not to notice the anxious doe peering at me from the shadows. The fawn cried like a baby as I threw my heavily bandaged stump under her chest, lifted slightly and untangled her hoof with my good hand. Anyone coming upon the scene would have surely thought I had lost my mind. As we both fell to the ground, the mama leapt over the fence squealing at the top of her lungs. Here I was, this old broad lying in a field, flat on my back in my pajamas, caressing a spotted fawn with half an arm, while Keesha wagged her tail and slurped my face in utter joy.

"Okay, okay, Mama, we're leaving," I yelled to the doe. With that she and her child ran off into the aspens without a by-your-leave. I couldn't help but laugh out loud and boast to Keesha as I rolled over and got to my feet. "Holy smokes girl, I've been home less than a day and already I'm a hero. I can do anything, even save a life."

And save lives I did as the years have flown by. I was, and still am, slightly insecure, and every time I get to feeling that life has dealt me a bum blow, I look around at others in such terrible trouble and thank God for allowing this wretch to live and love all who enter her life. We know not from where God sends his creations to heal souls when all seems lost. That little fawn will always be in my prayers, for she was a part of my healing that fateful day. Thank you, little fawn, thank you.

Kathe Campbell

Mountain Fever

There are people of good sense who do not grieve for what they have not, but rejoice in what they have.

Epictetus

The coup de grâce of our senior year at Oregon Episcopal School in Portland, Oregon, was an experiential program based in part on the Outward Bound philosophy, a twenty-seven-mile hike through the Columbia Gorge, the first event of its kind in the school's history. There was no such thing as a category for disabled teens on this adventure, and I was an amputee with many deformities.

Participation was voluntary, of course, and involved training in both endurance and rappelling. When the idea was presented to our senior class and our principal asked who *didn't* want to go, only one hand went up in the room, and it wasn't mine. Martha was healthy and capable, but she had no interest: "No way on earth I'm diving off cliffs, hauling a forty-pound backpack through a cold forest in the rain and cleaning bugs out of a sleeping bag in the middle of the night," she wailed. Everyone laughed, but seemed nonplussed and undeterred from what could befall us.

We were given a choice: final exams or the hike. Suddenly the room fell silent and everyone stared straight at me, their laser eyes like pin pricks in a voodoo doll. My classmates were waiting for my hand to go up in the nervous air. They stared so hard I was sure they could see my underwear. I said nothing. I didn't move.

I wanted to go so badly I could almost taste the moisture in the trees, but I feared that I would drain the patience and strength of my friends who had the luxury of taking navigation for granted. I knew it was a crazy idea because it held so much risk of disappointment, but I was determined to go. Later that day, after math class was over, I was walking by the faculty lounge and stopped to pick up a book I dropped. The door was barely cracked and I froze when I heard my name.

"Janet didn't raise her hand," said Sam Dibbins, our tennis coach.

"What the heck are we going to do? There's no way on this green Earth that girl can hike those trails, cross those creeks and carry forty pounds on her back with just one leg," said one of the science teachers. "If she collapses or takes a bad fall, we'll have to carry her out," he said. "It isn't prudent." Suddenly the room grew gravely quiet. "Maybe, if we're lucky, her father won't sign the permission form," he added.

As the conversation continued, they discussed the fact that Outward Bound was all about people pushing the limits, breaking set boundaries and realizing their potential.

"We'll figure it out," said Dibbins. "I say she goes! It may drag down the other kids, but it will also teach them teamwork." I limped off down the hall, hoping they hadn't heard the noisy click of my artificial knee.

One night during spring break, I waited until after dinner and took the permission form into my father's study. "What's this?" he asked.

"Oh, it's for an off-campus event," I said. "Just scribble your name. It's no big deal," I added, fumbling my words as I uttered this little white lie. He signed the form with the flick of his wrist and went back to sorting through his mail.

Since it was the month of May, we were hoping for nice weather; instead, we were met with relentless rain, so heavy it looked like falling apples against a backdrop of emerald silk. Between showers, we were surrounded by gnat clouds as thick as bedroom drapes. The forest was all-consuming to me, lush green ferns like peacock fans rustling in a light wind. The terrain wasn't terribly steep, but the hiking path was narrow and relatively untraveled. My body had never been free to write its own rules, and the uneven ground only exacerbated the problem. Each step was a problem to be solved. My friends kicked boulders and sticks out of my way as we hiked, in a vain attempt to prevent my falls. I was always on the ground and always wet from the moss, but the majesty of our surroundings and the smiles of my friends kept me afloat. They took turns helping me up. We dried my outer clothes at night by taking turns fanning them over what tiny campfires we could manage to keep ablaze.

At one point the trail narrowed to a foot-wide path of loose dirt, which was the only ledge we had against the wall of a very steep cliff. It was a long way down. The belly of the gorge looked like something out of a jungle movie on a wide, wide screen, but this was no movie we could turn off or ignore. Dibbons roped our backpacks together and we crossed it in a slow line, stomachs flat against the wall, one at a time, barely breathing as we moved. I tested each twig in the mountain's side for the surety of its hold. Most came out of the earth at the slightest pull. When I slipped, the others tightened the ropes in one quick, impulsive jerk, bringing me back to standing.

That night, when they thought I was fast asleep in our tent, two of the boys snuck in and took more weight out of my backpack. They sensed the fragility of my pride; they would do nothing to make me feel ashamed or burdensome. The second night of the trip, the temperature dropped and it began to snow—first in tiny white grains, then in doughy flakes larger than our fingertips. I was soaked to the proverbial bone from falling in creeks along the way, and that night they stripped me naked and put me in someone's dry sleeping bag. Two of the others had to double up in one. (You don't take extra bags on a hike like this!) In a pretty short time, laughter was echoing through the frosted trees as the two of them squirmed and jostled for a little precious space inside one bag.

Because of the weather, some of us were in grave danger of frostbite, and so we had to hike out in the middle of the night anyway. Because our trip had been cut short, our teachers promised us another one in the summer—a hike in the Wallowa Mountains, where we would get to rappel.

Graduation night, in front of hundreds of parents and relatives, I received more awards than my hands could carry down the aisle, and my father, sitting in the audience at Trinity Church, listened as the principal told the story of our hike and our choir sang "Amazing Grace."

When it came time for the second hike, Dad signed the forms with a flourish of pride, and I crossed out any "I can't" memories from my childhood.

Janet Buck

The Miracle of Dr. Steiner

I can't go on. I go on.

Samuel Beckett

On the night of November 1, 1957—the day after Halloween—Davey Steiner took his little sister, Susie, trick-or-treating. His sister had been ill the night before, Davey explained to each neighbor, so he wondered, on his sister's behalf, whether they had any treats left.

In addition to his kindness, Davey showed unusual intelligence—enough to earn straight As, participate in medical research while still in high school, score a perfect 1600 on his SAT exams and gain admission to Yale University—the first person in his working-class family to attend college.

David decided to become a physician. For him, the study and practice of medicine provided a way to use his body and soul in the service of others. While at Yale, David met and fell in love with Cindy, whose interest in law matched David's passion for healing. David was admitted to Yale's Medical School and Cindy would later begin her studies at the School of Law. After a storybook courtship, they became engaged on Valentine's Day.

Five days later, after David and Cindy returned home from a visit with his family, David called to let his parents know they had arrived home safely—then they went for a walk to get some fast food.

As they set out, nineteen-year-old Brian Doley slammed the door of his girlfriend's house after a terrible argument. He was angry, drunk and soon behind the wheel of his car.

David doesn't remember what happened that night, but others have pieced it together: He and Cindy were in a crosswalk when Doley, in a drunken stupor, appeared from nowhere, his car careening towards them. David's instinctive action was to push her as hard as he could out of the path of the car. She suffered a fractured leg as the right bumper hit her, then the car crashed squarely into David's pelvis, sending him flying through the air. His limp and broken body landed sixty feet away, and his head smashed into the curb.

At the hospital, doctors would not answer Cindy's pleas for news of David's condition—they had nothing to tell her yet. What could they tell an already-traumatized young fiancée? That David hovered between life and death? That they had seen many others with less severe injuries die? That if he lived, he might have no brain function?

A doctor called David's parents to tell them their son might not survive the night.

When they arrived, ashen and exhausted by fear and grief, they learned only what the doctors could surmise: that David had multiple fractures, including his pelvis and thighbone, with other internal trauma. But worst of all, he had a serious skull fracture and likely brain injury. As soon as he was stabilized, he would go into surgery to relieve cranial pressure. He wasn't expected to live, but if he did . . . his parents remember one physician's words: "I can't guarantee how smart he'll be."

Such trauma sends ripples into the larger world. Events are set in motion that also change the lives of other families and individuals. Susie was pulled out of class and told that her brother had been seriously injured; she caught the next plane to New Haven. David's father took a leave from work; even after he returned to work, he drove back to New Haven every weekend for the months that followed. Laura, David's younger sister, had arrived with her parents on that first frantic night, leaving behind her school, seventh-grade friends and life. She would stay to attend a new school in New Haven. David's mother and little sister moved in with good-hearted friends and relatives who lived near the hospital. His mother arrived every morning and didn't leave until visiting hours were over. Laura joined her mother after school. Once Cindy left the hospital on crutches, she continued her schooling, but visited regularly.

David's brain, once so brilliant, withdrew into a deep coma. There he remained for nearly four weeks while his mother and sister stood vigil, speaking and reading to him, comforting, encouraging and praying for him.

When David finally emerged from the coma, he was in almost constant pain. Because of the brain injury, however, his doctors could not give sedatives or painkillers. His mother remembers how her son's semi-conscious body would rock back and forth, back and forth, groaning in a litany of suffering. He tried many times to pull the tubes and wires out of his body, perhaps to die—anything to end the agony.

Maybe it's a blessing that the body exists only in the present and does not retain the memory of pain. Gradually, the physical suffering subsided, but David awoke with amnesia. He had no memory of who he was or who anyone else was. He did not remember his family and other loved ones, his friends and acquaintances, or his past. He knew no one; the people who spoke to him, held his hand and loved him were strangers. David also suffered from aphasia: He could talk, but the words he spoke (or heard) were mixed up and had to be deciphered. His first words made no sense until a doctor recognized them as the poetry of T. S. Eliot—words David didn't know he was even speaking, sounds boiling off from a misfiring brain.

Soon after, when Laura entered his room, David said, "Hi Laura!"

"You *know* me?" she asked

"Of course I do," David answered. But when his mother and a doctor joined Laura, David no longer recognized any of them. And when Susie visited during spring break, one of the nurses told her, "Your brother wants to speak with you." When Susie rushed into David's room he said, "Who are you? Where's Susie?" David's memory was returning, but only from childhood. Later, he remembered his first girlfriend, but Cindy remained a stranger to him.

Over time, David regained his childhood memories in threads and fragments. He was transferred to another hospital for rehabilitation, and there he trained as hard as any athlete, reclaiming his ability to walk and to move with agonizing slowness, slowly remembering his life and loved ones. When he finally recognized Cindy, his dear Cindy, it marked a turning point in his recovery and in hers.

In another bed in David's room lay a second patient with brain injuries strikingly similar to David's. Patient X was the brother of a well-known figure dedicated to his political rise. He visited only once. So it was that David, surrounded and supported by the presence of a loving family, made the long journey back, while his roommate, lying alone, passed into the mystery beyond this life.

David's story demonstrates not only his determination, but also speaks to the power of his family's love, dedication and sacrifice. Today, David and Cindy have celebrated many anniversaries together and raised bright and active children. Cindy finished law school and has assumed a position of high rank and responsibility in our nation's legal system.

And David? Well, this is the miracle of Dr. Steiner: He not only recovered his memory, and learned once again to walk and read and speak, he returned to Yale Medical School, completed his studies and went on to specialize in the field of psychiatry. He still practices today, a man of compassion, empathy and wisdom far beyond his years—for he has known the dark places of the psyche; he has been to hell and back.

David's long road back to a life of service was a journey no less heroic than that of any Olympian athlete. His devoted family share in their son's miracle: His life and work, made possible by their faith and Cindy's love, continue to make a difference in this world.

Joy Millman

"It's so nice to meet you—
you look so much better than your X rays."

8

LIFE
CHANGES

*Live the best way you can; then stay close
enough to your children for it to rub off.*

Anne Ortlund

Choosing Life

Nothing in life is more corroding than habit.

Gertrude Atherton

For nearly twenty years my life revolved around two things: smoking cigarettes—and trying to quit smoking cigarettes. It was a vicious circle, one I couldn't break.

When I married Cassie ten years ago, I crumpled up my pack of cigarettes and swore I was quitting.

When we bought our first house eight years ago, I marked that rite of passage by pulverizing my pack of cigarettes with my shoe heel.

When my son, Cole, was born five years ago, I slam-dunked my cigs into a garbage can.

And when my daughter, Olivia, was born three years later, yet another pack of butts bit the dust.

I even began working out fanatically—lifting weights and running five days a week, rain or shine. I lost forty pounds and developed a rock-hard physique, but I never was able to outrun those cigarettes.

Smoking is an insidious habit; it scrambles your brain. Rationally, you know cigarettes are lethal—but every cell in your body screams out for that nicotine, skewing judgment and priorities. So I kept puffing away, the life slowly and invisibly being sucked right out of me.

One day the willpower I had lacked arrived with brusque force, from a most unexpected place: an unclouded corner of my son's mind.

As Cassie was driving Cole home from kindergarten, they passed a cemetery, which prompted the boy to ask: "Mom, what's under tombstones?"

She pondered the question for a few moments, trying to think of a delicate answer. Realizing there was no delicate answer, she bluntly said, "Dead people."

"Is that where Dad's going to be because he smokes?" Cole asked.

"I hope not," Cassie replied.

"Dad shouldn't smoke," Cole said, his voice rising in anger. He kicked the back of the front seat. "Dad's stupid for smoking. When I'm twenty, he'll be dead."

Cassie was speechless, stunned by Cole's intuitiveness. Then, just as quickly as he had exploded, he composed himself. "I hope he comes back as a ghost and talks to me," he said placidly. "Like Obi-Wan Kenobi did to Luke Skywalker in *Star Wars*."

When I arrived home from work that evening, Cassie recounted the story to me. Never one to mince words, she stared right into my eyes and said, "He's already written you off, Will. He's figured things out in his mind, come to terms with the fact that you won't be around. And if he can only have you as a ghost, that's what he'll take."

Call it an epiphany. Although Cole hadn't said anything I didn't already know, his words—delivered so honestly and innocently, as only a child can do—distilled everything into a simple, unavoidable truth. Smoking could only lead to one conclusion, and when they placed me under that tombstone, life would have to go on without me. If I couldn't even fool my own five-year-old kid, why was I continuing to try to fool myself?

Cole was, however, off the mark on one important count: As

far as I knew, that ghost deal was a long shot at best. I wasn't coming back as some suburban Jedi Knight, a flickering ray of light in a golf shirt and khakis, dispensing pearls of wisdom to Cole and Olivia on how to combat the perils of their young adult lives. They'd be on their own.

Later that evening, I found Cole lying on the couch in the family room watching *Monsters, Inc.*

"Cole," I said. "I've been thinking about what you said to Mom today, and I'm going to quit smoking. But I need your help. It's too hard to do alone."

The seconds ticked by as he hatched his plan. His lips were pursed, a sure sign that he was deep in thought. Finally, he spoke. "Okay. Here's what we'll do: every morning and every night, I'll tell you not to smoke."

"You'll do that?" I said.

"Yes."

"Promise?"

"Yes."

"Sounds like a plan."

And, by God, it was. Every time I had an urge to smoke, I fought it off with thoughts of tombstones and Obi-Wan Kenobi and a little boy trying desperately to help his old man out of a jam. Those visions were like a psychic, industrial-strength nicotine patch.

So here I am, checking off the days that I've been cigarette-free. I miss those darn things, but I'm choosing life over the alternative. After all, my kids need me—although not nearly as much as I need them.

William Wagner

"God bless Sister, God bless Mommy,
God help Daddy."

Reprinted by permission of George Crensahw, Masters Agency.

Message in a Body

I believe that the physical is the geography of the being.

Louise Nevelson

Have you completely lost your mind? I asked myself as I walked down the hall to the office of my boss. In my right hand I clutched the resignation letter I had typed the night before.

No, you haven't, the small part of me that wasn't scared to death whispered back. *Remember what happened a few months ago?*

Oh yes, I remembered it well.

I had worked for the same company for over a decade, my dedication and long hours finally paying off when I was promoted to upper management while still young. I had tons of responsibilities, and there were deadlines and daily crises. The stacks of paper on my desk grew taller as the weeks passed, and phone calls, faxes and e-mails dominated my life. I took great pride in my work, and mailed home some business cards to my parents so they could see the title under my name.

One by one, relationships with friends dwindled as I lived and breathed my job. It had become my whole life, and I gave it 110 percent. I pumped myself up with caffeine during the day and took over-the-counter sleep aids to fall asleep at night. I had five kinds of headache remedies and dozens of antacids in my purse as I pushed myself beyond my limits. I started keeping a pad and pen near my bed so I could take notes during those middle-of-the-night anxiety attacks that started to plague me.

Finally, my body said, *No more!* I had taken three days off and planned to go to Florida and soak in the tranquility of sun, ocean and beach, but the morning I was scheduled to leave I couldn't even get up. My body refused to move. I was utterly exhausted and drained. I slept all day, getting up only to eat before collapsing back into bed. The next day the same thing happened. I tried to bribe my body by imagining a dazzling mental slide show of our vacation, but my body said, *Thanks, but no thanks. I need to be where I am.*

By the third day I was scared. After forty-eight hours of almost nonstop sleep I was still exhausted and unwilling to move, so I called my doctor, and his office worked me into their schedule.

I lay on the examining table while a technician ran blood tests. I caught a glimpse of myself in a mirror and was shocked—an older woman stared back at me. *Who are you?* I wondered. She didn't answer. The doctor came back in and pronounced me the healthiest sick person he had ever seen. "You have hyperstress," he said, and wrote a prescription.

"What am I supposed to take?" I asked. In a barely legible scrawl he had written on the pad: "Get a different job."

That day I made a promise to myself: *I will carve out time for myself every day. When the clock says it's 5 P.M., I will leave, no matter what.*

The first day back at work I had to force myself to do it, and was actually shocked when the sky didn't fall. What a revelation!

I started walking my dogs again, trying to pay them back for all the times I'd left them. I picked up my journal, blew dust off the cover and began writing. Words came slowly at first, then more freely as my inner voice was finally allowed to speak. During the next three months it said: *quit your job,* over and over again.

I'd been working since I was seventeen, part-time to put myself though college, and then full-time immediately after graduation. Now I had a strong feeling there was a person under all those diplomas and titles who was literally dying to get out. So, with no firm plans for the future, I gave a thirty-day notice and then spent that month alternating between panic, regret and hysteria. The real shocker—that I was easily replaceable—came when the company filled my position two weeks after my notice. The last day on the job I looked into the bathroom mirror and asked: *Who are you?*

The silence was deafening.

Suddenly, I had no job on which to hang my identity; I was putting all my trust in the great unknown, and I was truly scared. But there was also a strange, previously unknown faith buoying me up, telling me, *Don't be afraid. Everything will work out. Believe in yourself!* I clung to that like a frightened child to her mother's hand.

Finally, I was free to embark on my journey of self-discovery. After a while, I realized I'd never really forgotten who I was—I had just covered it up with work, work and more work. As I took long, slow walks in the woods, I rediscovered my inner core. I listened to my body and slept when it was tired, ate when it was hungry. I reconnected with friends, read dozens of books and wrote in my journal.

That faith did not fail me. Two months later, a friend heard of a low-stress job and helped me get an interview. I got the job— and a hefty pay cut as well—but I don't regret it for a second. That eight-week sabbatical changed my life and taught me that a life without balance isn't worth living—it isn't even livable! I felt a profound gratefulness to my body for sending me such a clear message.

I had dipped my hand in the well of restoration, and I will never forget it. I had finally learned to define myself from the inside out, rather than the outside in.

Kelly L. Stone

"First of all, relax."

Reprinted by permission of George Crenshaw, Masters Agency.

A Cheerleader for Fitness

Life is what we make it. Always has been, always will be.

Grandma Moses

In California, over seventy-three years ago, health-crusading nutritionist Paul C. Bragg told his audience they could reverse their physical problems by eating right and living a more healthful lifestyle. Those words struck a chord in a desperate, sickly young boy sitting nearby. His name was Jack LaLanne.

Jack's mother and her fifteen-year-old son had arrived late and had to sit on the stage close to Bragg in front of some 1,000 people. Jack remembers: "The last thing I wanted was anyone looking at me, and now I was sitting in front of a huge audience. It was the most embarrassing, humiliating time of my life. I thought they were all staring at me, unaware that most of the audience had health problems as well.

"My mother forced me to go. I had dropped out of school for almost a year because I was so ill. Shy and withdrawn, I avoided seeing people and especially hated being seen: I had pimples and boils, was thin, weak and sickly, and wore a back brace and glasses.

"I also had blinding headaches every day. I wanted to escape my body because I could hardly stand the pain. My life appeared hopeless until I heard Dr. Bragg tell us that we could be born again, into a new body. He wasn't a lecturer on religion, but he certainly had an evangelist's spirit—and he preached a new way of living—something I desperately needed."

After the lecture, Jack and Paul Bragg met in Bragg's dressing room and talked for an hour—the beginning of an inspiring, lifelong friendship.

Bragg asked Jack, "What do you eat for breakfast, lunch and dinner?"

"Cakes, pies and ice cream," Jack answered.

"Jack," he said, "You're a walking garbage can."

He told him healthy, positive alternatives to practice, and that night Jack says he got down on his knees by the side of his bed and prayed.

He didn't say, *God, make me a Mr. America.* Instead, he asked for a new beginning: *God, please give me the willpower to refrain from eating unhealthy foods when the urge comes over me. And please give me the strength to exercise even when I don't feel like it.*

There hasn't been a jelly donut in Jack's life since Bragg told him, "The best part of a donut is the hole." Bragg promised that if Jack would exercise and eat a proper diet, he could achieve good health, so Jack, with great determination, set out to build a totally new Jack LaLanne. He discovered that the Berkeley YMCA had a set of weights and began experimenting with them. Before long, Jack achieved the muscular healthy body of his dreams. Gray's Anatomy was his second Bible. He attended Chiropractic College and graduated, but was more interested in helping people before they became ill. He opened the first modern health studio in 1936, paying $45 a month rent in downtown Oakland, and began to formulate a basic approach to physical fitness and nutrition. His methods were scientifically sound. He developed the first models of exercise equipment that are standard in health spas today, such as the first leg-extension machine and the first weight selectors—using pulleys. Through determination and excellent advice, Jack became a nationally known cheerleader for a healthy lifestyle.

In the almost sixty-eight years since he opened his first gym, he has spread his gospel of fitness through nutrition and exercise, in lectures, a thirty-four-year television show and in a variety of extraordinary—some say superhuman—physical feats. These include 1,033 push-ups in twenty-three minutes, and swimming from Alcatraz to San Francisco in freezing ocean water while handcuffed and shackled. He lived what he taught, and his strong body reflected his dedication: a forty-eight-inch chest and a twenty-eight-inch waist. On his seventieth birthday, Jack celebrated with a mile-and-a-half-long swim in Long Beach Harbor, in which he towed seventy rowboats filled with seventy people—handcuffed and feet shackled.

Jack LaLanne pioneered health and fitness gyms and has a number of nutritional and exercise products, plus a juice machine, on the market, all of which have made him a wealthy man—although he cares little for material rewards. He is gratified that physical fitness and nutrition have become a huge growth industry, because he believes that the emphasis on exercise and a healthful, natural diet creates a stronger, smarter, better America. "With healthier citizens, we unburden society from sickness, and reduce the medical bills that are draining people's savings and causing so much grief."

He points out, "Those who begin to exercise regularly, and replace white flour, sugar and devitalized foods with live, organic, natural foods, begin to feel better immediately. I can serve as a living example of the transformations possible through a changed lifestyle. If Dr. Bragg hadn't changed my life at fifteen, I believe I may have been dead at seventeen."

His personal regimen includes a healthful diet, vitamin and mineral supplements, and a rigorous workout each day. He starts exercising at 5 A.M. because it's a challenge. "Many people think I'm some kind of superman because I like the results of a workout. To leave my wife in a warm bed to go down to a cold gym at 5 A.M. is not something I relish, but when I finish, I think, *Jack, congratulations—you did it again.* And everything else is easy in comparison. It takes pride and discipline."

Jack LaLanne, now close to ninety, still practices what he preaches for a healthy body and soul. Full of life and spirit, he exclaims, "I love inspiring people to be healthy, happy, stronger and better!"

Patricia Bragg

Lady Godiva and the Bee

Nature doesn't move in a straight line, and as part of nature, neither do we.

Gloria Steinem

Lady Godiva sashayed up the trail in front of me, the sun shimmering on her white coat. Her hips swayed and tail wagged as she sniffed the scents of hikers, other dogs and moose that had walked this trail before us. I had rescued this furry Samoyed from the Humane Society, and was going to change her name until I learned that the historical Lady Godiva had been a heroine who rode her horse in the nude to save her village from oppressive taxation.

My Lady Godiva was also a heroine: She had rescued me from depression and isolation following my divorce. I barely had the energy to work on my computer, and spent the rest of the time curled up in a fetal position on the couch, watching whatever happened to be on television. But Lady demanded at least two vigorous walks a day, saving me from life as a couch potato. Her curiosity and zest for life were contagious, propelling me into the Wasatch Mountains and back into the world.

Today, the spring air was crisp and clear, the sky too blue to be real, and aspen leaves had begun to uncurl into chartreuse circles. The spicy scent of pines and pinions was intoxicating as we hiked for more than an hour, about a third of the way up a steep mountain. I needed to get back to work and didn't feel like struggling to go higher.

I called Lady Godiva. She sat down and stared at me. Usually she was happy to turn around and get a treat, but today her reluctance was evident.

I called again, and Lady came back slowly for her dog biscuit. We walked about twenty feet downhill toward home when the bee from hell appeared. It was about the size of a child's fist—I had never seen one as large. It circled a few feet from my body, buzzing like a cake mixer. I froze.

Although startled, I wasn't afraid. I knew it wouldn't sting me unless it felt threatened. Lady and other animals had taught me that all creatures are intelligent and respond to our thoughts. If we send kind thoughts, animals won't hurt us. Native Americans know this, and they avoid rattlesnake bites by greeting snakes as brothers, not as enemies. So, standing motionless, I sent the bee a mental greeting. The bee continued to circle.

After a few minutes, I took a step down the trail again. The bee circled closer, and the buzzing grew louder. I stepped back, and its circles widened. What was going on? *What am I supposed to do?* I turned around and took another step up the trail, toward the mountaintop. The bee disappeared.

I turned back towards home, and the thing reappeared, buzzing a foot from my face.

The universe sends us signs, often in ordinary ways, so I decided to experiment. Toward home, and it reappeared. Up the mountain, and it vanished. Why?

Lady bounded up the trail, barking for me to follow. I obeyed. *Was climbing this mountain some kind of test?* I wondered. *Was there someone I was supposed to help, some challenge to be overcome, a lesson to be learned?* Familiar anxiety churned my stomach. *What if I couldn't do it—whatever it was? What if I wasn't good enough? Worse: what if the bee doesn't mean anything, and I'm crazy?*

I pushed through my fear by pumping up the trail, even as the path grew steeper and I had to stop to catch my breath. The peak still seemed far away, and I was afraid it would be too late when I reached the top—I would then have to hurry down the mountain in the darkness.

Lady ran back toward me, startling me out of my worries with a couple of sharp barks. I looked up. Bright bluebells waved in the breeze near the edge of the precipice, which overlooked a valley of aspen trees, their new green leaves dancing in the sunlight. A stream fed by melted snow gushed through the meadow below. I didn't have time to stand and appreciate the beauty; I had to get up the mountain. I had to find out what I was supposed to do.

Thoughts of that mission, whatever it might be, kept me ascending for another hour, and without warning we emerged from forest darkness into a clearing filled with sunshine at the summit.

A glorious panorama of mountains, hills and valleys in shades of greens, yellows and browns melted into a Monet painting. A hawk screeched above, the sun illuminating its red tail as it soared in lazy circles. Lady leaned quietly against my leg, letting me soak in the beauty.

Filled with unfamiliar peace and gratitude, I was afraid to move, afraid it was too good to be true. Then I remembered: *What was my mission? What have I been sent here to do?* Worry pushed peace aside.

A soft voice floated into my mind—the still, small voice I'd come to recognize, which was always gentle and kind, and never critical. *Do nothing.*

My words burst out in the golden silence: "What do you mean . . . nothing?"

Silence.

What does "nothing" mean? There must be a purpose.

Then the thoughts filled my body and soul like music: *Enjoy. Be. Just Be. I don't have to do anything. I don't have to prove I'm good or perfect. I don't have to save the world. I just have to enjoy life and drink in the beauty around me every day. I only have to be.*

Laughter erupted from deep inside, releasing fears. I yelled, "Bee, I got your message!" Lady barked with delight, and we danced together on the summit as the sun blazed from gold to red.

As we started for home, there was so much beauty to see that I forgot I was tired—I forgot to even think. I inhaled the pungent scent of sage and smiled at the carpets of wildflowers. If I missed squirrels chattering, or a robin flying to her nest with a worm, Lady reminded me. She led me home just as the indigo-sky darkened and night enfolded us.

Lynne D. Finney, J.D., M.S.W.

It Happened One Autumn

In every real adult, a child is hidden that wants to play.

Friedrich Nietzsche

I've been seduced again by the boy next door.

It doesn't happen often, but he does have a way about him. I'm sitting in my office, nose to the grindstone, shoulder pressed to the wheel, struggling to meet deadlines without much success. My brain seems to have slipped into neutral, gone on vacation—oh, you get the idea. So I'm busily shuffling stacks of paper and writing fevered motivational notes to myself: *Finish proposal!!!*—as if the number of exclamation points will resurrect my will to work.

In the midst of this busy inactivity, I hear a knock on my door. I open it, turn my gaze downward and see Tyler, my young neighbor, and he's holding a football. Somewhat redundantly, he says, "You want to come out and play football with me?"

Tyler is eight, but he knows a playmate when he meets one. The day I moved in, Ty and his brother Jay came over and helped me unload boxes from my U-Haul. After we finished, I bought them each a burger and a root beer. After that, during those first few weeks in my new place, when I needed duct tape or another curtain rod, Ty and Jay were more than willing to accompany me to Wal-Mart and show me the best toys.

Jay is eleven and a cool guy—too cool, actually, to meander over to the lady next door to see if she'll come toss a football with him. Tyler, however, has no such inhibitions. He sees that I have not one, but two bicycles; that I go for walks every day; and that some evenings I sit on my porch and strum on my guitar. So I am, in his eyes, okay.

"Ty," I say, doing my best to be a grown-up, "I really would like to, but I've got to work."

Tyler holds up a piece of white plastic. "Look," he says, as if this piece of conversation will make all the difference: "I got a new tee. I can kick and you can catch."

"Tyler," I repeat slowly, to impress upon him the urgency of my situation. "I have a deadline. That means I have to get this in the mail tomorrow."

"Fifteen minutes," he says steadily, locking my gaze with those cornflower blue eyes.

My children always knew they could do this, too. What kind of signals do I give out, I wonder, that apparently say, "Press on, she can be had"?

I stand in the door, looking at him, considering. *Okay*, I tell myself, *I can go play with Tyler for fifteen minutes and eat dinner at my desk—it's not as if I'm making any progress anyway.*

"All right," I respond, wagging a finger. "Let me get my shoes on. But just fifteen minutes. I *mean* it." Tyler never sees the wagging finger; he's already doing a little end-zone victory dance on my porch.

As I slip on my shoes, my dog enters stage left, positively effervescent. When Bob-Dog sees lace-up shoes come out, he knows the leash is next and then, let the good times roll. So out we go into the front yard—Bob-Dog, Tyler and me. The crystalline air is fresh, cool, filled with the scents of autumn. Leaves crinkle under our feet as Ty kicks off and I dash within the general vicinity of the ball.

"You have to catch it," he says, as if I needed this solemn bit of coaching.

"Thank you, Tyler," I say, as I take up my position down field again.

This time, I catch it and it's my turn to throw. As usual, I toss the football about three feet in front of me. Tyler lopes up beside me in that easy manner of the natural athlete. "The way to do it," he says, picking up the football and demonstrating, "is to twist at the waist before I throw. That way I use more than just my arm."

I try it and I am astounded—I throw the ball halfway across my yard. Not great, but . . . not utterly pathetic. I try again. Tyler is all over the encouragement thing.

"Way to go!" he says, with absolute sincerity. "Here—throw it all the way down here!"

And so it goes, for about an hour. Finally, my conscience catches up with me. Breathing hard, I tell him it's time to stop.

"Okay," he says, "After you catch one more." He's on very solid turf with that one. He knows I only catch about one out of ten. He tosses. I miss and shag the ball. He tosses, I miss and shag the ball. He tosses and finally I say, "Look, kiddo, I really have to go to work."

He kicks a few leaves and says, "Heck," but then he runs toward the driveway. "Throw long!" he shouts over his shoulder. I do. He misses and I laugh.

Entering the warmth of my house, I remove my jacket—it smells like autumn. My face is cool and I am happy.

Within minutes of sitting down, in a slap-my-forehead, V-8 moment, I suddenly see what my project was missing. Why hadn't I realized that before? Maybe because my body was telling me what my brain didn't want to hear—that recess is important, no matter how old we are or how serious our work becomes.

It's autumn. Front-yard football is best at this time of year and must be savored when in season, just like tomatoes in August or hot cider in December.

I hope I always have a Tyler in my life to remind me that all work and no play make Jill a grumpy girl. I hope that no matter how old I get or how serious I become, that I'll allow myself to be coached—even if the coach is only eight and I can't tell if it's freckles or chocolate milk splattered on his nose.

K. C. Compton

Back from the Heights

As we are liberated from our own fear, our presence automatically liberates others.

Marianne Williamson

On the day my son Alex was born, if you let him hold onto your little fingers he would stand up. I didn't realize how unusual that was until years later, when my scrawny little teenager wanted to pack his harness, his shoes, his chalk and ropes, and go climb an Alp.

Every time Alex went to the climbing gym, I thought he'd get tired of it. I secretly hoped something would deter him, but I couldn't say no because it was the only thing he loved to do. I couldn't say no to the look in his eyes, and I couldn't refuse when he pleaded with me to let him accept his buddy Pierre's invitation to visit the Swiss Alps. Not even when I knew it meant he would be invited to climb with Pierre's father, Philippe. How could I tell Alex that the sole, driving passion of his life happened to terrify his mother?

If I had seen the "rock" they were going to climb that sunny day, I never would have agreed. Philippe had assured me it was within my son's ability.

The Monolith (how could I not have wondered why it was

called that?) rose straight up from the floor of the National Park of Haute Savoie, cleaving the sky like a skyscraper—a three-hundred-foot vertical sword of pale granite.

I gasped. "That?" I pointed as all my rock-climbing fears coalesced into one giant, monolithic terror. They couldn't be up *there*—Alex would never do anything so foolhardy. There was no way that this—this *giant*—was within my son's ability.

"*Regardez!*" Shouts of, "Look!" People milling about at the foot of the mountain had noticed two climbers clinging to its side, moving very slowly, barely visible. A crowd began to form as I walked farther around the base of the rock, my neck already sore from looking up.

"People way up there!" someone commented in French, pointing skyward. Expecting the worst, I felt a stab of guilt. I should have known where they were going. I should have stood my ground and said "No." Now my folly could cost my son and his friend's father their lives.

In the still Alpine air, we could hear the smallest sounds clearly. Alex's voice sounded so small, so unsure, as he responded to Philippe's directions. Although Alex's French was fine, Philippe was speaking English to him just to be on the safe side. The safe side! This irony wasn't lost on me as I clenched and unclenched my fists and tried to breathe slowly.

A murmur surged through the now sizable crowd. "*Ce n'est pas des Français, ça.* "They aren't French," someone said. "They're speaking English." More mumbling, then a group of heads nodded in mutual judgment: "Those English are crazy!"

English or not, the crazy pair continued slowly, haltingly, up the sheer side of the rock. Why would *anyone* want to hang onto the side of a slippery wall of stone like that?

But Alex wasn't looking down; he was looking up at Philippe who was shouting directions down to him as my son followed him skyward.

Voices were building again—someone had made another discovery.

"There's a little *boy* up there." That revelation seemed to touch a chord among all the adults, and heads were shaking vigorously as voices grew more adamant.

"Where is that boy's mother?" said one observer. "How could she let him do such a thing?"

How, indeed, I thought, hoping the nausea would pass.

The silence that followed made me aware that the onlookers had shifted their focus away from the thousand-foot-high rock. Someone had noticed I was lingering nearby, not joining in. Others had come and gone, but I had stayed, alone and silent, staring at the tiny figures. They were looking at me, the lone suspect, the bad mother. A few dared to smile in sympathy or amusement. I smiled back.

"*C'est mon fils,*" I finally admitted. "That's my son." When I explained in French why the climbers were speaking English, heads bobbed silently. "*Ah, Americans.*" That, apparently, explained everything.

There was something else in their eyes, in their stance, in the way they glanced upward as we spoke. Their accusations, uttered before they had known I was present, spoke of good sense and caution and caring, but now their smiles, their wistful peering up the side of the monolith, whispered something louder than our fears.

I squinted upward and felt my smile return, my heart begin to calm. That was my son up there, the one everyone was watching, the one doing what we earthbound beings feared, or perhaps never dared to dream—following his passion to the heavens.

At last, when he and Philippe, in rope-bound slow motion, landed safely back on earth at the foot of that granite monster, the crowd erupted with applause for the little boy who had conquered it. The tears I brushed away before greeting the triumphant climbers were not from fear. I was proud of him—of his courage and what he'd done.

Alex's smile was unlike any I'd ever seen: It radiated a quiet pride that came from his supreme accomplishment. Not an accomplishment I wished for him, but one he had chosen for himself. He had set his own hurdle and overcome it. Wasn't that the true measure of success?

At home, Alex still couldn't seem to pick up his socks, remember to put his dirty clothes in the hamper or clean up his kitchen clutter. But here, on his own sacred ground, fighting the battle he'd chosen for himself, he had mastered the mountain and found the measure of himself.

I can't promise I will never again worry about his safety. What mother could? But from that day on, those feelings lessened as I conquered my own fears at the base of *le Monolithe*.

Dierdre W. Honnold

Ready to Fly

Angels can fly because they take themselves lightly.

G. K. Chesterton

I entered her hospital room with her chart tucked under my arm. She looked up at me with tears in her eyes. "I want you to do something for me," she said.

"What is that?" I asked.

"Tell me how to be healthy and happy—the way you are." She took a few breaths to calm herself, then continued: "It seems like I keep having some kind of health problem or drama in my life that holds me back. Why can't I be like everybody else and just get on with my life?"

"Jean," I said, taking her hand. "You *can* be like everyone else. After all, you have a body and a mind; you want to be loved and appreciated and understood—just like everyone. We're more alike than we are different."

I pulled back the covers to examine Jean's surgical wound. As I removed the dressings, I reflected on the mysteries of healing. Long ago I had realized that my job as a doctor goes far beyond the procedures or medicines I offer my patients. I might carry around a bag full of bandages, but patients themselves hold the keys to their healing. Why some people get better and others don't remains mysterious and unpredictable.

I knew Jean well. Over the years she had seen me many times, and each time I would open my "bag of tricks"—new prescriptions for her heart problem, for high blood pressure; a new bandage for her knees.

And now the latest procedure—surgery to remove part of her stomach to help her lose unwanted weight. She weighed over 300 pounds, causing terrible stress on her heart, joints and most of all, on her husband and family. I was ready for the upcoming challenges with her recovery. Jean would, as she had in the past, demonstrate some kind of postoperative difficulty: pain, poor healing, you name it. She would then expect me to offer a magical cure. I wondered when it was that she had decided to give away her innate power to be strong, healthy, vibrant and happy. It seemed she most needed to see herself as a victim.

I replaced the dressing, then sat down and looked deeply into her eyes. "I remember when I was six years old," I said. "Back then, Superman was my hero. I never missed watching him on television, and I learned to read by figuring out the words in Superman comic books. My mom was quite a seamstress, so she whipped together some Superman costumes for my brother and me, as well as for a couple of the neighborhood kids.

"I still remember the feeling of power when I slipped into that suit. I felt as if I was transformed into Superman himself—I could run faster than any kid on the block with my cape flying in the wind. Even kryptonite couldn't slow down this superguy.

"Then one day I decided it was time to *fly*. So I climbed up on the roof of my grandmother's house in my costume, grabbed my cape and jumped. I can still remember feeling the wind rush through my hair and my heart pounding."

"What happened?" Jean asked.

"When I hit the ground, a new appreciation for reality—and gravity—struck me. Fortunately, it was a low, one-story structure. I limped into the house, my Superman suit all smudged by my crash landing, crying in an un-Superman way. Reluctantly, I told my mom what had happened. She just smiled, gave me a hug, cleaned off my suit and sent me back out to play. She knew I had to decide for myself how I would fly in life.

"Anyway, that was a long time ago, but I never forgot . . ."

"Forgot what—how much it hurt?" Jean asked.

"No—I never forgot how great it feels to fly!"

The next day I discharged Jean from the hospital.

Weeks later, she appeared in my office for a postoperative appointment. My mouth dropped open when I entered the examining room: there stood Jean—now a much lighter person—wearing a Superwoman costume.

Still smiling at me, she said, "I'm ready to fly."

Dane E. Smith

Coming Back to Life

The body is wiser than its inhabitants. The body is the soul. We ignore its aches, its pains, its eruptions, because we fear the truth. The body is God's messenger.

Erica Jong

For almost fifteen years, I've worked as a personal development leader in Britain, specializing in eating disorders—mainly overeating—and helping people take charge of their bodies and their lives. I've been privileged to work with thousands of people whose progress has provided endless delight over the years. Yet, of all the stories I recall, the one of Gina Logan really stands out.

Gina first came to my weekly classes back in 1991. At twenty-six years old, she was overweight by over a hundred pounds, unhealthy and obviously extremely out of shape. The day after attending her first class, Gina called to tell me that she enjoyed my talk. Then she began to cry, and finally broke down completely. She was clearly depressed and desperate. We spoke for nearly an hour. At conversation's end, she sounded ready to take action to improve her life.

She attended my classes for five consecutive weeks and reduced her weight by sixteen pounds. Then she left the program. A couple of months later, Gina called. It was a familiar litany that I'd heard many times before: She had regained the weight she lost and was feeling terrible remorse. After some gentle probing on my part, she confessed that her main weakness was alcohol, and that everything had progressed well until she was invited to a party where she drank too much. The day after the party, Gina binged on junk food and never regained control of her eating and drinking.

She rejoined the program—and this time lost less than twenty pounds before dropping out. Six months passed before Gina called me, sorrowfully asking if she could rejoin my classes. I told her that she was most welcome, but that she would not achieve or maintain her goals if she kept quitting. When the same pattern reasserted itself—and it would, she should have no illusions about that—she would tend to lose control again. And if alcohol set off a binge, she would have to be prepared to avoid it completely.

After a brief pause, Gina said, "I'm telling you right now, Joanne—I can't do it."

"Why not?" I asked. "Are you an alcoholic?"

"No. It's just that . . . it's just . . . ," I heard her crying softly. "It's just that I hate myself so much, I don't have the confidence to go anywhere unless I've had a few drinks."

"How's your confidence the next morning when your hangover's throbbing and you want to eat everything in sight? How's your confidence when you face the consequences of your binges?"

"You don't understand," said Gina crying, "I'm in so much pain, I just need a few drinks to make me feel normal."

"So you're incapable of socializing without drinking alcohol?"

"Well . . . yes," she replied.

"Well, if you can't go out without drinking, I'm going to suggest—"

"What—that I don't go out at all?" she said, like an adolescent in a shouting match with a parent.

"I'd never suggest you shouldn't go out. Instead of bars and nightclubs, find other places to go. To change your life you need to change your patterns, even if that means breaking away from your current circle of friends. So go out and have fun with people—but go to the cinema, the theater or the gym."

"The gym?" she screamed, horrified. "The gym? With this body? Are you off your head? Have you noticed the size of me? I wouldn't be seen dead in a gym."

"Then start by walking the length of the promenade, and walking back. Begin by doing whatever you can."

"It's not going to happen," she said adamantly.

"Then I'm refusing to work with you. There's no point in us even continuing the conversation." Acting tough when your heart's as soft as mine is the most difficult part of my life, but there are times we have to be tough to be kind.

"Well that's rich, isn't it?" she said without missing a beat. "So what am I expected to do now?"

"Nothing's expected of you, Gina—you do exactly what you want to do. It's your life, your choice. You can drink yourself into oblivion, or you can come back when you're ready to commit to a different choice. Think it over. If you truly want to change your body and your life, there are no instant solutions. It will take you about a year to reach your ideal weight. One year, Gina. You'll need to keep a low profile for a while and change your social scene. But the clubs aren't going anywhere—and when you've reached your goal you won't need alcohol for confidence anymore."

Two years passed before I saw Gina again. She showed up in my class, and she was ready to fight.

Gina decided to fight the good fight. She gave up alcohol and broke away from her old circle of friends. She improved her daily diet, bought a pair of running shoes and started walking. Eventually, she progressed to the gym. Big time.

Gina lost 120 pounds in just over a year and kept it off. I've seen some amazing transformations over these years, but hers was exceptional, because as well as taking the action required to change her body, she made the most crucial change of all— she faced herself, her fears and weaknesses, her shadows and her shame. She reinvented herself.

As she was nearing the last phase of her weight loss, we went power-walking uphill together. She laughed as I remarked she hadn't even broken a sweat.

"You know, Joanne," she said, grinning from ear to ear, "your hikes are just too easy for me now!"

"Well, don't let me hold you back, Miss Gina!" I waved her on, and on she went.

Later, Gina revealed something else: "I've ended my relationship with John," she said seriously. "I've never told anyone this, but he punched me around a bit, and I'm not standing for it anymore. I'm not standing for a lot of things I tolerated before. . . ."

She took a deep breath before continuing, "He seems threatened by the fact that I've given up alcohol and seems to resent my weight loss. I realize now that I put up with John because I never felt I deserved any better. That's changed now. I moved out last month and found my own apartment. And I've been thinking about going to college. What do you think?"

I stopped and met her gaze. "That's an excellent idea."

For years, Gina had indulged in alcohol, junk food and self-pity, convinced that she was a hopeless case—that she was "born to be fat." Such beliefs conveniently allowed her to justify her laziness. But her spirit was strong, and with patience, perseverance and the appropriate discipline, she improved her body and her life.

I got a letter from her last year. She returned to Scotland and went back to college. She now works for one of the country's most successful entrepreneurs, earning enough money for a down payment on her first home. What thrills me the most— icing on the cake, so to speak—is that Gina is earning extra money teaching aerobics. This from a woman who wouldn't be seen dead in a gym.

Today, on my desk, I still have a small, framed picture—a gift she gave me. The inscription she wrote for me reads, "To teach is to touch a life forever." Gina Logan has touched my life forever, too. There's nothing a teacher treasures more than to see a pupil succeed.

Joanne Reid Rodrigues

Reprinted by permission of Martha Campbell.

The Only Way to Begin Is to Begin

Everyone who got to where they are had to begin where they were.

Richard Paul Evans

January is a good time for beginnings, so for years I have had the habit of seeing all my assorted doctors soon after the New Year. This means two weeks of being poked, prodded and probed by internists, gynecologist and radiologists while clad in a paper dress that makes me feel like a large lamb chop in a badly made frill. When it's all over I feel virtuous, reassured that I am not dead and able to make intelligent decisions about how to stay that way for a while longer.

Despite being too fat for my height or too short for my weight, I've always had low blood pressure and cholesterol, a slow pulse, lots of energy and the ability to wrap my legs around my own head—a pointless and unaesthetic exercise, perhaps, but it keeps me limber and frightens off burglars.

However, throughout most of 1996, problems I confronted in writing my new book had squashed my usual optimism. It was all I could do to maintain the discipline of writing something every day. My few healthy habits vanished. I stopped my daily walk and/or swim, and I was living on ice cream, pork rinds and mayonnaise. This regime soon made me feel rotten—lethargic, creaky and even more depressed. My arthritic joints ached and I was chomping Rolaids by the handful as I watched daytime television—for a writer, a sure sign of physical, mental and spiritual decay.

I went to a New Year's Eve party at a friend's house, stayed the night to avoid the drunks on the highways and got to bed around two. When I awoke at 6 A.M., as usual, I lay there, staring at the ceiling and thinking about my life. When the others got up we sat blearily around the living room with mugs of coffee, and someone asked, "Has anyone made any New Year's resolutions?"

"I have," I said into the laughter. "I'm going to walk for twenty minutes four days a week, and eat five servings of fruits and vegetables every day." This rather dull statement was greeted with polite murmurs, and the discussion turned to the more interesting subject of what to have for breakfast.

I began the month with my customary round of doctors, and found to my horror that I was in even worse shape than I thought. My blood pressure and cholesterol were sky high, and I had gained twenty pounds in a year. No wonder my knees hurt. I was now carrying the equivalent of an extra person on my belly, thighs and buttocks. This news, instead of depressing me further, made me angry—not with myself, not at the doctors, not even at the evil publishers and editors who had made my life so miserable. I was just plain *angry*. And that anger spurred me to action.

I drafted Sally, my new internist, into my war on the midlife blahs. I told her I didn't want any advice about diet and exercise; I had been reading and writing about food and fitness for years. I needed her to monitor my blood pressure and cholesterol, but mostly I wanted her moral support. Sally is much younger than I, and I think she was taken aback at first by the large, belligerent, extraordinarily naked woman on her examining table, but she agreed to see me once a month for a checkup and chat, and soon she became my strongest ally.

I began walking every day, twice around the half-mile circle near my apartment. The twenty-minute walk made me breath-less at first, and I could hear my knee joints clicking with every step. I could also hear the seductive voice in my head whisper-ing a million reasons *not* to walk, but I usually managed to ignore it.

I'm an excellent cook, so the large quantities of vegetables and fruits I added to my diet tasted great. I hadn't eliminated or restricted any food, so I never felt deprived. What I *did* feel was gassy. My digestive system, startled by all this roughage after so many years of fatty, salty, sugary smoothage, expressed itself in loud seismic rumblings and explosions. It's a good thing I'm not a smoker; a lighted match in my apartment would have vaporized the whole east end of town.

After a few weeks, however, this side effect passed (so to speak), and I began to feel better. I wasn't 100 percent consis-tent; I had occasional relapses into excessive amounts of fudge ripple ice cream and television, but most days I walked and ate my greens.

My weight dropped from month to month, sometimes quickly, sometimes not. The blood pressure and cholesterol proved more stubborn, but after six months, the changes began to show.

It has been eight months now. My blood pressure is normal, and I've lost forty pounds. I can see my feet without bending over, and my knees don't hurt. A mile is an easy walk, and I danced all night at my nephew's wedding with hardly a creak or gasp. The demons of depression, with their weapons of fatigue, apathy, insomnia and doubt still plague me now and then. Publishers are as obtuse as ever, and I still have days when walking, broccoli and coherent sentences are all beyond my reach. Boring consistency will never be one of my problems.

But at fifty-two I'm doing okay. The world looks good to me most of the time, and the face in the mirror pleases me. I like the feel of a brisk walk in the rain. I happily fry up a whole head of rapini with garlic and olive oil to eat with crusty bread. I'm strengthened by the love and support I get from friends, family and a doctor who takes the time to listen. I rejoice in small things: my cat washing her face in a sunny window, a dark red nasturtium blooming on my balcony, a phone call from my sister, an hour over coffee with a new friend.

I will never be the kind of Lycra-clad ascetic who actually likes steamed tofu and working out. I will always prefer lying in a hammock with a cat, a book and a large bag of Oreos. But once I'm out I enjoy my walk, and a baked potato with a glass of buttermilk tastes very good when I'm hungry. A good night's sleep, silent knee joints and a cheerful vitality feel much better than my sad, sluggish state of a year ago—occasional demons notwithstanding.

My New Year's resolution demanded not a destination, but a journey that, like all journeys, began with one small step. I have no advice for others—no maps, prescriptions or platitudes—no idea of where I will end up, or how I'll get there. I only know that the trip is worth taking, the scenery is always interesting and the only way to begin, is to begin.

Luisa Gray

My Visions with Soup

We must take care to live not merely a long life, but a full one; for living a long life requires only good fortune, but living a full life requires character.

Seneca

Twenty-five years ago I was at a turning point. I had to rethink everything: I was the single mother of two children, still working in our adversarial legal system as a family attorney, doing research, writing, lecturing . . . and I was exhausted. I was grieving over the sudden death of both my parents, looking for a life companion I yearned for, not paying attention to what I ate and not sleeping enough. In short, living in an unsustainable way.

I became so ill that I felt as if I would not survive, and one day I nearly collapsed. I realized I had to make fundamental changes in how I treated my body, how I lived, where I lived and how I spent my time—my life energy. It was all so huge, so overwhelming: I didn't know what direction to go in and couldn't figure out what my next step should be.

One day I did something I had never done before. I took a blank piece of paper, closed my eyes and without any plan or agenda simply began to write in stream of consciousness style, imagining where and how I'd like to be in five years. The first image that came to mind was that I would be living with a wonderful man who loved and respected me—and who cooked. I had painted myself into a corner with my feminist beliefs: I did not and could not play the traditional "helper" role. I wanted a man who would be a real partner in every way, and who didn't expect "a little woman in the kitchen." I imagined that he would be an artist or a writer. He would love me and my children, and support my work—as I would support his. Above all, he would be a good man, a kind and truly spiritual person, someone who cared about others as well as himself. And yes, he would care about the world, too. I was very clear about all these qualities for the first time in my life, and very clear that neither success nor looks were what counted. But where was this man?

I'm not a visual person, but this time the images in my mind's eye were surprisingly clear: I saw us in a house with wood paneling, in a quiet place, surrounded by trees and flowers, near a stream. It would be very unlike the frantic pace of life in Los Angeles. I saw myself writing, writing, writing.

I wondered why I had jotted all this down in a blaze of what I assumed was romantic fantasy, and I put the paper aside. The strange thing was, though, I began acting in ways I hadn't anticipated, because the vision stayed in my mind and influenced what I did.

So I took the plunge and gave up the security of a regular income—my law practice. I started to take walks, rest more and lie down during the day—things I had never done before. I paid more attention to the messages my body was sending me, and began to see a most remarkable physician, an eighty-five-year-old doctor who lived 100 miles away and made house calls: Dr. Henry Bieler, the author of one of the groundbreaking books on natural healing, *Food Is Your Best Medicine*. When he came to make a house call, something no doctor in Los Angeles did any more, he always brought some variation of his recipe for cleaning out toxins: his famous Bieler soup, an odd blend of zucchini, green beans and parsley. It may not sound appealing, but since conventional medicine hadn't helped, I was willing to test anything. And I began to feel better.

I wrote steadily now, not just in fits and spurts. I got a contract for my first book, and set aside everything that didn't support my dreams, including friends who were not congruent with my new, healthier lifestyle. One day I hired a typist to help me complete my book, although it meant spending money I was concerned about using up. It turned out to be a terrific investment though: Not only did I complete the book much faster, but my typist introduced me to David.

Had I not been at this turning point in my life, I wouldn't have been so quick to recognize he was the right man for me. He wasn't the glamorous L.A.-style guy I had often been attracted to in the past. Had we met earlier in my life, we joked later, I would not have recognized that he was the man I'd been waiting for all my life—a writer and an artist, the kind and caring man of my vision.

This is the part that still amazes me—David and I ended up sharing a wonderful, wood-paneled house surrounded by trees and flowers, where I wrote *The Chalice & The Blade* and other books. It has been twenty-one years now since we met.

We even got the stream, except that it wasn't quite what I thought it would be: it turned out to be directly under the house, because our basement floods every rainy season. But that's another story, perhaps one in which we may have to be very careful about the details of our vision.

I'm still eating lots of soup—not exclusively Dr. Bieler's soup any more, but chicken soup, prepared by my husband, who is an excellent cook. And yes, it is *very* good for my soul.

What is best for my soul is the feeling of gratitude I have that, in my moments of deepest despair, I finally wrote my own life script and learned how to get in touch with my deepest self by listening to my body. I needed to find the wisdom and the courage to make real changes and experience my full potential.

Riane Eisler

$\overline{9}$

ON GRATITUDE

There shall be eternal summer in the grateful heart.

Celia Thaxter

The Red Ribbon

A series of failures may culminate in the best possible result.

Gisela M. A. Richter

Everyone wants to win a first-place blue ribbon, to be the best in something. Even kids in kindergarten want that blue ribbon. In sports, I was never a blue-ribbon person. In a race I was always last. In baseball I was likely to be hit on the head or drop the ball. In basketball I was fine as long as there weren't other players on the court with me. I don't know where I got my horrible sports ability, but I got it—and got it early.

During the spring of my kindergarten year, our class had a field trip to a park in a town about twenty miles away. Making that drive now is no big deal, but when you're six and you've lived in a town of 300 people all your life, going to a big town of a couple of thousand people is a major event. I don't remember much of that day, but I'm sure we ate our little sack lunches, played on the swings and slid down the slide—typical six-year-old stuff. Then it was time for the races.

These were no ordinary races. Someone had come up with the idea to have picnic kind of races, like pass the potato under your neck and hold an egg on a spoon while you run to the finish line. I don't remember too much about those, but there was one that I will never forget—the three-legged race.

The parents decided not to use potato sacks for this particular event. Instead, they tied our feet together. One lucky little boy got me for a partner. Now what you have to know about this little boy is that he was the second most athletic boy in our class. I'm sure he knew he was in trouble the second they laced his foot to mine. As for me, I was mortified. This guy was a winner. He usually won at everything, and I knew that with me tied to him he didn't have a chance.

Apparently, he didn't realize that as deeply as I did at the time. He laced his arm with mine, the gun sounded and we were off. Couples were falling and stumbling all around us, but we stayed on our feet and made it to the other side. Unbelievably, when we turned around and headed back for home, we were in the lead! Only one other couple had a chance to win, and they were a good several yards behind us.

A few feet from the finish line, disaster struck: I tripped and fell. We were close enough that my partner could have easily dragged me across the finish line and won. He could have, but he didn't. Instead, he stopped, reached down and helped me up—just as the other couple crossed the finish line. We received a small red ribbon for coming in second.

I still remember that moment, and I still have that little red ribbon. When we graduated thirteen years later, I stood on the stage and gave the valedictory address to the same group of students, none of whom even remembered that moment anymore. I told them about the young boy who had made a split-second decision and decided that helping a friend get on her feet was more important than winning a blue ribbon. I said, "One of the boys sitting up here on the stage is that young boy, but I won't tell you which one he is." I wouldn't tell because in truth, at one time or another, all of them had been that little boy—helping me up when I fell, taking time out from their pursuit of their own goals to help a fellow person in need.

And I told them why I'd kept the ribbon. "You see, to me that ribbon is a reminder that you don't have to be a winner in the eyes of the world to be a winner to those closest to you. The world may judge you a failure or a success, but those closest to you will know the truth. That's important to remember as we travel through life."

You may not have a red ribbon to prove it, but I sincerely hope you have at least a few friends who took time out from their pursuit of the world's blue ribbons to help you. I'm thinking those friends will be the ones who really count—I know that such a friend was the one who counted the most to me.

Staci Stallings

Alex and His Magic

*I am sure there is Magic in everything, only we
have not sense enough to get hold of it and make
it do things for us.*

Frances Hodgson Burnett

"Willie! Wait for me!" cried five-year-old Alex, maneuvering
his bicycle across a busy street in Anchorage, Alaska, trying to
keep up with his older brother. He never saw the car until it
was too late. The impact sent his bicycle flying, and moments
later, Alex was raced to the hospital in an ambulance.

For the next thirty days, his family hovered at his bedside
while doctors assessed the extent of the damage as they eased
his pain. The prognosis was bad: Alex would be permanently
paralyzed from the neck down—the same fracture actor
Christopher Reeve would suffer a few months later. For the rest
of his life, Alex would be in need of around-the-clock care and
a ventilator to breathe for him. He would also need complicated
surgeries and a breathing tube in his trachea. Alex was flown to
a hospital that specialized in pediatric trauma cases in Seattle.

He had been there for ten days when one of the specialists
asked me, as the hospital's resident storyteller, if I would work
with him, warning me that Alex had no body movement, could

barely nod his head "yes" or "no," and could only whisper a word or two. His face registered no emotion, but his eyes seemed responsive.

Before the accident, he had been an effusive, talkative child, one of seven children, ready to comment on everything both in English and his native Spanish. Now. . . . almost nothing. Alex's mother led me to his bedside. Staring up at me was a beautiful child with raven black hair and penetrating black eyes framed by thick dark lashes. The only sound in the room was the bellowing rhythm of the ventilator that allowed him to breathe.

"Alex," I said softly. "Would you like me to tell you a story?"

He said nothing, but nodded slightly.

"This is an old, old story about a man who sold caps. It's called 'Caps for Sale,' and it goes like this . . ."

I told him the folktale of a peddler who fell asleep under a tree with hats on his head. When he woke up, his hats were gone. He found them on the heads of monkeys seated in the branches above him. The story is filled with their sounds and with repetitive dialogue, such as, "You monkeys, you! Give me back my hats!" To illustrate the story I used actions ranging from the peddler stacking his hats on his head to shaking his fists and stamping his feet at the mischievous monkeys.

I watched Alex's eyes follow my fingers when I pointed up at the imaginary monkeys in the imaginary tree. Twice, I saw his mouth try to move, to make a sound. I asked him if he'd like another story, and he nodded slightly.

"Alex, I think you might know this one. It's called 'The Three Bears.' Do you know it?" A nod.

When I came to the line, "One day the Mama Bear was making some—" and before I said "porridge," I stopped as his mouth opened and he whispered, almost inaudibly, "soup."

Taking my cue from him, I answered, "Yes, that's right, Alex. Soup," and continued, "But that soup was too—" and waited. Sure enough, he whispered, "hot!" The story had wrapped itself around him, and he was ready to take control. Using the tube in his trachea, he began to fill his lungs with oxygen to support what he needed to say next. His lips slowly formed every word, and he said, "The Paaapa Bear (inhale) and the Maaama Bear (inhale) and the Baaaby Bear (inhale) went for a waaalk (inhale) in the woods."

We witnessed a miracle: the first sentence he had spoken since the accident over a month ago! Tears flowed down his mother's face and mine as Alex continued the story.

I went to his room every day after that and told him folk, fairy and literary tales. He retold these to everyone else, much to their delight. He did not allow the hospital staff to poke, prod or change a dressing without hearing a story first, and they never complained about the lengthy process. They became like little children as he enchanted them. He also insisted they tell the stories to others.

One of the stories was "The Little Old Lady Who Wasn't Afraid of Anything," which he changed to "I ain't afraid of nothing!" He repeated those words every time his healing process offered him new challenges.

One day I was about to leave his room when he said excitedly, "Michale, I want to tell you a story!"

"You do?"

"Yes," he said, beaming. "From inside my head." He started in the time-honored tradition, "Once upon a time . . . ," and suddenly I heard the words inside my head: *Write this story down*. I stopped him, ran out of the room and grabbed a notepad from the nurse's station, invited them, a doctor and therapist in, and soon nine people surrounded Alex's bed, gently calling forth his story through their enthusiastic listening. I wrote down every word. He had successfully transported us all to that place where time stands still and miracles happen. When he finished, we broke into thunderous applause, Alex obviously loving our adoration.

I turned the notepad toward him, flipping the pages. "Alex, these are your very own words. *You are a writer! A storyteller!*"

"I am?" A huge grin flashed across his face.

"You are. And I'm going to put your story on my computer, print it out, and it will be your very first book. We will now call you Alex Guerrero, author and storyteller!"

"Really?" He had to repeat the words "author" and "story-teller" so they could sink in.

"Alex . . ." I said, leaning forward so it looked like I was peering into the top of his head.

"What, Michale?"

"Alex . . . I see hundreds more stories inside your head." He rolled his eyes up, attempting to see what I saw.

"Are you *sure*?"

"I'm sure, sweetheart. I'm *very* sure."

After that, when anyone walked into his room, Alex would say, "I'm going to tell you a story from inside my head. Write it down." Soon his original stories lined the walls of his room. He loved me to act them out, as I galloped about whinnying like a horse or snorting like a pig. He loved being in control of another person in this antiseptic environment where so very much was beyond his control.

It was through the power of storytelling that he also began to create meaning out of his accident. One day he said to his mother, "Mommy, a long time ago, when I was inside your tummy, I was happy. Why was I born?"

The answers to that question lie deep inside him. When he's ready, he'll tell them through metaphors and stories.

Alex left Children's Hospital two months later, using his head to expertly maneuver his electric wheelchair. Dozens of our cheering medical staff lined the halls, giving voice to our love and commitment to his continued healing.

He had discovered something magical during his rehabilitation: He was not bound by a body that held him captive. Through his imagination, love and the power of story, he could travel anywhere in the universe and back again. And so, I discovered, can we.

Michale Gabriel

Pop Pop's Promise

Happiness lies in the consciousness we have of it.

George Sand

When I was a little girl my grandfather, Pop Pop, used to tell me that every part of life held the promise of something good. He said if I believed in that promise, sooner or later I would find a good thing even in life's roughest situations. When I was young, it was easy to believe what my grandfather told me, especially when the two of us spent time together on his farm in Virginia's Shenandoah Valley. The gentle greeting of a milking cow, the fragrance of freshly turned earth in the garden and the unspoiled sweetness of a newborn kitten taught me the truth in my grandfather's words.

Still, as a child born with cerebral palsy, I thought I'd found something my Pop Pop had gotten wrong. He had said *"everything* in life holds the promise of something good."

His words made sense when it came to newborn kittens and fresh gifts from the garden, but not when it came to cerebral palsy. I couldn't find a single good thing in my disability. It meant physical pain; frightening operations, difficult therapy and the frustrating realization that no matter how hard I tried, there were things that I just could *not* do. I used to watch other children walk smoothly across a room, but when I tried to do the same, my muscles refused to cooperate. My body behaved like a complicated toy that never worked the way I wanted it to. I underwent my first operation before I was two. By the time I was sixteen, I had endured a dozen surgical procedures on my feet, ankles, thighs, calves and even my eyes. Cerebral palsy did not fade away with surgery, therapy or braces, and it didn't fade away with prayers hung on every star in the heavens.

Walking was an overwhelming task. It demanded determination, concentration and luck. If I had all of these, I could usually move across a room without crashing into anything. For me, that was graceful. Far too often, my poise faltered in midstride and I'd tumble to the ground like some weary, wind-tossed butterfly.

With time and practice, I learned to manage—somewhat. Still, my greatest struggle was that cerebral palsy had a terrible hold on my heart. I tried to act happy and secure, but beneath my smile I felt guilty and afraid. Even saying the words "cerebral palsy" made me redden with shame. I believed my worth was measured not by the way I lived, but by the way I walked. I was afraid that other people would see my disabled body and decide there wasn't enough to love in the person they saw. That fear surrounded me like a huge stone wall, and I couldn't open up to other people. I could not believe in the person I was created to be—I could only hide behind that wall of fear.

Since my grandfather said that everything in life held the promise of something good, I wanted to believe him, but after many years of trying, I couldn't find anything good about having to live in my body. Then, when I was twenty-three, something good found *me*.

Slugger was a lively young Labrador, a handful of sunshine-colored fluff. Doggy delight bubbled up inside him and escaped in a constant stream of puppy wiggles. When Sylvia Fisher of Caring Canine Companions saw Slugger, she knew he was destined to make a difference. Sylvia enlisted the help of Vicki Polk and many other Caring Canine Companions volunteers. Thanks to the tireless dedication of these people, the bright-eyed puppy was transformed into a skilled service dog.

I'll always remember the moment when I met Slugger for the first time. His tail waved an easy hello and his brown eyes sparkled with friendly curiosity. At that moment I fell in love. He was the most incredible animal I could have imagined, but I soon discovered there was even more to him than I could have guessed. Much more! As a certified service dog, Slugger had mastered basic obedience. He knew how to retrieve dropped items, open doors and bark on command. He had even learned to provide support while navigating steps and hills with his handler.

It had taken two years for Slugger to learn the skills essential for a service dog; it took the two of us several months to uncover the secret of successful teamwork. We graduated together in 1993, and although he and I still had a lot to learn from each other, I knew this dog would make a difference in my life. At the time, I had no idea how great that difference would be.

My partnership with Slugger brought a new freedom to my life. When we began our career as a service dog team, I was completing my master's degree at James Madison University. With Slugger by my side, tasks like carrying heavy textbooks and walking across a crowded campus became easier than I had ever dreamed they could be. I no longer had to rely on other people to give me a hand when I was going up a hill. If I dropped a pencil during one of my classes, he quickly retrieved it. On many occasions, Slugger even kept me from falling on icy steps and rain-soaked sidewalks.

My service dog brought me the gift of physical freedom. Even more precious than that, however, was the gift he brought to my heart. Slugger touched me with an extraordinary love—a love that kept pace when my heart danced, and held steadfast when I stumbled. In sweet, unspoken ways, that love eased the pain in my heart, and his devotion taught me to believe in the person I was created to be. I learned to define myself not by what I had to overcome, but by what I had the courage to become.

Slugger and I have lived and worked together for nine years.

In his gentle way, my service dog continues to share his Labrador lessons, and they have made me a wiser person. Thanks to him, I understand that blond fur on a dark skirt makes a wonderful fashion statement. I've discovered that every good partnership requires give and take. I have learned that a gift is most beautiful when it is shared. And now, at last, I understand what my grandfather meant when he said that every part of life holds the promise of something good.

Leigh B. Singh

Both Sides Now

After my mother passed away, my dad tried even harder to stay healthy and active. Each morning, until the weather turned too cold, he swam in the turquoise pool in the complex where he lived. Each day—no matter how he felt—he swam one more lap than the previous day, just to prove there was always room for improvement. Every few days he reported the new number of laps to me, pride edging his voice. I would answer truthfully, "Golly, Dad, I don't know if I could still swim that many!"

By his late seventies, in spite of swimming and working six days a week, my dad had noticeably dwindled in strength and energy. By age eighty-one he was in poor health and had to retire. He pretended he didn't need to lean heavily on me for support as we walked slowly, and I pretended not to notice. His mind was clear, but congestive heart problems and disabling arthritis had worn him down. One day he said, "In case of an emergency I do *not* wish to be kept alive by any extraordinary means. I've signed an official paper to this effect." He smiled his wonderful, broad grin and said, "I've been blessed to have had your mother as my wife and you as my only child, and I'm ready to go."

Less than a month later he had a heart attack. In the emergency room, he again reminded his doctor and me of his

wishes, but I couldn't imagine—in spite of this latest crisis—
that he wouldn't always be saying, "Have I told you yet today
that I adore you?"

He was miserable in intensive care; tubes seemed to come
from every opening. But my dad still had his sense of humor,
asking me, "Does this mean we can't keep our lunch date
tomorrow?" His voice faltered.

"I'll be here to pick you up and we'll go someplace special." I
answered, a lump in my throat.

Dad refused to look at me for the first time in his life and
turned toward the blank green wall next to his hospital bed.
There was a painful silence between us. He said, "I don't want
you to remember me like this. Promise me you won't, darling!
And please go now—I'm so miserable."

That night, back at the hospital with my husband, the atten-
dants wouldn't let us in to see him. "He's having a little problem," one said. "Please wait in the visitors' lounge and we'll call
you as soon as possible."

I sat holding my husband's hand for about ten minutes.
Suddenly, a jolt shook me and I felt my heart stop beating. "Oh,
honey," I said. "Daddy just died. I felt it!" I jumped up, rushed
down the hall to intensive care and began knocking on the
door. "Let me in to see him," I begged.

"He just died a moment ago," one of the nurses answered.
"Please go back to the lounge and we'll come get you in a few
minutes." They blocked the door so I couldn't rush in.

It had seemed to me that this beloved man could never die.
He had been such a solid, loving presence in my life. In spite of
what the nurse had said, my heart refused to believe he died so
suddenly. I raged inside, believing I had let my dad down by
not being at his side, holding his hand and telling him of my
love as he had passed on. *That's the way it* should *have been,* my
inner critic scolded. *You* should *have told him how much you loved
him, as he had always told you. You* should *have been there for him. It
would have meant a lot to him. That's what you* should *have done!* And
I felt the relentless heaviness of guilt mingled with grief.

Knowing I'd been an attentive and loving daughter wasn't

enough as the months and years wore on. Nothing made a dent in my stubborn conviction that I hadn't been there when he'd needed me the most.

Now a dream has set me free.

After a dozen years, my father came to visit me in a dream and tell me his side of the story:

> *You know I worked long past retirement age, and when my knees just couldn't carry me anymore, I felt disgraced by being so weak. Most of all, I never wanted you to see me as a helpless old man dying in a hospital bed. It would have hurt too much to have you there. So I'm telling you the truth, my darling daughter: I know you loved me as I loved you. And I did not want you there at my death, and I did not want you holding my hand when I died. That was what you wanted, not what I wanted. My death was perfect, just the way it was. There are two sides to everything—even death.*

Bobbie Probstein

Gratitude

I climb up a mountain to breathe in the air,
and leave behind, with each step, one more useless care.
The sun ripples like laughter across the wide sea.
I smile at a flower and it smiles back at me.
The wind lifts a scent from the meadow below,
and reminds me of the first girl I kissed, long ago.
I kneel in the heather, feel my spirit expand.
A bright butterfly stops to rest on my hand.
The clouds, ever present, yet no two the same,
give lively imaginations a game.
"Look! A sailboat! A rabbit! An angel! A swan!"
And it's the best kind of game because no one's ever wrong.

Everyone should have a secret place like my hill,
just to rest and let the mind roam free where it will,
far away from the traffic, the noise and the dust,
in the crystal clear sunshine of a world they can trust.
Turn your heart to the beauty that's in and around you.
Walk gently, with love, and the same will surround you.
You will surely see further the farther you go,
and remember, it's pain which helps us to grow.
For with all of its sadness, its heartache and strife,
with all of its sorrow, it's a wonderful life.
Yes, with all of its sorrow, it's a wonderful life.

Mark Rickerby

Grateful Life, Joyous Passage

Why not enjoy yourself? Your life is here and now. Birth is not a beginning; death is not an end.

Lama Thubten Yeshe

Thirty-five years go, during a Michigan winter, I shot two rabbits in the woods near my home. When I made the incision to skin the second animal, the room filled with a putrid smell— I literally jumped back from the animal. In the process, I nicked myself with my hunting knife. The small cut on my hand infected me with what the doctors diagnosed as tularemia. Within days, my "cold symptoms" turned into a 105-degree fever. I was rushed to the hospital and zipped inside a plastic body bag filled with ice.

I went into a coma just the same. At that point, the strangest thing happened: I had a clear sense of leaving my body. I observed my physical suffering with divine detachment, taking none of it seriously. I was able to move about freely, but part of me felt attached to my body as though by an invisible thread. I found myself staring into a startlingly bright tunnel of light— the same tunnel described by many in the years since then.

With a sense of quiet exhilaration, I approached the tunnel

and saw it opened into endless space. Then I stopped and turned around to see my body, packed in ice. I noticed my father sitting in a chair near the bed, crying. I had never seen my father cry, and it disturbed me. I remember trying to communicate with him, to comfort him. I couldn't figure out at first why he was upset; then I realized my body was dying, my soul withdrawing. From my vantage point, sorrow made no sense. It all seemed entirely natural, simple and ordinary.

The gaunt-looking body in the bed took shallow breaths, and I was able to identify it as my body. I understood that I had a decision to make—to live or to die. It seemed arbitrary at that moment. I felt attracted to the brilliant light, but was drawn back, in part, by sympathy for my father. So, being sixteen at the time, I decided to stick around and find out what life was all about.

Having made the decision to stay, I began a journey I might *not* have chosen had I known what I was getting into. Upon returning to my body, I found I had to work harder than I'd ever worked before. The body was badly damaged by the disease: My hair had fallen out; I looked like a skeleton; I was blind; and my senses were mixed up. Sounds sometimes manifested as images in my brain; light might translate into physical sensations.

The physical world at that time made only minimal sense.

As months passed, my sight returned and my senses straightened themselves out. But thanks to the "rabbits' revenge," as I now call it, I never again saw life with the same eyes.

My near-death experience was repeated twelve years later after a motorcycle accident. It wasn't until ten years after *that* scary incident that I seriously asked myself why such experiences were given to me. I was working for a publisher at the time who asked if I'd be interested in editing a manuscript. It turned out to be a book on death and dying, and it was the catalyst for examining my own experiences with death.

Over time, I began talking with what I took to be an imaginary character in my psyche, who introduced himself to me as

"Alex." I was an author now (*The Well Body Book* with Mike Samuels), and had earned my Ph.D. By all accounts I was a rational human being, so I treated Alex as my muse, or a foil with whom I could converse and ruminate. Then Alex started making suggestions, such as "Stop here and visit Ann. She's having a difficult time."

Amused by this oddity, I did stop by. Ann opened the door almost immediately and stared at me in disbelief: "I've just been thinking about you," she said. "I was about to call you." Ann told me a mutual friend of ours had died a few days before in a violent accident. "Since he died," Ann said, "it's like he's always here, nagging at me. I don't know what to do."

Alex gave me detailed directions: "The next time her dead friend nags her, Ann should go to a quiet place, sit down and just be with him—talk with him as if he were physically present. Give him permission to leave this life. Ask him if there is any unfinished business he needs her to finish for him."

A week later Ann called to tell me it had worked. Whether my (Alex's) advice was my own subconscious wisdom that helped put her mind to rest, or whether our friend's soul was able to finally let go and leave, I cannot know for certain. But after some of my experiences, it seemed as credible an explanation as any.

Many adventures with the living and dying followed. I will share a special one with you. The evening my mother died, I was holding her hand. My mother's eyes dropped shut, and I decided to close mine as well. As I did so, a tremendous feeling of peace spread over me. Speaking only in my mind, I said, *I think it's time for you to go.* I opened my eyes. My mother was looking right past me, her eyes alert and happy.

"All right," she said, answering what I had only said in my mind. A coincidence?

"Go toward the light," I said.

She turned her head slightly up, to the right. Her face lit up. I had the clear impression she was greeting someone she was pleased to see. In a soft, calm voice, I repeated these words, "Go lightly, lightly, lightly."

I felt her hand in mine, but she was slipping away, like an airplane fading away, growing smaller, becoming a dot, a blur. Then she was gone. Her soul had left her body—of that I had no doubt. Yet she looked radiant.

I said a little prayer, though I don't recall the words.

My mother's gravestone bears the following epitaph: "A grateful life, a joyous passage." It tells the story well.

And so, I end, as all stories end, with a farewell and a reminder: "Go towards the light. Go lightly, lightly, lightly."

Hal Zina Bennett, Ph.D.

Say Yes! To Life!

My motto is, wake up and have a good day, have a good time, no matter what goes wrong, and turn that into something good. Come out smiling, come out having a good time.

Magic Johnson

Breast cancer has offered me a great opportunity for discovery. In fact, I can go so far as to say that breast cancer has been one of the most enriching experiences of my life. Now please don't think I'm crazy. Let me explain.

For many years before my illness, I was teaching my students how to say "Yes!" to life—how to say "Yes!" to whatever life hands them and how to find the beauty in a situation, no matter how difficult it may be. I had learned this philosophy of life by reading and re-reading *Man's Search for Meaning* by Viktor Frankl, a book that describes his experiences in a World War II concentration camp. Frankl had seen and experienced the worst life had to offer, yet he also learned that the one thing no one could ever take away from him was his reaction to whatever life handed him. And his choice was to react to his horrible experiences in a way that brought much enrichment to his life and to the world.

After the first reading of this inspiring book, I said to myself, *If he can say "Yes!" to something as horrible as a concentration camp, which included the worst kind of treatment one can imagine and the loss of his loved ones, then I can say "Yes!" to anything.* And I've tried to live my life with a great big "Yes!" in my heart ever since.

So there I was lying in my hospital bed many years ago, saying to myself, *Okay, Susan, you have a choice now. Are you going to see yourself as a victim, or are you going to say "Yes!" and find the blessing in something as frightening as breast cancer.* With my "Yes!" philosophy, I thankfully chose the latter. Trust me when I tell you I didn't understand immediately what possible blessings there could be in breast cancer, but when I set my sights on looking for the blessings instead of the negatives, I found so many— and I am still counting.

Let me share some of these blessings with you.

I was dating my present husband, Mark, at the time. I wasn't quite sure where I wanted this relationship to go. I was a "no need" woman, incredibly independent. He was a workaholic; work coming before everything. When I was diagnosed with breast cancer, he was able to see my vulnerability and dropped everything to be with me. I was able to see the incredible nurturer that emerged from deep within his soul, and I let myself take in all the gifts of love and caring he was giving. This experience was so meaningful to the both of us that we decided we wanted to spend the rest of our lives together. So Mark and I got married. Now, many years later, it remains a marriage made in heaven.

What else did I learn? I learned that sexuality had nothing to do with a breast. I never had a breast reconstruction after my mastectomy because I did not want my body to suffer any more trauma. When I look in the mirror, I do not feel mutilated—as some magazine articles suggest I should feel. Rather, I look at that scar and breathe a sigh of relief and gratitude knowing I've conquered a disease. I celebrate the fact that I am now healthy. And I feel just as sexual as I did before the mastectomy. I learned that sexuality is an attitude, a way of being. It has nothing to do with a breast. In fact, Mark says I look like a sexy pirate!

Another blessing. When Mark used to travel a lot on business, as a joke, I would often put one of my spare prostheses in his suitcase with a love note. He often bragged that he was the only man he knew who could take his wife's breast with him whenever he went away! Dare I reveal it? Yes. He calls me his "titless wonder!" And I never cease to be thrilled by my title. I feel special.

At the time of my diagnosis, I also asked myself if there were any negative emotions I was holding within that could cause disease in my body. As I looked, I couldn't help but notice I was still holding on to a lot of old anger. While I liked being angry—it was a very powerful feeling!—I decided it was time to let the anger go and deal with the fear and pain that was lurking behind it. I learned that anger can be a cop-out for not taking responsibility for my actions and reactions in life. I stopped casting blame. I took charge of my life. I honored who I was, and I learned how to open my heart. Wow! What a difference an open heart makes in your life! It lets in the sunshine instead of the gloom. My letting go of my anger was also the impetus for writing my second book, *Opening Our Hearts to Men.*

Then there was the time I went for a mammogram. As I was paying my bill, the cashier said it was $120. She looked again and said, "Wait. It's only one side. That's $60." And I shouted, "Yes! I even get to save some money!"

And then there's my teaching. Often when I talk about saying "Yes!" to life, a student will say, "That's easy with the little things. But what about the big things, such as cancer." It's here that I can say, "You sure *can* say 'Yes!' to cancer. I did!" And I tell my story.

And then there's the issue of aging. Someone asked me recently if aging bothered me. I said, "Are you kidding? Once you've had cancer you celebrate every birthday with much greater joy than you ever did before. And so do the many people who love you."

In many ways, cancer is like a wake-up call. It says one never knows how much time one has left in life. So we should stop focusing so much on the future and pay more attention to the simple pleasures of everyday life. That's what I have learned to do: that first cup of coffee in the morning—"Yes!" . . . the hot shower on the back—"Yes!" . . . the purr of the engine when the key is turned in my car—"Yes!" . . . the beautiful sun warming the very depths of my being—Heaven!

I discovered that it's not the grand splashes of brilliance that define a beautiful life. It's the simple pleasures of the moment. Cancer has taught me a beautiful lesson indeed. And it was this discovery that eventually led to my book, *End the Struggle and Dance with Life.*

I know it's very easy to say "Yes!" when things go right for us. But the trick is learning to say "Yes!" when things *seem* to be going badly. We can only do this when we realize there are blessings inherent in all things and that our task is to find those blessings. This attitude of "Yes!" makes all the difference between a life filled with misery and scarcity, or a life filled with joy and abundance. I am forever thankful that I learned I had a choice. We all have that choice.

Susan Jeffers, Ph.D.

The Spirit of Body and Soul

It is not the critics who count;
not the ones who point out how
the strong stumbled,
or where the doer of deeds
could have done better.
The credit belongs to those
who are actually in the arena—
who strive valiantly;
who fail and come up short
again and again;
who know great enthusiasm
and great devotion;
who spend themselves in a worthy cause,
and who, at the best,
know in the end the triumph
of high achievement;
and who, at the worst,
if they fail, at least fail while
daring greatly,
so that their place shall never be
with those timid souls
who know neither victory nor defeat.

Theodore Roosevelt

More Chicken Soup?

Many of the stories and poems you have read in this book were submitted by readers like you who had read earlier *Chicken Soup for the Soul* books. We publish at least five or six *Chicken Soup for the Soul* books every year. We invite you to contribute a story to one of these future volumes.

Stories may be up to 1,200 words and must uplift or inspire. You may submit an original piece, something you have read or your favorite quotation on your refrigerator door.

To obtain a copy of our submission guidelines and a listing of upcoming *Chicken Soup* books, please write, fax or check our Web site.

Please send your submissions to:

Chicken Soup for the Soul
P.O. Box 30880, Santa Barbara, CA 93130
fax: 805-563-2945
Web site: *www.chickensoup.com*

Just send a copy of your stories and other pieces to the above address.

We will be sure that both you and the author are credited for your submission.

For information about speaking engagements, other books, audiotapes, workshops and training programs, please contact any of our authors directly.

Supporting Others

In the spirit of supporting others, a portion of the proceeds from *Chicken Soup to Inspire the Body and Soul* will be donated to the Special Olympics.

The Special Olympics provides sports training and competitions year-round and are cost-free to all persons eight years of age and older with mental retardation. There are over 1 million athletes participating in Special Olympics programs throughout the world.

Special Olympics helps persons with mental retardation to find and fulfill their unique roles in the Circle of Life. Special Olympics respects the unique qualities that every life brings to the world. Their organization makes it possible for its athletes to develop their talents and abilities so that they might experience the everyday joys that many people take for granted.

Special Olympics, Inc.
1325 G. Street, NW, Suite 500
Washington, DC 20005
Phone: 202-628-3630
Fax: 202-824-0200
www.specialolympics.org

Who Is Jack Canfield?

Jack Canfield is one of America's leading experts in the development of human potential and personal effectiveness. He is both a dynamic, entertaining speaker and a highly sought-after trainer. Jack has a wonderful ability to inform and inspire audiences toward increased levels of self-esteem and peak performance.

He is the author and narrator of several bestselling audio- and videocassette programs, including *Self-Esteem and Peak Performance, How to Build High Self-Esteem, Self-Esteem in the Classroom* and *Chicken Soup for the Soul—Live*. He is regularly seen on television shows such as *Good Morning America, 20/20* and *NBC Nightly News*. Jack has co-authored numerous books, including the *Chicken Soup for the Soul* series, *Dare to Win* and *The Aladdin Factor* (all with Mark Victor Hansen), *100 Ways to Build Self-Concept in the Classroom* (with Harold C. Wells), *Heart at Work* (with Jacqueline Miller) and *The Power of Focus* (with Les Hewitt and Mark Victor Hansen).

Jack is a regularly featured speaker for professional associations, school districts, government agencies, churches, hospitals, sales organizations and corporations. His clients have included the American Dental Association, the American Management Association, AT&T, Campbell's Soup, Clairol, Domino's Pizza, GE, ITT, Hartford Insurance, Johnson & Johnson, the Million Dollar Roundtable, NCR, New England Telephone, Re/Max, Scott Paper, TRW and Virgin Records. Jack is also on the faculty of Income Builders International, a school for entrepreneurs.

Jack conducts an annual eight-day Training of Trainers program in the areas of self-esteem and peak performance. It attracts educators, counselors, parenting trainers, corporate trainers, professional speakers, ministers and others interested in developing their speaking and seminar-leading skills.

For further information about Jack's books, tapes and training programs, or to schedule him for a presentation, please contact:

Self-Esteem Seminars
P.O. Box 30880
Santa Barbara, CA 93130
phone: 805-563-2935 • fax: 805-563-2945
Web site: *www.chickensoup.com*

Who Is Mark Victor Hansen?

In the area of human potential, no one is better known and more respected than Mark Victor Hansen. For more than thirty years, Mark has focused solely on helping people from all walks of life reshape their personal vision of what's possible. His powerful messages of possibility, opportunity and action have helped create startling and powerful change in thousands of organizations and millions of individuals worldwide.

He is a sought-after keynote speaker, bestselling author and marketing maven. Mark's credentials include a lifetime of entrepreneurial success, in addition to an extensive academic background. He is a prolific writer with many bestselling books such as *The One Minute Millionaire, The Power of Focus, The Aladdin Factor* and *Dare to Win,* in addition to the *Chicken Soup for the Soul* series. Mark has also made a profound influence through his extensive library of audio programs, video programs and enriching articles in the areas of big thinking, sales achievement, wealth building, publishing success, and personal and professional development.

Mark is also the founder of MEGA Book Marketing University and Building Your MEGA Speaking Empire. Both are annual conferences where Mark coaches and teaches new and aspiring authors, speakers and experts on building lucrative publishing and speaking careers.

His energy and exuberance travel still further through mediums such as television (*Oprah,* CNN and *The Today Show*), print (*Time, U.S. News & World Report, USA Today, New York Times* and *Entrepreneur*) and countless radio and newspaper interviews as he assures our planet's people that *"you can easily create the life you deserve."*

As a passionate philanthropist and humanitarian, he's been the recipient of numerous awards that honor his entrepreneurial spirit, philanthropic heart and business acumen, including the prestigious Horatio Alger Award for his extraordinary life achievements, which stand as a powerful example that the free enterprise system still offers opportunity to all.

Mark Victor Hansen is an enthusiastic crusader of what's possible and is *driven* to make the world a better place.

Mark Victor Hansen & Associates, Inc.
P.O. Box 7665 • Newport Beach, CA 92658
phone: 949-764-2640 • fax: 949-722-6912
FREE resources online at: *www.markvictorhansen.com*

Who Is Dan Millman?

Dan Millman is a bestselling author whose books include *Way of the Peaceful Warrior, Sacred Journey, No Ordinary Moments, The Life You Were Born to Live, The Laws of Spirit, Everyday Enlightenment* and *Living on Purpose*. His books are read by millions of readers in twenty-eight languages.

Dan graduated from the University of California at Berkeley, where he studied psychology and excelled in sports (former world trampoline champion, inducted into the USA Gymnastics Hall of Fame). He later served as gymnastics coach at Stanford University, then as a professor at Oberlin College.

Dan traveled around the world studying various forms of yoga, martial arts and other practices with an unusual array of teachers. Over time, he began to write and speak about ways to cultivate a peaceful heart with a warrior's spirit, using the challenges of daily life as a means of personal evolution and global transformation.

Dan's talks and seminars continue to influence leaders in business, health, psychology, education, politics, sports and the arts. His approach to living has helped countless men and women clarify and energize their personal and professional lives.

Dan has spoken at national and international conferences as varied as Apple University, United Bank of Switzerland (UBS), the Center for Professional Development and the International Conference on Business and Consciousness. He has lectured at institutions such as Luton University in England and the University of California at Berkeley.

As a dedicated husband, father, grandfather, writer and speaker, Dan continues to reach across generations to redefine the meaning of success and to demonstrate how to live a more spiritual life in the material world.

For further information about Dan's books and seminars, or to schedule him for a presentation, please contact:

Peaceful Warrior Seminars
Phone: 415-491-0301
Fax: 415-491-0856
E-mail: *wpw@danmillman.com*
Web site: *www.peacefulwarrior.com*

Who Is Diana von Welanetz Wentworth?

Diana von Welanetz Wentworth is an author of award-winning books and a popular public speaker and television host.

Her books include the best-selling *Chicken Soup for the Soul Cookbook* with Jack Canfield and Mark Victor Hansen. With her late husband, Paul von Welanetz, she wrote and published six cookbooks, including *The Pleasure of Your Company* (Atheneum, 1976), winner of the French Tastemaker Cookbook of the Year award, and *The Von Welanetz Guide to Ethnic Ingredients* (Jeremy P. Tarcher, 1983), considered the classic reference for international ingredients. Other books include *With Love from Your Kitchen, The Art of Buffet Entertaining, L.A. Cuisine* and *Celebrations*.

Diana and Paul hosted their own long-running daily television series, *The New Way Gourmet*, which was broadcast internationally on the Cable Health and Lifetime networks to millions of viewers.

Diana was also founder, with Paul, of the Inside Edge, a visionary enterprise that helped launch the careers of many of today's most celebrated authors and speakers, including Jack Canfield, Mark Victor Hansen, Louise Hay, Susan Jeffers and Barbara DeAngelis. (To receive information on the Inside Edge Foundation for Education, in Irvine, California, and to listen to renowned speakers via the Internet, please visit their Web site at *www.insideedge.org*.)

Diana's romantic memoir, *Send Me Someone: A True Story of Love Here and Hereafter* (Renaissance/St. Martin's Press), was featured nationally on television and in *People* magazine.

Diana lives in southern California and is married to Ted Wentworth. Both are listed in *Who's Who in America*.

Diana is a dynamic and insightful speaker with a gift for telling stories. She loves speaking to women's organizations. To schedule Diana for a speech, please contact:

The Wentworth Group
P. O. Box 5758
Balboa Island, CA 92662
Phone: 949-720-9355 • Fax: 949-720-9356
Web site/E-mail: *www.sendmesomeone.com*

Contributors

Several of the stories in this book were taken from previously published sources, such as books, magazines and newspapers. These sources are acknowledged in the permissions section. If you would like to contact any of the contributors for information about their writing or would like to invite them to speak in your community, look for their contact information included in their biography.

The remainder of the stories were submitted by readers of our previous *Chicken Soup for the Soul* books who responded to our requests for stories. We have also included information about them.

Father, husband, brother, friend, surfer, sailor, travel photographer and documentary filmmaker—and organ donor—all characterize **Erik Arnesen's** personal and career profile. You can find him in his studio in Venice, California or at *www.amfoto.com*.

Sheila Ascroft runs her own writing and editing business in Ottawa, Ontario. She has worked as a newspaper reporter, book editor at Parks Canada, and is currently associate editor of an architecture preservation magazine. She continues to pursue further cycling challenges. Contact her at *sheilaascroft@rogers.com* or *http://members.rogers.com/sheilaascroft*.

Lane Baldwin is a professional musician, writer, speaker and business consultant. He and his wife, Eva, have dedicated their lives to promoting spirituality, servant-leadership and living with others in harmony. They live with two dogs and one misguided cat. Learn more about his endeavors by visiting *www.lanebaldwin.com* and *www.2baldwins.com*.

What a joy it is for **Donna Barstow** to draw and write cartoons! Her quirky drawings appear in over 200 publications, including *The New Yorker, The Los Angeles Times, Reader's Digest, Harvard Business Review,* law publications, etc., and in many calendars, books and greeting cards, including other *Chicken Soup* books. Her own calendar, *What Do Women REALLY Want?* is in Barnes & Noble. Her favorite topics are relationships, computers, pets and mayhem. You can see more of Donna's work at *www.reuben.org/dbarstow,* and please write to her at *dbarstow@hotmail.com*.

Donna Beales is many things—wife, mother, Episcopalian, artist, writer, jeweler and amateur magician—but mostly she's an ordinary person trying to make sense of this wondrous journey we call life. Secondarily, she's a professional librarian at Lowell General Hospital, where she helps others be well. She lives in Lowell, Massachusetts.

Hal Zina Bennett, Ph.D. has over thirty successfully published books to his credit, including *Write From the Heart: Unleashing the Power of Your Creativity*. As one of the most sought-after writing coaches in the U.S., his clients have published over 200 successful books. For information about his services, visit his Web site at *www.HalZinaBennett.com*.

Robert Bishop has been active in the martial arts for over twenty years. All of his adult life has been guided by intense interest in personal growth. He is a coauthor (with Matt Thomas) of the book *Protecting Children from Danger: Building Self-Reliance and Emergency Skills Without Fear*.

Sheri Borax graduated from Tufts University and taught kindergarten/first grade for ten years, then went into residential real estate and development. She has been happily married for thirty-eight years and has two grown children whom she adores. She is an active member of International Dyslexia Association and AIPAC.

Patricia Bragg is an internationally recognized inspiring health author and daughter of world-renowned life-extension specialist and originator of health stores, Paul C. Bragg. They coauthored the *Bragg Self-Health Books* which are gifts for life and promote health and longevity. The Bragg Healthy Lifestyle has inspired millions, including the ageless Jack LaLanne, Clint Eastwood and the Beach Boys. Patricia spreads the gospel of good health worldwide through Bragg Health Crusades, radio shows and the bestselling *Bragg Books*. View them on *www.bragg.com* or contact Health Science, 1-800-446-1990. Contact Patricia at *patricia@bragg.com* or fax 805-968-1001.

Janet Buck is a six-time Pushcart nominee. Her poetry and essays have appeared in *Pedestal* magazine, *Red River Review,* the *American Muse* and hundreds of journals world-wide. In October 2003, Gival Press will release her second print collection of poetry, *Tickets to a Closing Play.* E-mail her at *jbuck22874@aol.com.*

Kathe Campbell and her husband, Ken, live on a 7,000-foot mountain near Butte, Montana, where they have raised national champion spotted asses. The Campbells have three grown children and eleven grandchildren. Kathe has contributed to news-papers and national magazines on the subject of Alzheimer's disease. She has been a prolific left-handed writer of the month at *www.2theheart.com, www.Heartwarmers, www.Petwarmers.com, www.sevenseasmagazine.com* and various other e-zines. She is cur-rently featured in *Chicken Soup for the Grandparent's Soul,* and her Montana artwork serves as stationery at *www.outlookstationery.com* and *www.thundercloud.net/stationery.*

Martha Campbell is a graduate of Washington University, St. Louis School of Fine Arts, and a former writer/designer for *Hallmark* cards. She has been a freelance cartoonist and book illustrator since 1973. She can be reached at P.O. Box 2538, Harrison AR 72602, 870-741-5323 or *Marthaf@alltel.net.*

Dave Carpenter has been a full-time cartoonist since 1981. His cartoons have appeared in such publications as *Harvard Business Review, Barron's, The Wall Street Journal, Reader's Digest, Good Housekeeping,* and *Better Homes and Gardens.* Dave can be reached at *davecarp@ncn.net* or through his Web site at *www.carptoons.com.*

Shawn Childress is a photographer in Austin, Texas. His photography ranges from Weddings to Architecture. His extensive travels have been shown in various Austin loca-tions such as Apple Bar in downtown Austin. His wedding work has taken him to Sweden, Italy and New York City. View his work or contact him at *www.shawnchildress.com.*

In her eighty-five zestful years, **Emily Coleman** has graduated with honors from UCLA, raised two boys, completed one marriage, led workshops around the world for singles, had numerous love affairs and has written three books. Nowadays, she occasionally coaches midlife women on *Growing Old Disgracefully*—the title of her memoir, a book in progress.

K. C. Compton is a writer and editor with more than twenty years experience working for daily newspapers. Formerly managing editor for *Mother Earth News* magazine, she now is editor in chief for *The Herb Companion* and *Herbs for Health* magazines. Her email address is *kc@kccompton.com.*

Donna St. Jean Conti received her Bachelor of Arts in communications, with high honors, from California State University, Fullerton, in 1988. Donna is a marketing communications/public relations professional and enjoys spending time with her family, writing short stories, walking, hiking, reading and gardening. Please e-mail her at stconti@cox.net.

George Crenshaw is an old pro with a long track record of success. He is an ex-Walt Disney animator and a magazine cartoonist with top sales for three decades. The creator of NUBBIN by King Features, creator of GUMDROP by United Features, creator of MUFFINS by Columbia Features, creator of BELVEDERE by Post Dispatch Features and the president of Post Dispatch Features, Masters Agency, Inc.

Jean Deeds was fifty-one years old when she gave up a successful career to spend six months hiking the Appalachian Trail. Since her journey, she has written a book, *There Are Mountains to Climb,* been featured in a television documentary and made hundreds of presentations about her adventure. E-mail her at *jeandeeds@hotmail.com.*

Roberta R. Deen was born into a military family, traveled extensively and graduated from UCLA. She taught kindergarten/first grade for thirteen years before becoming the chef at the Premier Caterer in Los Angeles. She now owns her own company, Capers Catering. She writes when the muse lights on her shoulders and indulges in black-and-white photography. Contact her at: *capers@pacbell.net.*

Mary Desaulniers, a retired secondary-school teacher, is now an Herbalife distributor. She is able to indulge in protein shakes, running and food because weight is no longer an issue. Please e-mail her at *mdesaulniers@yahoo.com.*

Sanford Drucker created the Chicago Four-Year City College Committee. Drafted in June 1941, he served three years in active combat in the Aleutian Islands without a day off, returned to graduate from Stanford University and became an investment banker. Retiring in 1970, he founded *www.livingtreasures.org* and cofounded *www.VivoMetrics.com* and *www.VeteranStories.org.*

Riane Eisler is best known for her bestseller, *The Chalice and the Blade,* translated into nineteen languages, *Tomorrow's Children, Sacred Pleasure* and *The Power of Partnership,* a highly acclaimed guide to personal, cultural and political transformation. She keynotes conferences worldwide and is president of the Center for Partnership Studies. Contact her at the center at *www.partnershipway.org.*

Gail Eynon received her Bachelor of Arts in psychology from the University of Hawaii at Hilo in 1990. She works with terminally ill patients of all ages in Hilo. Gail enjoys writing and playing with her two grandsons. She is in the process of writing her first two nonfiction books.

Lynne D. Finney, J.D., M.S.W., is an award-winning author, attorney, therapist and motivational speaker who helps people live more fulfilling lives. She presents workshops nationwide and has appeared on 200 radio and TV shows. Lynne's self-help and inspirational books include *Windows to the Light* and *Reach for the Rainbow.* She also has a CD, *Connecting with the Universe.* Visit her at *www.lynnefinney.com.*

Don Flynn lives in Connecticut with his wife, Susan, and sons, Kyle and Shaun. He wishes to say, "Sue, I love you with all my heart!" Readers can find great online support and information about melanoma at: *www.mpip.org.*

Toni Fulco has authored over 150 articles and poems in national magazines and anthologies. She raises cockatiels at home and is known locally as "the bird lady" for her affectionate, talkative, hand-fed babies. Toni, recovering from a stroke, can be reached at #10 R Own Lake, Stroudsburg, PA 18360.

Michale Gabriel is an award-winning storyteller, keynote speaker, recording artist, author and corporate consultant. She founded Young Storytellers for Peace U.S./USSR Exchange Program and the Storytelling Residency Program at Children's Hospital in Seattle. She consults with corporate clients including executives of The Boeing Company on how to communicate effectively in story form. Contact her at *michalegabriel@bigplanet.com*.

Mike Gold is a business executive for a software company in Austin, Texas, where he lives with his wonderful wife and family. He is working on a book about his experiences and enjoys presenting inspirational talks and trainings on developing inner strength and courage. Contact him at 512-258-4991, *mgold@austin.rr.com*.

Luisa Gray learned to read at the age of two—and has been reading ever since. She spent many years wandering through Europe, South America and the Middle East before settling in the United States. She collects recipes for unusual dishes (i.e., grasshopper tacos), and gardens enthusiastically, specializing in carnivorous plants.

Mark Grevelding is a fitness professional and freelance writer in Rochester, New York. His articles have appeared in various fitness publications, including *American Fitness* and *AWKA*, and on numerous Web sites, including his own. Please contact Mark through his Web site: *www.fitmotivation.com*.

Dee Hakala holds four certificates as a fitness instructor and personal trainer, including those from the American College of Sports Medicine and the American Council on Exercise. Chicago-based, she travels extensively spreading her "fitness for all" message as a professional speaker and consultant. Reach Dee at 630-853-4349, or through her Web site at *www.newfaceoffitness.com*, or by e-mail at *Deenfof@comcast.net*.

Kathleen Halloran lives in Northern California and is a very active grandmother. Kathleen also assists her sister Grace working with people with serious eye disorders. You can read her book, *Amazing Grace—Autobiography of a Survivor.* For more information or to contact Kathleen, visit *www.visualhealing.com*.

Nancy Harless is a nurse practitioner now exercising her menopausal zest through travel, volunteering and writing about those experiences and adventures. Most of her writing is done in a towering maple tree, in the treehouse built specifically for that purpose by her husband, Norm. She is currently writing a book about some of the strong and beautiful women she has met along her journey. E-mail her at *nancyharless@hotmail.com*.

Karen Hayse has a Master's of Education and has taught for fifteen years in Shawnee Mission, Kansas. She sticks by her daughter through rough times, and credits her husband, family, friends, and above all, God for making her life possible. *Klvs2write@aol.com*.

A UCLA graduate, **Ruth Heidrich** earned a bachelor's and master's in psychology, and a Ph.D. in health management. She's completed the Ironman Triathlon six times, and has won more than 900 trophies in triathlons, marathons and other races. She is a health and fitness advisor and still actively competes. Contact her at *www.RuthHeidrich.com*.

Leigh Hennessy grew up in Lafayette, Louisianna. She has a master's degree in communication and holds several world and national trampoline titles. Currently, she lives in Los Angeles and is working in the film industry as a stunt performer. Her list of credits includes over sixty feature films, television shows and commercials.

Dierdre W. Honnold is a teacher, writer, artist, musician, orchestra conductor and tour guide—but finds parenting and writing the most rewarding. More than 100 of her articles, stories and essays have been published on four continents (including *Chicken Soup for the Writer's Soul*). Her books, fiction and nonfiction, have won many awards. She loves to hear from her readers at *wordintl@cwnet.com*.

Susan Jeffers, Ph.D. is an international bestselling author and speaker. Her many books include *Feel the Fear and Do It Anyway*, (over 5 million copies sold), the award-winning *Embracing Uncertainty, Feel the Fear and Beyond, End the Struggle and Dance With Life, Opening Our Hearts to Men*, and *Dare to Connect*. Learn more at *www.susanjeffers.com*.

Bil Keane created *The Family Circus* in 1960 and gathered most of his ideas from his own family: wife Thel and their five children. Now read by an estimated 188 million people daily, nine grandchildren provide much of the inspiration for the award-winning feature. Web site: *www.familycircus.com*.

Cheryl M. Kremer lives in Lancaster, Pennsylvania, with her husband, Jack, daughter, Nikki, and son, Cobi. After working full-time for twenty years, she is now a stay-at-home mother. She spends her time crafting, writing and being a soccer mom. She also volunteers in her church's infant and toddler nurseries.

Wayne Allen Levine is a writer, poet, and public speaker. His first book, published by The Center Press, is *Forgiveness for Forgotten Dreams*, a collection of poetry. He resides in Southern California with his wife and two sons, and can be reached at *poeticsun@ earthlink.net*.

Patricia Lorenz keeps body and soul together by being an avid biker, swimmer, writer and speaker, and by following her dreams while she's still awake. Patricia is one of the top contributors to the *Chicken Soup for the Soul* books. She has written over 400 articles, was a contributing writer for fifteen *Daily Guideposts* books, and is an award-winning columnist for two newspapers. Her two latest books, *Life's Too Short to Fold Your Underwear* and *Grab the Extinguisher, My Birthday Cake's on Fire*, can be ordered through Guideposts Books at: *www.dailyguideposts.com/store*. To contact Patricia for speaking opportunities, e-mail her at: *patricialorenz@juno.com*.

Nichole Marcillac went on to win the overall state collegiate mountain bike title for 2000 and 2001. In 2001, she also placed second at the Collegiate National Championships in Plattekill, New York. Since then she has had numerous top finishes in national events and plans on turning pro in mountain biking in 2004 while continuing her academic career. She finds that the principles of relax, breathe and flow, transfer off the bike and into all facets of her life, including her academic pursuits. She received her Bachelor of Science in animal science from Cal Poly, San Luis Obispo, and is currently at UC Davis pursuing a Ph.D. Contact her at: *nmarcillac@ucdavis.edu*.

Joy Margrave is a freelance writer and project manager. Her writing specialty is nonfiction, but she has completed one novel and another is in the works. Active in the writing community, she is chairman of the Tennessee Mountain Writers, Inc., Board of Directors. She holds a master's degree and manages re-employment services for dislocated workers in addition to teaching management classes. Joy lives in East Tennessee with her husband Gary.

Marketing Director with Mototek, Inc. (*www.mototek.com*), **Genvièv Martin** is a freelance writer whose work is regularly published in the press nationwide. Genvièv holds a doctoral degree in international trade and foreign languages obtained summa cum laude from the University of La Sorbonne in Paris. Genvièv can be reached at *Mototekimports@aol.com.*

JoAnn Milivojevic is a Chicago freelance writer who loves to travel, exercise and eat! Her food, fitness and travel stories appear in magazines nationwide. She credits her dog, Tolstoy, for teaching her that roaming the great outdoors is as important to her writing career as tapping away on the keyboard. E-mail her at *joannmil@aol.com.*

Joy Millman is a graduate of Oberlin College. She lives with her husband in California, and has two grown daughters. She enjoys a busy and productive life, currently working with elementary school children in a library setting.

Catherine Monserrat, Ph.D., psychotherapist, educator and author, has worked in support of healing throughout her career. She has appeared on local and national television and is a popular speaker. Her latest book, *Cara's Journey Home: A Parable for Today's Woman,* explores the psychological and spiritual development of women. E-mail her at *drcmons@aol.com.*

Mary Marcia Lee Norwood speaks and writes about her life as a wife, mother, grandmother—and mother again at fifty! God's presence in her life has changed ordinary experiences into extraordinary adventures around the world. Marcia's writing has been published in newspapers, magazines and books. For speaking engagements, e-mail Marcia at *marcianorwood@mindspring.com.*

Marcia Horn Noyes is a former television reporter and newspaper journalist. She now writes inspirational articles for a variety of publications from her home in Golden, Colorado. She has run five marathons and is presently hoping to qualify for the Boston Marathon—another lifelong dream. E-mail her at *wingspire@aol.com.*

Adoley Odunton is a speaker, coach and author who empowers her clients to find success, balance and fulfillment. A former actress and producer, she lives in Los Angeles with her husband, Jim. She loves teaching yoga, traveling and dancing, and has just completed her first triathlon. Please e-mail her at *adoley@adoley.com.*

Perry P. Perkins was born and reared in the Pacific Northwest. He received his Foursquare pastoral license and also formed a touring theater group in 1992, where he met Victoria, his wife. His work has appeared in many outdoor sports and ministry magazines and Perry is available for freelance writing assignments. Contact him at *Perk@ perrysmail.com* or 503-816-5937.

Bobbie Probstein is the Associate Editor of this book. She has written *Healing Now: A Personal Guide Through Challenging Times* and *Return to Center: The Flowering of Self-Trust,* both illustrated with her photography, and her work is in many collections. She lives in Southern California with her husband Larry. Contact her at *yesbobbie@aol.com.*

Seventeen years old, sitting in his high-school library suffering from ADD (Adventure Deficiency Disorder), **Cory Richardson** decided to paddle around the continent. Although he had never been in a kayak, with determination and faith, he believed one becomes what they focus on. As a symbolic reminder of his mission and the person he wanted to be, Cory adopted the action hero persona MAX, an acronym for Motivational Academic Xperience. Inspiring others to live their dreams, *MAX @ School—Living an Adventure Novel* shares his educational journey through multi-media presentations at schools, community centers, prisons and on the Web at *SoloMAX.com*. Directing The FAR OUT School, MAX creates opportunities and provides tools for art and adventure promoting personal goal setting and environmental awareness. Contact him at *MAX@soloMAX.com*.

Mark Rickerby is a writer and Internet marketer living in Los Angeles, California. He enjoys road trips and hiking. Mark is currently collaborating with his father on a memoir, *The Other Belfast*. For more of his poems or work-at-home information, please contact him at *mrickerby@yahoo.com* or visit *www.ByeByeCommute.com*.

Joanne Reid Rodrigues is the founder of Slimming Together, a company dedicated to teaching others how to overcome weight issues. Joanne is an award-winning speaker and motivational force in the arena of nutrition and personal growth. Joanne's written work has appeared in magazines and newspapers across Britain and her first book is being released in the UK this year. She can be contacted via e-mail at *joanne@slimmingtogether.com*.

Erica Ross-Krieger is a life coach, artist and freelance writer. Writing and coaching with heart, Erica invites her worldwide clients and readers to come to life more fully. She's just finished writing her first book, *Seven Sacred Attitudes*, a collection of inspirational essays and provocative coaching inquiries. E-mail her at *erica@newattitudes.org*.

Richard Rossiter served in the celebrated Green Berets from 1966-69, received his MFA in 1977 from Western Washington University, became a personal trainer, Pilates instructor and owns Pilates of Boulder, Colorado. He is devoted to climbing, running, road bikes, motorcycles and longevity. He has nine books in print and is writing a novel. Contact him at *www.boulderclimbs.com*

George Salpietro continues to work at the Fidelco Guide Dog Foundation, now as Executive Director, making him the only blind person to hold such a position in any guide-dog school. Contact George at *gjskarl@fidelco.org*. For more information about the Fidelco Guide Dog Foundation, go to *www.fidelco.org*.

Rose Marie Sand is a freelance writer and producer with Shine Productions, LLC. Previously published in *Chicken Soup for the Traveler's Soul*, Rose is grateful to Dan Millman for his guidance and inspiration along her river of life and for sharing his birthday with her daughter and angel in heaven, Gina Marie. E-mail her at *rosesand@shinepresents.com*, and visit her Web sites at *www.sandenterprises.com* and *www.shinepresents.com*.

Harley Schwadron's cartoons have appeared in *Barron's, Wall Street Journal, Reader's Digest, Harvard Business Review, Good Housekeeping* and many others. He worked as a newspaper reporter, college alumni magazine editor and university public relations editor before becoming a full-time cartoonist. Phone/fax 734-426-8433 or write P.O. Box 1347, Ann Arbor, MI 48106.

Lori Shaw-Cohen has been a nationally and regionally published journalist and editor for more than twenty-five years. Formerly the managing editor of *Teen* magazine, she currently authors a weekly parenting column in Nashville where she moved with her husband and three children from Los Angeles in 1996. E-mail her at *ALoudVoice@aol.com*.

Kimberly Ann Shope just graduated with a double major and honors from the University of Texas in Austin, Texas. In 1990, her book, *A Bear Named Song*, was published by Standard Publishing Company.

Susan J. Siersma has contributed stories to numerous inspirational books. She hopes that her work lifts the spirits of others. Her family is her life and she dedicates her story in *Chicken Soup to Inspire the Body and Soul* to the memory of Mary Bennett. Susan welcomes correspondence at *ssiersma@msn.com*.

Leigh B. Singh is a writer and an advocate for people with disabilities. She became a published author at the age of fifteen. Her writing has appeared in magazines and newsletters across the country. Leigh enjoys exploring nature, reading, and relaxing with her Labrador. Please visit her at *www.Leighsingh.com*.

Dane E. Smith, is an oral and maxillofacial surgeon who practices on the southern coast of Oregon. His interest in personal growth and motivational training has brought him to write, facilitate and serve with the objective of attaining that goal. He can be reached at *genesisgame@earthlink.net*.

Author **Staci Stallings** has published numerous inspirational articles and inspirational romance novels—in print, e-book, e-zine and cyberserial form. Every day, her Web site—*www.stacistallings.com*—is frequented by visitors from around the globe. Staci's newsletter *On Our Journey Home,* brings comfort and joy to a vast audience each month. As a monthly columnist for online publications such as *The Christian* magazine, Staci has been blessed to be a part of the cyberworld where the only border is your imagination. Staci lives in Amarillo, Texas, with her husband and three beautiful children. You can contact her at *info@stacistallings.com*.

Joyce Stark is a secretary but does as much writing as she can cram into her free time. She enjoys people and the stories they tell her, and aims to write full-time just as soon as she possibly can.

Inspired by his own study and recovery, **Leonard Stein** left his career as an attorney to become a chiropractor. He treats professional athletes and dancers with a specialty in complex injuries. The lives of his patients demonstrate that profound health and athletic excellence are ever present within each of us. He lives with his wife and their two children, and still runs long distances. He can be reached at 415-563-1655 or via e-mail at *ajasearch@aol.com*.

Kelly L. Stone is a professional counselor and writer who lives in Atlanta with four dogs and four cats. She has stories in *Chicken Soup for the Sister's Soul, Cup of Comfort for Mothers & Daughters* and *Cup of Comfort for Inspiration.* She is currently working on a novel. Visit her at *www.kellylstone.com*.

Mark Stroder is a reporter for *The Costco Connection* magazine, located in Issaquah, Washington. He spent four years as a freelance sports writer for the *Los Angeles Times.* He also has three sons under the age of ten, whom he hopes will follow many of the life principles of Coach Wooden.

Kimberly Thompson adapted "Tears and Laughter" form her book *Eric's Gift.* She owns a photography business with her husband in Florida and continues her writing with a second book, *Unwrapping Eric's Gift.* Kim enjoys playing in the mountains and on the beaches with her family. Contact her at *kimtfoto@tampabay.com*.

Christine Van Loo was a seven-time national champion sports acrobat, female Olympic athlete of the year and athlete of the decade. Currently she works as a professional freelance acrobat and aerial artist in movies, television and live shows. She also produces instructional videos called "Secrets of the Circus Acts Revealed."

William Wagner currently is writing a book based on his parenting adventures. You can e-mail him at *WWagner289@aol.com.*

Bob Welch is a columnist for *The Register-Guard* newspaper in Eugene, Oregon, and has been honored three times by the National Society of Newspaper Columnists. He has written seven books, most about family, fathering and faith. Contact him at *www. bobwelch.net* or *bwelch23@earthlink.net.*

Woody Woodburn is a sports columnist for the *Daily Breeze* in Torrance, California. He has won numerous national honors, including being named top-five in Column Writing by the Associated Press Sports Editors in 2002 and 2001. He also appeared in *The Best American Sports Writing 2001.* Woodburn, forty-three, who resides in Ventura with his wife and two teenage children, can be reached at *Woodycolum@aol.com.*

Permissions *(continued from page iv)*

Stretch Marks. From LIVING OUT LOUD by Anna Quindlen, coyright ©1987 by Anna Quindlen. Used by permission of Random House, Inc.

You Don't Have to Wear a Thong to Belong! Reprinted by permission of Dee D. Hakala. ©1997 Dee D. Hakala.

Soaring with Eagles. Reprinted by permission of Toni Fulco. ©1999 Toni Fulco.

Guiding Me Home. Reprinted by permission of George J. Salpietro. ©1999 George J. Salpietro.

Learning to Love Golf. Reprinted by permission of Patricia Lorenz. ©2003 Patricia Lorenz.

Letting Go. Reprinted with the permission from Simon & Schuster from JOURNEY TO IXTLAN by Thomas Crum. Copyright ©1997 by Thomas Crum.

The Week I Got My Life Back. Reprinted by permission of Adoley Odunton. ©1998 Adoley Odunton.

Relax, Breathe and Flow. Reprinted by permission of Nichole Marie Marcillac. ©2000 Nichole Marie Marcillac.

"Rags" to Riches and *Open Eyes and the Human Spirit.* Reprinted by permission of Woody Woodburn. ©2001 Woody Woodburn.

The Little White Shoes. Reprinted by permission of Catherine Monserrat, Ph.D. ©2001 Catherine Monserrat, Ph.D.

Mending the Body, Healing the Soul. Reprinted by permission of Sanford Drucker. ©2000 Sanford Drucker.

My Favorite Injury. Reprinted by permission of Leonard Stein. ©2000 Leonard Stein.

Angel to the Bone. Reprinted by permission of Lori Shaw-Cohen. ©2000 Lori Shaw-Cohen.

Inner Windows and *Both Sides Now.* Reprinted by permission of Bobbie Probstein. ©1998, 1997 Bobbie Probstein.

The Last Attack. Reprinted by permission of Wayne Allen Levine. ©1999 Wayne Allen Levine.

Maureen's Fears. Reprinted by permission of Joyce Stark. ©2002 Joyce Stark.

Input and Outcome. Reprinted by permission of Sheri Borax. ©2002 Sheri Borax.

Mountains to Climb. Reprinted by permission of Jean Deeds. ©1996 Jean Deeds.

Exploring Limits. Reprinted by permission of Sheila Ascroft. ©1998 Sheila Ascroft. Originally titled: "The Longest Ride" from the *Ottawa Citizen* newspaper, June 8, 1999; pp. B10 and B11.

Living Life to the Fullest. Reprinted by permission of Cory Richardson. ©1997 Cory Richardson.

A Fall from the Sky and *Coming Back to Life.* Reprinted by permission of Joanne Reid Rodrigues. ©2003, 2000 Joanne Reid Rodrigues.

Into the Unknown. Reprinted by permission of Richard Rossiter. ©2001 Richard Rossiter.

Zen in the Art of Survival. Reprinted by permission of Genvièv Martin. ©2002 Genvièv Martin.

Growing Old Disgracefully. Reprinted by permission of Emily H. Coleman. ©1998 Emily H. Coleman.

Mirror, Mirror. Reprinted by permission of Joy T. Margrave. ©1998 Joy T. Margrave.

My Candle Burns at Both Ends. . . . Excerpted from *First Fig.* ©1922, 1950 by Edna St. Vincent Millay.

Rite of Passage. Reprinted by permission of Robert Bishop. ©2002 Robert Bishop.

Of Needs and Wants. Reprinted by permission of Bob Welch. ©1999 Bob Welch. From *Where Roots Grow Deep.* Published by Harvest House of Eugene, Oregon.

Tears and Laughter. Reprinted by permission of Kimberly Thompson. ©2001 Kimberly Thompson.

Diary of a Yoga Retreat. Reprinted by permission of JoAnn Milivojevic. ©2000 JoAnn Milivojevic.

A Matter of Weight. Reprinted by permission of Mary Desaulniers. ©2002 Mary Desaulniers.

Granny's Last Cartwheel. Reprinted by permission of Nancy Harless. ©2001 Nancy Harless.

One Price. Reprinted by permission of Roberta R. Deen. ©1995 Roberta R. Deen.

From Prison to Ph.D. Reprinted by permission of Kathleen Halloran. ©2000 Kathleen Halloran.

Dusting Off. Reprinted by permission of Kimberly Ann Shope. ©1998 Kimberly Ann Shope.

Faster and Higher. Reprinted by permission of Mark Richard Grevelding. ©2000 Mark Richard Grevelding.

Living His Dream. Reprinted by permission of Susan J. Siersma. ©2002 Susan J. Siersma.

There's a Lot Going on up There. Reprinted by permission of Cheryl M. Kremer. ©2000 Cheryl M. Kremer.

Phoenix Rising. Reprinted by permission of Michael Warren Gold. ©2003 Michael Warren Gold.

A Matter of Perspective. Reprinted by permission of Donna L. Beales. ©2001 Donna L. Beales.

The Canyons of My Heart. Reprinted by permission of Rose Marie Sand. ©2002 Rose Marie Sand.

Jessica's Story and *Alex and His Magic.* Reprinted by permission of Michale Gabriel. ©1999 Michale Gabriel.

A Surprise Wedding. Reprinted by permission of Donald K. Flynn. ©2001 Donald K. Flynn.

Life Lessons. Reprinted with permission of *The Costco Connection.* Excerpted from "Life Coach" by Mark E. Stroder; March, 2002, *The Costco Connection.*

What Did You Do for Someone Today? By Jack McConnell, M.D. From *Newsweek,* June 18, 2001, "My Turn" column; pg. 13. All Rights Reserved. Reprinted by permission.

The Beautiful Girl in the Mirror. Reprinted by permission of Mary Marcia Lee Norwood. ©2002 Mary Marcia Lee Norwood.

Style. From KITCHEN TABLE WISDOM by Rachel Naomi Remen, M.D., copyright ©1996 by Rachel Naomi Remen, M.D. Used by permission of Riverhead Books, an imprint of Penguin Group (USA) Inc.

If You Think You Can, You Can. Reprinted by permission of Christine Van Loo. ©2003 Christine Van Loo.

Little Angel in Heaven. Reprinted by permission of Gail L. Eynon. ©2002 Gail L. Eynon.

On My Own. Reprinted by permission of Leigh Hennessy. ©2000 Leigh Hennessy.

A Gift of Spirit. Reprinted by permission of Lane Baldwin. ©1999 Lane Baldwin.

"Michigan, You Walk a Long Way." Reprinted by permission of Donna St. Jean Conti. ©2002 Donna St. Jean Conti.

A New Definition of Health. Reprinted by permission of Erica Ross-Krieger. ©2001 Erica Ross-Krieger.

My First Miracle and *Ready to Fly.* Reprinted by permission of Dane Edward Smith, D.D.S. ©2001 Dane Edward Smith, D.D.S.

The Fawn. Reprinted by permission of Kathe Campbell. ©2002 Kathe Campbell.

Mountain Fever. Reprinted by permission of Janet Buck. ©2002 Janet Buck.

The Miracle of Dr. Steiner. Reprinted by permission of Joy Millman. ©2000 Joy Millman.

Choosing Life. Reprinted by permission of William J. Wagner. ©2002 William J. Wagner.

Message in a Body. Reprinted by permission of Kelly L. Stone. ©2002 Kelly L. Stone.

A Cheerleader for Fitness. Reprinted by permission of Patricia Bragg. ©2003 Patricia Bragg.

Lady Godiva and the Bee. Reprinted by permission of Lynne D. Finney, J.D., M.S.W. ©2002 Lynne D. Finney, J.D., M.S.W.

It Happened One Autumn. Reprinted by permission of Kathryn Compton. ©2000 Kathyrn Compton.

Back from the Heights. Reprinted by permission of Dierdre W. Honnold. ©2002 Dierdre W. Honnold.

The Only Way to Begin Is to Begin. Reprinted by permission of Luisa Gray. ©1998 Luisa Gray.

My Visions with Soup. Reprinted by permission of Riane Eisler. ©1999 Riane Eisler.

The Red Ribbon. Reprinted by permission of Staci Stallings. ©2003 Staci Stallings.

Pop Pop's Promise. Reprinted by permission of Leigh B. Singh. ©2003 Leigh B. Singh.

Gratitude. Reprinted by permission of Mark John Rickerby. ©2002 Mark John Rickerby.

Grateful Life, Joyous Passage. Reprinted by permission of Hal Zina Bennett, Ph.D. ©1999 Hal Zina Bennett, Ph.D.

Say Yes! To Life! Reprinted by permission of Susan Jeffers, Ph.D. ©1997 Susan Jeffers, Ph.D. *From Feel the Fear . . . and Beyond.* ©1997, Susan Jeffers, Ph.D.